CREATING SMART CITIES

In cities around the world, digital technologies are utilized to manage city services and infrastructures, to govern urban life, to solve urban issues and to drive local and regional economies. While "smart city" advocates are keen to promote the benefits of smart urbanism – increased efficiency, sustainability, resilience, competitiveness, safety and security – critics point to the negative effects, such as the production of technocratic governance, the corporatization of urban services, technological lock-ins, privacy harms and vulnerability to cyberattack.

This book, through a range of international case studies, suggests social, political and practical interventions that would enable more equitable and just smart cities, reaping the benefits of smart city initiatives while minimizing some of their perils.

Included are case studies from Ireland, the United States of America, Colombia, the Netherlands, Singapore, India and the United Kingdom. These chapters discuss a range of issues including political economy, citizenship, standards, testbedding, urban regeneration, ethics, surveillance, privacy and cybersecurity. This book will be of interest to urban policymakers, as well as researchers in Regional Studies and Urban Planning.

Claudio Coletta is research manager in the Urban Studies Institute at the University of Antwerp. His research focuses on urban phenomena at the intersection between technology, narratives and practices. His current interests address algorithms and automated urban management, the temporal dimension of smart cities development, and experimental urbanism.

Leighton Evans is a Senior Lecturer in Media Theory at Swansea University. His research focus is on phenomenology and digital media, with interests in locative media, virtual and augmented reality, the experience of labour in data intensive environments and the subjective experience of technological implementation.

Liam Heaphy is a postdoctoral research fellow in the School of Architecture, Planning & Environmental Policy at University College Dublin. His research draws on science and technology studies, planning, architecture and history to examine the relationship between urban science and urban form, with a particular focus on sustainability and spatial planning.

Rob Kitchin is a professor and ERC Advanced Investigator at the National University of Ireland Maynooth. He is principal investigator of the Programmable City project and co-PI of the Building City Dashboards project. He has published widely across the social sciences, including 26 authored/ ... and book chapters.

REGIONS AND CITIES

Regions and Cities
Series Editor in Chief
Joan Fitzgerald, *Northeastern University, USA*

Editors
Maryann Feldman, *University of North Carolina, USA*
Ron Martin, *University of Cambridge, UK*
Gernot Grabher, *HafenCity University Hamburg, Germany*
Kieran P. Donaghy, *Cornell University, USA*

In today's globalised, knowledge-driven and networked world, regions and cities have assumed heightened significance as the interconnected nodes of economic, social and cultural production, and as sites of new modes of economic and territorial governance and policy experimentation. This book series brings together incisive and critically engaged international and interdisciplinary research on this resurgence of regions and cities, and should be of interest to geographers, economists, sociologists, political scientists and cultural scholars, as well as to policymakers involved in regional and urban development.

For more information on the Regional Studies Association visit www.regionalstudies.org

There is a 30% discount available to RSA members on books in the Regions and Cities series, and other subject related Taylor and Francis books and e-books including Routledge titles. To order just e-mail Joanna Swieczkowska, Joanna.Swieczkowska@tandf.co.uk, or phone on +44 (0)20 3377 3369 and declare your RSA membership. You can also visit the series page at www.routledge.com/Regions-and-Cities/book-series/RSA and use the discount code: RSA0901

CREATING SMART CITIES

Edited by Claudio Coletta, Leighton Evans, Liam Heaphy and Rob Kitchin

Routledge
Taylor & Francis Group

LONDON AND NEW YORK

First published 2019
by Routledge
2 Park Square, Milton Park, Abingdon, Oxon OX14 4RN

and by Routledge
52 Vanderbilt Avenue, New York, NY 10017

Routledge is an imprint of the Taylor & Francis Group, an informa business

British Library Cataloguing in Publication Data
A catalogue record for this book is available from the British Library

Library of Congress Cataloging-in-Publication Data
Names: Coletta, Claudio, editor. | Evans, Leighton, 1979- editor. | Heaphy, Liam, editor. | Kitchin, Rob, editor.
Title: Creating smart cities / edited by Claudio Coletta, Leighton Evans, Liam Heaphy and Rob Kitchin.
Description: Abingdon, Oxon ; New York, NY : Routledge, 2019. |
Series: Regions and cities ; volume 131 | Includes bibliographical references and index.
Identifiers: LCCN 2018031048| ISBN 9780815396246 (hardback) | ISBN 9780815396253 (pbk.) | ISBN 9781351182409 (ebk.) | ISBN 9781351182393 (PDF) | ISBN 9781351182386 (epub) | ISBN 9781351182379 (mobi)
Subjects: LCSH: Smart cities. | Municipal engineering. | City planning.
Classification: LCC TD159.4 .C74 2019 | DDC 307.760285--dc23
LC record available at https://lccn.loc.gov/2018031048

ISBN: 978-0-8153-9624-6 (hbk)
ISBN: 978-0-8153-9625-3 (pbk)
ISBN: 978-1-351-18240-9 (ebk)

Typeset in Bembo
by Taylor & Francis Books

Printed and bound in Great Britain by
TJ International Ltd, Padstow, Cornwall

CONTENTS

PART III
Conclusion   **217**

FIGURES

TABLES

CONTRIBUTORS

Julian Agyeman, Urban and Environmental Policy and Planning, Tufts University, USA.

Claudio Coletta, Urban Studies Institute, University of Antwerp, Antwerpen, Belgium.

Ayona Datta, Department of Geography, King's College London, UK.

Martin Dodge, Department of Geography, University of Manchester, UK.

James Evans, School of Environment, Education and Development, University of Manchester, UK.

Leighton Evans, Media and Communications, Swansea University, UK.

Liam Heaphy, School of Architecture, Planning and Environmental Policy, University College Dublin, Ireland.

Shazade Jameson, Tilburg Institute of Law, Technology and Society, Tilburg University, the Netherlands.

Andrew Karvonen, Division of Urban and Regional Studies, KTH Royal Institute of Technology, Sweden.

Rob Kitchin, Maynooth University Social Sciences Institute, Maynooth University, Ireland.

Brice Laurent, Centre de Sociologie de l'Innovation, Mines ParisTech, France.

Thomas Lodato, Center for Urban Innovation, Institute for People and Technology, Georgia Institute of Technology, USA.

Duncan McLaren, Lancaster Environment Centre, Lancaster University, UK.

Chris Martin, School of Earth and Environment, University of Leeds, UK.

Maria Helen Murphy, Department of Law, Maynooth University, County Kildare, Ireland.

Carmen Pérez del Pulgar, Institute of Environmental Science and Technology and Barcelona Lab for Urban Environmental Justice and Sustainability, Universidad Autonoma de Barcelona and Hospital del Mar Medical Research Institute, Spain.

Sung-Yueh Perng, Department of Sociology, Tunghai University, Taichung, Taiwan.

Réka Pétercsák, School of Business, Maynooth University, Ireland.

David Pontille, Centre de Sociologie de l'Innovation, Mines ParisTech, France.

Christine Richter, Department of Urban and Regional Planning and Geoinformation Management, University of Twente, the Netherlands.

Jathan Sadowski, School of Architecture, Design and Planning, University of Sydney, Australia.

Taylor Shelton, Department of Geosciences, Mississippi State University, USA.

Félix Talvard, Centre de Sociologie de l'Innovation, Mines ParisTech, France.

Linnet Taylor, Tilburg Institute of Law, Technology and Society, Tilburg University, the Netherlands.

James Merricks White, Maynooth University Social Sciences Institute, Maynooth University, Ireland.

Alan Wiig, Urban Planning and Community Development, School for the Environment, University of Massachusetts Boston, USA.

1

CREATING SMART CITIES

Rob Kitchin, Claudio Coletta, Leighton Evans and Liam Heaphy

Introduction

Many cities around the world are presently pursuing a smart cities agenda in which networked ICTs are positioned and utilized to try to solve urban issues, drive local and regional economies, and foster civic initiatives. Regardless of whether cities have formulated and are implementing smart city visions, missions and policies, all cities of scale utilize a number of smart city technologies (e.g., intelligent transport systems, urban control rooms, smart grids, sensor networks, building management systems, urban informatics) to manage city services and infrastructures and to govern urban life (see Table 1.1). In this sense, we are already living in the smart city age, with assemblages of networked technologies being used to mediate many aspects of everyday life (e.g., work, consumption, communication, travel, service provision, domestic living), with the trend moving towards ever more computation being embedded into the urban fabric, previously dumb objects and processes becoming 'smart' in some fashion, and services being shaped by or delivered in conjunction with digital platforms (Kitchin and Dodge 2011). Smart city agendas corral the development and use of these technologies into a rhetoric and agenda in which digital technologies are championed as commonsensical, pragmatic solutions to all the ills of city life.

The smart city agenda builds upon and extends a longer history of computationally networked urbanism that has been in progress from the early 1970s and variously labelled 'wired cities' (Dutton et al. 1987), 'cyber cities' (Graham and Marvin 1999), 'digital cities' (Ishida and Isbister 2000), 'intelligent cities' (Komninos 2002), 'networked cities' (Hanley 2004), 'sentient cities' (Shepard 2011), among others (Kitchin 2014; Willis and Aurigi 2018) and overlap with other popular, current city framings (e.g., resilient cities, sustainable cities, safe cities, eco-cities). In contrast to earlier formulations of networked urbanism, smart cities as a concept, an aspiration and an assemblage of products, rapidly gained traction in industry, government and academia from the late

TABLE 1.1 Smart city technologies

Domain	Example technologies
Government	E-government systems; online transactions; city operating systems; performance management systems; urban dashboards
Security and emergency services	Centralized control rooms; digital surveillance; predictive policing; coordinated emergency response
Transport	Intelligent transport systems; integrated ticketing; smart travel cards; bikeshare; real-time passenger information; smart parking; logistics management; transport apps; dynamic road signs
Energy	Smart grids; smart meters; energy usage apps; smart lighting
Waste	Compactor bins and dynamic routing/collection
Environment	IoT sensor networks (e.g., pollution, noise, weather; land movement; flood management); dynamically responsive interventions (e.g., automated flood defences)
Buildings	Building management systems; sensor networks
Homes	Smart meters; app-controlled smart appliances

Source: Kitchin (2016)

2000s onwards to become a global urban agenda (see Willis and Aurigi 2018). In large part, this is because it has been actively promoted by a well-organized epistemic community (a knowledge and policy community), advocacy coalition (a collective of vested interests) and a cohort of embedded technocrats in new governmental roles (chief information officers, chief technology officers, chief data officers, data scientists, smart city policy specialists, software engineers and IT project managers) (Kitchin et al. 2017). Beyond city administrations, many consultancies are offering specialist smart city services, tech companies have created new smart city units/divisions and universities have founded smart city research centres. In just a handful of years, a number of smart city consortia of aligned actors have been formed at different scales (global, supra-national, national and local), each claiming to provide authoritative, neutral, expert advice, resources and partnerships that can cut through the complexities of managing cities by using digital technologies to solve difficult issues/problems (Kitchin et al. 2017).

Given this step change in activity and the embracing of smart city rhetoric and the formulation of associated policy and funding programmes by governmental bodies, the emerging market for smart city technologies, and the potential consequences with respect to urban living, management and governance, not unsurprisingly the concept of a smart city and the drive to create 'actually existing smart cities' (Shelton et al. 2015) has attracted much media, scholarly (including fundamental and applied research), policy and corporate attention. However, the focus, intention and ethos of smart city ideas, approaches and products remain quite fragmented and often quite polarized across and within these domains.

On the one side are those that seek to develop and implement smart city technologies and initiatives, often with little or no critical reflection on how they fit into and reproduce a particular form of political economy and their wider consequences beyond their desired effects (such as improving efficiency, productivity, competitiveness, sustainability, resilience, safety, security, etc.). Typically, this grouping is composed of scientists, technologists and technocrats working in universities (in disciplines such as Computer Science, Data Science, Civil Engineering), companies and government. When challenged about some of the underlying assumptions used in developing their technologies, or the problematic ways in which their inventions are being used, they try to side-step the critique by claiming that: they employ a mechanical objectivity in their work, thus ensuring that it is neutral and non-ideological; they are developing what society, the market and city administrations want or need; and they are not responsible for how their products are used in practice. Their role is to create technologies that solve instrumental problems, such as how to make a process more sustainable, efficient or cost-effective, not to evaluate whether it is the most appropriate solution or to address wider social, political and philosophical issues of fairness, equity, justice, citizenship, democracy, governance and political economy (though they may try to utilize these notions in promoting/marketing their solution); those are the remit of practitioners, policy-makers, politicians and social movements.

On the other side are those that critique such initiatives from political, ethical and ideological perspectives, focusing on issues of power, capital, equality, participation, citizenship, labour, surveillance and alternative forms of urbanism, but provide little constructive and pragmatic (technical, practical, policy, legal) feedback that would address their concerns and provide an alternative vision of what a smart city might be. Much of this critique has emerged from the social sciences (especially Geography, Urban Studies, Science and Technology Studies, and Sociology) and civil organizations. They contend that smart city technologies are never neutral, objective, non-ideological in nature, both with respect to how they are conceived and developed, and how they are promoted. Smart city technologies, they argue, prioritize a technological solutionist approach to issues (Morozov 2013; Mattern 2013), rather than solutions that are more political, fiscal, policy, deliberative and community development orientated, and they inherently have certain values embedded in them which produce particular kinds of solutions (Greenfield 2013). The smart city, they contend, facilitates and produces instrumental, functionalist, technocratic, top-down forms of governance and government (Kitchin 2014; Vanolo 2014); is underpinned by an ethos of stewardship (for citizens) or civic paternalism (what is best for citizens) rather than involving active citizen participation in addressing local issues (Shelton and Lodato, this volume; Cardullo and Kitchin 2018); and often provides 'sticking plaster' or 'work around' solutions, rather than tackling the root and structural causes of issues. With respect to how they are promoted, smart city initiatives often leverage from neoliberal arguments concerning the limitations of public sector competencies, inefficiencies in service delivery and the need for marketization of state services and infrastructures. Public authorities, it is argued, lack the core skills, knowledges and capacities to address pressing urban issues and maintain critical services and infrastructures. Instead, they need to draw on the competencies held within industry and academia that can help deliver better solutions through public–private partnerships, leasing, deregulation and market competition, or outright privatization (Kitchin et al. 2017). In turn, the logic of a reliable, low-cost, universal government provision in the public interest is supplemented or replaced by provision through the market, driven in part or substantively by private interests (Graham and Marvin 2001; Collier et al. 2016). Luque-Ayala and Marvin (2015: 2105) thus argue there is 'an urgent need to critically engage with why, how, for whom and with what consequences smart urbanism is emerging in different urban contexts'.

Smart city protagonists then are largely divided into those that advocate for the promise or warn of the perils of smart cities (see Table 1.2). That said, we would acknowledge that this division is somewhat of an over-simplification. Over time, many of those promoting smart cities have come to recognize that they need to be more mindful of critiques, often trying to reframe smart city interventions in ways that are more citizen-centric and complementary to other approaches for tackling urban issues – though often it is the discursive framing that is recast, rather than the fundamental principles and implementation of technologies/initiatives (Kitchin 2015a). Moreover, they have come to realize that implementing a smart city initiative/strategy consists of a complex set of tasks and politics that are difficult to resolve in practice and require multi-stakeholder negotiations, policy changes and investments to address. For example, beyond the concerns that critics typically focus on (as set out in Table 1.3) the 42 interviewees – from local government, state agencies, business, universities, civic bodies active in smart city initiatives in Dublin – that were interviewed in a sub-project of The Programmable City project[1] discussed over 60 different issues that can be characterized as 'critique, challenges and risks' with regards to Dublin becoming a smart city. Nearly all of these are practical, pragmatic, organizational and institutional in nature (concerning issues such as personnel capacity/ competency, funding/procurement, processes and procedures, structures, coordination, priorities, strategy, leadership, policy/law, competing interests, etc.), rather than being political or ideological (see Table 1.3). Similarly, many critics have recognized that smart city technologies do provide workable solutions for some urban issues, are often well-liked by citizens, and such technologies are not only here to stay but are going to become more entrenched in the future. Their focus of attention is thus on modifying the formulation and ethos of smart city initiatives and implementing them in ways that minimize perils, rather than seeking their abandonment.

The collection of essays in this book seeks to bridge the gap between advocates and critics by critically examining the production of smart cities and suggesting new visions of smart urbanism that seek to gain some of the promises of networked ICT while addressing some of their more problematic aspects. Indeed, it is fair to say that none of the contributors are against the use of new innovative technologies *per se* to help mitigate urban issues, but they are all cautious and concerned about how smart city initiatives envisage and deploy technologies and re-imagine how cities should be governed and managed. Thus conceived, the book explores the various critiques of smart city rhetoric and deployments *and* seeks to suggest social,

TABLE 1.2 The promise and perils of smart cities

Promises[2]	Perils[3]
Will tackle urban problems in ways that maximize control, reduce costs, and improve services, and do so in commonsensical, pragmatic, neutral and apolitical ways through technical solutions.	Treats the city as a knowable, rational, steerable machine, rather than a complex system full of wicked problems and competing interests.
Will create a smart economy by fostering entrepreneurship, innovation, productivity, competitiveness, and inward investment.	Promotes a strong emphasis on technical solutions and overly promotes top-down technocratic forms of governance, rather than political/social solutions and citizen-centred deliberative democracy.
Will enable smart government by creating new forms of e-government, new modes of operational governance, improved models and simulations to guide future development, evidence-informed decision making and better service delivery, and by making government more transparent, participatory and accountable.	Solutions treat cities as ahistorical and aspatial and as generic markets, promoting one-size fits all technical fixes rather than recognizing local specificities.
Will produce smart mobility by creating intelligent transport systems and efficient, inter-operable multi-modal public transport, better and dynamic routing and real-time information for passengers and drivers.	The technologies deployed are positioned as being objective, commonsensical, pragmatic and politically benign, rather than thoroughly political, reflecting the views and values of their developers and stakeholders.
Will make smart environments by promoting and creating sustainability and resilience and the development of green energy.	Promotes the corporatization and privatization of city services, with the developers of smart city technologies capturing city functions as market opportunities which are run for profit rather than the public good, and potentially create proprietary technological lock-ins.
Will create smart living by improving quality of life, increasing choice, utility, safety and security, and reducing risk.	Prioritizes the values and investments of vested interests, reinforces inequalities, and deepens levels of control and regulation, rather than creating a more socially just and equal society.
Will produce smart people by creating a more informed citizenry and fostering creativity, inclusivity, empowerment and participation.	The technologies deployed have profound social, political and ethical effects: introducing new forms of social regulation, control and governance; extending surveillance and eroding privacy; and enabling predictive profiling, social sorting and behavioural nudging.
	The technologies deployed potentially produce buggy, brittle and hackable urban systems which create systemic vulnerabilities across critical infrastructure and compromise data security, rather than producing stable, reliable, resilient, secure systems.

Source: Based on analysis in Kitchin (2015b), see endnotes 2 and 3 for specific sources of promises and perils.

TABLE 1.3 Critique, challenges and risks in seeking to become a smart city

• Antagonism/conflict/misunderstanding between stakeholders	• Mismatch needs/solutions
• Best practice	• Multinational/jobs focused
• Business case issues	• Need action not talk
• Capacity issues/staffing	• Need alignment with wider planning
• City complex systems	• Need bespoke solutions
• City requires stability/risk adverse	• Need champions
• Communication to public	• Need CIO, CTO, CDO
• Competing interests	• Need for education/data literacy
• Competitiveness	• Need for joined-up thinking/ coordination
• Creating impact	• Need for strategy/sense of direction
• Cultural mindset	• Non-interoperability/lack of integration
• Data dumps/quality/governance	• Not using locally-sited industry
• Data protection/privacy	• Path dependency
• Data security	• Political geography of city
• Digital divide/inclusion	• Poor choice/implementation
• Drift in roles	• Privatization
• Endless experimentation/pilots	• Procurement issues
• Future proofing	• Proprietary systems/data
• How to prioritize/assess proposals	• Resistance
• Ignores planning system/process	• Scepticism
• Internal politics/inertia	• Setbacks
• IP, NDAs and legal issues	• Solutionism
• Lack of clear route to engagement	• Standardization/standards
• Lack of economy of scale	• Surveillance
• Lack of inclusion of citizens	• Sustainability
• Lack of investment/finance	• Too many barriers to implementation
• Lack of national level support	• Unanticipated consequences
• Lack of openness	• Under-utilization of installed tech
• Lack of opportunities	• Unofficial state aid
• Lack of proper implementation	• Upgrade treadmill
• Lack of transparency	• Variances between local authorities
• Lack of trust in government	• Vendor-led rather than city- or citizen-led
• Legacy infrastructure	• Wasting investment
• Local authorities lack nimbleness	• Weak governance/leadership

Source: MAXQDA coding of Rob Kitchin's Dublin interviews (conducted 4th February to 7th May 2015)

political and practical interventions that would enable better designed and more equitable and just smart city initiatives. In particular, the essays explore the benefits of smart city initiatives while recasting the thinking and ethos underpinning them and addressing their deficiencies, limitations and perils. The essays were initially drafted in advance of an invited workshop that took place in September 2016 as part of a European Research Council funded project, The Programmable City (ERC-2012-AdG-323636).

The political economy of smart cities

The first half of the book considers issues of political economy, including how smart cities are framed and promoted, how they are sustained by and reproduce particular formations of power and regulation, and how they shape patterns of economic development. The chapters highlight how smart cities need to be reimagined in new ways that enable technologies to be deployed to aid city management but which are less technocratic, more inclusive in orientation, and do not simply serve the interests of capital and elites.

In Chapter 2, Jathan Sadowski calls attention to the ways in which the smart city is not merely an assemblage of technologies, but rather a concerted attempt to enact a neoliberal transformation of urban governance. He divides his analysis into two parts. In the first, he contends that the push for smart cities has been driven by two sets of processes: austerity and accumulation. In a time where cities are starved of resources they are forced to seek to do more with less and compete in the global marketplace for investment. Technological solutions offer cities a pathway towards efficiency, entrepreneurialism and economic development. At the same time, these technologies provide a means of generating and accumulating a massive amount of data about people, places and systems that underpin a new data-driven economy, which is also reshaping the operation of urban governance. These twin drivers (re) produce technocratic, neoliberal urbanism. In the second part of the paper, he sets out an alternative view, contending that 'the smart city is a battle for our imagination' and it is necessary to offer other ways to re-imagine and reframe more progressive smart cities. The model he offers, the Digital Deal, is modelled on the New Deal policies that were implemented in the United States during the Great Depression. Whereas the New Deal was based on the three principles of relief, recovery and reform, the Digital Deal he advocates for is based on participation (by citizens in visioning and programmes), protection (from the excesses of data accumulation) and progress (towards a more a just, equitable, prosperous city for all). Without new visions and politics of smartness, he argues that city leaders and decision makers are provided with limited and limiting urban imaginaries of the present and future city.

Over the past decade there have been a number of initiatives to create standards for smart cities and their associated technologies. James Merricks White explores two key questions with respect to such standardization projects: what do smart city standards attempt to standardize? and, what do they hope to achieve by doing so? He argues that standards seek to map out and formalize the systems that compose smart city assemblages. This is important, as producing and adopting standards enables the mediation of the relationship between supply and demand in the market for city services and technologies by providing certainty in knowledge and systems, stability in consumer demand, and permits benchmarking and interoperability and the breakdown of system silos. He contends that the creation of standards is shaped by three orders of knowledge – systems theory, neoliberalism and governance – each of which he details with respect to a different standard making initiative: City Protocol Anatomy, BSI PAS 181 and ISO 37120. He then describes points of contradictions and conflicts in what he calls the 'field of possibilities'. These show standardization to be an intensely political and normative act that posits ideas about how the world is and ought to be. His chapter highlights one aspect of the political work undertaken to produce particular visions of smart cities, namely putting in place technical specifications for particular technologies and guidelines for how smart cities should be measured and governed. An alternative vision for smart cities needs to undermine or operate in this terrain if it is to provide a counter to the present dominant vision, for example, setting out standards for the ethical use of smart city technologies and embedding privacy-by-design and security-by-design as core orientations (see Kitchin 2016).

Alan Wiig provides a detailed case study of the surveillance capitalism that lies at the heart of much smart city technology. His focus is the city of Camden in New Jersey, United States, a city that has been in decline for decades and is blighted by high rates of deprivation and crime, but whose waterfront is being regenerated through $800 million in public and private investment, with another $1.2 billion being invested elsewhere in the city. A key part of the strategy to encourage and protect such investment, and to re-imagine the city, has been the rollout of an automated, militarized surveillance and policing system. This has included the use of an 'Eye in the Sky' camera network, an interactive community alert network (an anonymous, online neighbourhood crime watch), automated license plate readers that can track vehicle movement, and a body-worn camera programme for police officers, with the data flowing into an urban control room and into predictive policing software. Here, economic development and a militarized surveillance grid and policing practices are synergistically intertwined, with the city becoming a market for repurposed military technologies and expertise, and the securitized city protecting the interests of capital and enabling orderly and planned economic development. This is a city of cybernetic control that seeks to capture and contain undesirable behaviour. While Camden is a relatively exceptional case in terms of its scope and depth, the assemblage of technologies detailed are being deployed extensively across cities, particularly in North America, and provide a salutary example of how surveillance capitalism is being used to produce securitized smart cities. There is clearly much to be concerned about with respect to civil liberties and new forms of city governance in such an assemblage, but as yet there have been little sustained interventions to reverse such deployments where they have been rolled out.

Félix Talvard also considers the links between economic development and smart cities, but does so by focusing on the assembling of economic performance and social inclusiveness, rather than securitization. His case example is Medellín in Colombia, a city once ranked as one of the most dangerous on the planet. However, whereas the Camden example ensnares the local population in a grid of control designed to shackle their actions, Medellín has sought to enrol public and private actors to build consensus on how the city should be organized politically and economically. Talvard focuses on one key initiative, *Medellinnovation*, a specially designated district that acts as a site of urban experimentations and seeks to attract transnational investment. Unlike other smart districts that seek to minimize or control who lives in them, *Medellinnovation* is located in an existing neighbourhood and engages with the local community, with a stated aim of serving them rather than producing gentrification that pushes existing residents away from the area. In this sense, the community are invited into the practices of urban experimentation and learning taking place. However, while Medellín has sought to become what city administration terms an 'inclusive and competitive smart city', Talvard details how it still delivers a 'rather paternalistic and market-oriented notion of smartness' and follows a linear path of development that favours the interests of commercial actors. He thus concludes that despite the emphasis on social inclusion, it appears that there has been a 'corporate capture of the public interest masquerading as local development'. However, he contends that the situation is more complex in practice, with the city authorities aware of such criticism and having sought to counter 'smart imperialism' by adapting rather than copying best practices from elsewhere. Despite the specific governance and funding circumstances of Medellín, it is clear that some of the normative ideas being developed and practised in the city are transferable elsewhere (indeed this is the ambition of the city administration). It would, for example, be interesting to see how they would be grounded in a city like Camden.

Similarly, Liam Heaphy and Réka Pétercsák examine the creation of a smart district in an area of brownfield sites and old working class residential neighbourhoods in the Dublin docklands. Formally designated as a 'strategic development zone' (SDZ), the area is a site of urban regeneration in which a cluster of mostly foreign direct investment ICT and finance multinationals are mixed with high-end apartment complexes and heritage and leisure amenities. It has recently been designated the 'Smart Docklands', an innovation zone for trialling new urban technologies by university research centres and private enterprise. While local authorities are still regarded as the main providers of city services, the emerging platform of engagement in the area seeks to reshape how services are delivered through new forms of partnerships between city authorities, local start-ups and multinationals. The chapter highlights two important aspects that are often missing from smart city research to date. First, the need to place smart city developments into a longer historical context. Smart Docklands is the latest phase in a much longer trajectory of urban and economic development framed within an evolving political economy. Rather than start their discussion of the emerging smart district with its formal inception in 2016, they begin with the foundation of the state in 1922. Second, the need to understand the complex organizational and political work required to initiate, mobilize and sustain initiatives such as Smart Docklands that involve multiple stakeholders who have different motivations and aims. They note that the initiative consists of an ecosystem of vested interests that must try to find common ground and work in concert to achieve its ends. These are tasks that require much liaison and coordination, and are prone to inertia and failure, especially when formal processes and legal and financial frameworks are missing or partners do not understand or appreciate the roles and constraints each is operating under. They conclude that the challenge for smart cities initiatives is not only to develop and trial new urban technologies, but to determine the optimal operational practices and organizational frameworks to enable collaborative innovation. This includes local residents, not simply public and private stakeholders.

For Brice Laurent and David Pontille, the real-time policing in Camden, Medellinnovation in Medellín and Smart Docklands in Dublin are forms of city experiments – a form of urban trialling and testbedding in which new forms of 'smart' governance and economic development are being deployed in real-world contexts. Here, the city becomes a living lab in which experimentation is practised as systems are developed and refined. In both cases, the technologies and organizational practices are still prototypes, being actively developed based on performance, feedback, analysis and reflection. In their chapter they advocate that smart cities are considered as consisting of city experiments, as specific initiatives that can be made sense of through a Science and Technology Studies approach that focuses on understanding their constituent elements and processes – experimenters, experimental subjects and objects, laboratories and audiences – as well as their consequences. They illustrate their ideas with respect to two case studies: Virtual Singapore, a dynamic three-dimensional simulated city model and collaborative data platform produced through a public–private partnership, and MuniMobile, an app developed by the San Francisco Municipal Transportation Authority and a non-profit organization that enables fare purchase and trip planning. By focusing on specific initiatives, their praxes, politics and interlinkages to other experiments, rather than on the broad sweep of smart cities writ large, they argue it becomes possible to more clearly understand their nature and implications. In essence, they are advocating that a deeper understanding of how smart cities are created requires an epistemological shift in how we frame and unpack the projects and technologies at work.

Andrew Karvonen, Chris Martin and James Evans discuss one form and example of city experimentation in their chapter on the role of universities as sites and conductors of experimental smart urbanism. They note that universities are often ideal living labs for urban trials because they are large, single-owner sites that are managed in-house, thus avoiding the political and administrative issues of using public spaces managed by local authorities, they can leverage the research and teaching expertise of their staff and actively contribute to those endeavours, and they have well-established and trusted links to city administration, companies and civil society groups. In this sense, following Laurent and Pontille, university living labs have well-defined and bounded experimenters, experimental subjects and objects, laboratories and audiences. They focus their analysis on the roles of the University of Manchester (UoM) and Manchester Metropolitan University (MMU) in the Triangulum project and the wider Corridor Manchester, a knowledge-intensive urban development zone extending south from the city centre. They conclude that while university campuses present many opportunities for developing and experimenting with smart urbanism, and create a number of beneficial effects such as building stronger linkages between stakeholders and shaping local urban development, their wider spillover effects with regard to local residents and driving smart urbanism elsewhere in the city have so far been more limited. A key question thus remains as to how to translate testbed urbanism conducted in 'smart districts' into mainstreamed smart urbanism available to all. This is a key challenge for producing more inclusive smart cities.

Smart cities, citizenship and ethics

As Dan Hill (2013) and a number of others (Gabrys 2014; Datta 2015; Cardullo and Kitchin 2018) have argued, the vision and deployment of smart cities and the forms of citizenship they enact predominantly produce technocratic forms of governance that only pay lip-service to meaningful citizen participation. In addition, as Kitchin (2016) details in depth, there are several ethical implications arising from the assemblage of smart city technologies, including forms of dataveillance, social sorting and redlining, predictive profiling and anticipatory governance, nudge and behavioural change, control creep, and system security. These issues of citizenship and ethics are a significant blind spot in much smart city rhetoric, and if addressed are usually only done so through lip service. As the chapters in this part highlight, creating inclusive and principled smart cities means a radical rethink in how smart cities are framed and implemented.

In the opening chapter, Christine Richter, Linnet Taylor, Shazade Jameson and Carmen Pérez del Pulgar note that while digital devices and infrastructures are becoming ever more embedded into everyday life, and administrations rollout smart city initiatives, we still know relatively little about citizens' perceptions of such technologies. While there is some research concerning specific technologies and platforms, they contend that we know very little about people's everyday experiences, thoughts, concerns and emotions concerning the entire coded assemblage encountered daily. To address this lacuna, they conducted interviews with twenty expert stakeholders and conducted focus groups with different constituencies in Amsterdam, including non-natives, ethnic and religious minorities, people who try to minimize their digital footprint, regulated professions such as sex workers, freelance technologists and school children. Their participants articulated a set of concerns characterized by ambivalence and insecurity and expressed through four tensions: convenience of use and risk of being tracked; visibility as citizens and the invisibility of watchers; individualized data sharing and structural forces of digitalization; and the community of digital citizenry and fragmentation and individualization of human concerns. These concerns are only partially addressed by administrations and companies, who continually push the boundaries of datafication and data-driven governance and products. In turn, citizenship has become highly individualized, with collective community responses fractured and uncoordinated, so while citizens hold many concerns these rarely translate into political action. They contend that a truly smart city would enable public concerns to be articulated and the use of digital technologies would be rearticulated to take account of them. In other words, the smart city needs to find an effective means to shift citizens from users and consumers to active stakeholders in order to become more democratic in nature.

Ayona Datta, in her examination of smart citizenship in the drive to create 100 smart cities in India, notes a similarly benign, post-political conception of citizenship – though one rooted in India's postcolonialism and the nationalism of the present ruling party. She details how the consultation process used by cities in the process of producing their applications to the government's smart city challenge (that selected which cities would leverage funding and political support to become a smart city) not only set the parameters of how the cities would be developed, but set the ideals for the smart citizens that would develop, live and work in them. Through a series of online surveys, competitions and infographics, citizens are encouraged to perform in ways designed to reproduce the discursive rhetoric they are being asked to comment on. This produces what she terms 'hashtag citizenship' – a set of jingoistic memes that discursively frame the ideal qualities of a smart citizen (e.g., 'green, honest, polite, social, bright, healthy and virtuous', who seek to 'be the change, stay on course, feel the need, meet the world, yearn to learn, follow the sun, and pass it on'). This is a digital citizenship of passive contribution and consumption, rather than rights and entitlements. Moreover, given the use of online e-government platforms and social media to undertake the consultations, the audience was largely self-selected to be those who already possessed digital skills and were users and developers of ICTs. Such citizens – mainly young, male and middle-class – are more likely to be open to the idea that ICT can be used effectively in the management of cities, and at the same time excluded many along lines of class, caste and gender. She concludes that the process of creating smart cities in India has become 'synonymous with the production of a postcolonial technocratic subjectivity', with production of citizenship practices moving from civil and political society to digital space. This redrawing of the political limits of citizenship shifts the boundaries of urban participation and democracy, and who gets to embody and perform being a citizen in a smart city. Her analysis highlights the need for sustained critical reflection on who smart cities are being built for, not only in India but globally.

In their chapter, Taylor Shelton and Thomas Lodato draw on fieldwork conducted within Atlanta's task force for smart cities to examine what they term the 'actually existing smart citizen'. That is, how citizens are imagined and citizenship enacted in historically and geographically specific ways within Atlanta's smart city vision and programmes of the city. They detail that while the city administration and companies often talked of producing a citizen-focused smart city, in practice citizens were included as two empty signifiers (both of which were also evident in Datta's Indian cities). The first is what they term a 'general citizen', wherein the citizen is framed as a catch-all community of seemingly homogenous residents and visitors. Here, the city administration and companies envisaged the smart city from within the frame of stewardship (delivering on behalf of citizens) and civic paternalism (deciding what's best for citizens). Here, citizens are generic recipients or consumers of services, rather than being meaningfully involved in their design and deployment. The second is the 'absent citizen', referring both to all those diverse communities that hold differing identities, values, concerns and experiences to the 'general citizen' (which is largely framed as white, male, heterosexual, able-bodied and middle class) and to the absence of citizens from the processes of formulating and implementing smart city strategies and programmes. Indeed, there were no citizens beyond those employed as city administrators, stakeholders and vested companies at the events they attended in Atlanta, nor were there elected officials that citizens have chosen to represent them. They conclude with two contentions. First, that a truly citizen-focused smart city would adopt strategies to include citizen participation in their visioning. Second, that the path to just, equitable and democratic cities may well require a radical rethink of the present market- and technology-centric formulation of smart cities than simply adding citizens and stirring can supply. The challenge then in creating smart cities is to reimagine citizenship beyond its present formulations.

Sung-Yueh Perng documents the politics and praxes of urban and public experimentation that actively involves citizens collaborating with local government. His chapter takes as its case study the work of Dublin City Council (DCC) Beta, an initiative in the local authority that seeks to develop and implement what Halpern et al. (2013 term 'test-bed urbanism'; that is, experimental interventions in the urban milieu designed to produce new products and practices. In the case of DCC Beta it is interventions that will improve the lives of local residents, but also enhance the work of the local authority. In particular, Perng focuses attention on a 'collaborative infrastructuring' project in which the local residents, artists, hackers from Code for Ireland and city staff worked together. The project involved painting what seem like mundane street infrastructure – traffic light control boxes. However, these boxes attract graffiti and stickers which, as well as being ugly, produce a cleaning cost. Enabling artists to paint the boxes, and producing an app that would allow people to find them, would provide a public exhibit for the artist, enhance the visual appearance of the area, strengthen place identity and save the council money. As he details, undertaking collaboration and experimentation, and aligning diverse viewpoints and practices is not straightforward, but can be immensely productive in terms of enhancing a sense of participation, value and trust in urban management and development. He concludes that the process of collaborative infrastructuring, while not without its challenges, has the potential to create a more inclusive means of creating smart cities.

Similarly, Duncan McLaren and Julian Agyeman examine the constitution of more citizen-orientated smart cities through the lens of sharing. Noting the various criticisms of smart cities detailed in other chapters in the book, they examine the notion that smart cities should become sharing cities. They show how the ethos and practice of sharing comes in different guises, detailing four broad types: commercial, monetized platforms (e.g., Uber and Airbnb); not-for-profit, peer-to-peer and communal platforms (e.g., Streetbank and Freecycle); commercial, social-cultural (rather than exclusive platform mediated) exchanges (e.g. Enspiral and Bitcoin); and communal, social-cultural exchanges such as sharing within families and communities. They note that these forms of sharing produce different forms of smart sharing city models, with commercial platforms prevailing in Anglo-Saxon cultures, while in Latin cultures, especially in South America, urban commoning is facilitated. Elsewhere in Europe and Asia, a range of hybrid forms exist. In the final part of the chapter, they compare what they term 'smart sharing cities', ones that prioritize the values of smart cities, such as being efficient, functional and well-controlled, designed to produce economic development and treating people as consumers, with 'social urbanism' that holds the values of being effective, diverse and resilient, designed to produce social inclusion and treating people as citizens. They contend that rather than producing smart cities rooted in the values of the sharing economy and serving the interests of elites and corporations, smart cities should be fair, just, equitable, sustainable and democratic, grounded in the ideas of social urbanism.

In contrast to the focus on citizenship, Maria Helen Murphy considers the privacy implications of smart cities from the perspective of the law, and in particular the new EU General Data Protection Regulation. She notes that the smart city poses particular problems for data protection and privacy because the issues of notice and consent are difficult to deal with in practice as people move through environments saturated with networked sensors, actuators and cameras that generate huge volumes of data about them. She maps out some of these challenges, existing approaches to dealing with them and the approach advocated by the GDPR and its likely effects. In particular, she considers the introduction of a privacy-by-design mandate and the role that pseudonymiation might play as a privacy enhancing technique. These two approaches to protecting privacy are framed as 'positive-sum', in that they are pro-privacy but also pro-progress and the use of smart city technologies. However, she notes that while their use will be beneficial, they are not a panacea for the data protection and ethical challenges of smart cities. Of course, GDPR also relates solely to the Member States of the EU and significant privacy infringing practices will continue within and across other countries.

Leighton Evans takes a different tack, considering privacy from a phenomenological, behavioural, epistemological and practical perspective. In other words, rather than focus on the law and how privacy can be regulated in an era of smart city technologies, he draws attention to how the nature of privacy is being transformed, with the nature of the public and private sphere altering. He contends that traditionally privacy has been spatially separated, with spaces such as the home being private spheres. In the era of pervasive and ubiquitous computation, wherein networked computation becomes embedded into all manner of previously analogue objects and systems, and computation is available anywhere and on the move, spaces that were previously private are now becoming subject to a surveillance gaze that operates on an almost continual basis. Privacy then is transformed from a property of spatial boundaries, to one of orientation towards technology. Smart city technologies then are transforming not only the limits of privacy, but the very notion of privacy itself. In creating smart cities, such considerations have to date been absent or been dealt with fairly lackadaisically, yet they raise fundamental ethical and moral concerns. Indeed, as Kitchin (2016) details, the ethical implications of smart cities are profound and require redress in ways that extend beyond legal remedies if the trust of citizens in such endeavours is to be maintained, especially in the wake of a series of data breaches and scandals such as the Snowden revelations and Cambridge Analytica's misuse of personal information.

As well as creating privacy risks and harms, smart city technologies are also vulnerable to security risks. In Chapter 16, Martin Dodge and Rob Kitchin examine the paradox that creating smart cities is promoted as a means to effectively counter and manage risks to cities, yet the technologies used create new vulnerabilities and threats by making city infrastructure and services open to hacking and cyberattacks, malware and viruses, and software bugs and data errors. They identify five forms of vulnerabilities with respect to smart city technologies – weak software security and data encryption, the use of insecure legacy systems and poor ongoing maintenance, system interdependencies and large and complex attack surfaces, cascade effects, and human error and deliberate malfeasance of disgruntled (ex)employees – and detail illustrative examples of security breaches. In the latter half of the chapter they explore how these vulnerabilities are presently being tackled via a technically-mediated mitigation approach, how this might be extended to include a wider set of mitigation tactics, and how such tactics might be enacted and enforced through market- and government-led regulations. In addition, they make the case for a more radical preventative strategy to security. They conclude that unless sufficient attention is paid to improving the cybersecurity of smart cities we will create fragile urban systems that are vulnerable to severe disruption – which, ironically, is far from the anticipated disruptive innovation smart city technologies are meant to produce.

Conclusion

Whether the term 'smart cities' will have longevity or be replaced by another label, the use and promotion of networked ICTs in managing and governing cities, fostering economic development and mediating everyday life are set to continue into the future. Indeed, urban systems and infrastructure, and many of the tasks undertaken daily, are already reliant on and overdetermined by digital technologies (Kitchin and Dodge 2011). How these technologies are conceived, developed, promoted and implemented matters to future urbanism – how cities will be planned, built and run. It is important then that critical attention is paid not only to the technical and instrumental aspects of creating smart cities, but also their politics, ideology and ethics. As the essays in this collection highlight, there is a need to consider how smart cities can be reimagined, reframed and remade, both in general terms and with respect to specific issues and initiatives.

This is a task that Rob Kitchin tackles in the concluding chapter. He details six ways in which smart cities can be productively recast that seek to leverage the benefits of using urban technologies while reimaging and reframing how they are conceived and pursued and remaking how they are deployed so they are underpinned by an alternative rationale and ethos that is more emancipatory, empowering and inclusive. Three of his suggestions concern normative and conceptual thinking with regards to goals, cities and epistemology, and three concern more practical and political thinking and praxes with regards to management/governance, ethics and security, and stakeholders and working relationships. His contribution does not seek to be prescriptive, but rather aims to provide conceptual and practical suggestions and stimulate debate about how to productively reimagine smart urbanism and the creation of smart cities.

The essays in this collection provide a springboard for the kind of debate we think is needed if we are going to produce smart cities that serve all of their citizens and tackle urban issues effectively. While some might bemoan that there is already too much dissent and critique of smart cities, we would disagree. Urban centres are the places where most people on the planet live and where most work and consumption happens. It is vital that we seek to create effective, attractive and inclusive smart cities, rather than ones that perpetuate or deepen inequalities by serving only some interests. That means identifying shortcomings in present approaches and proposing alternative visions and agendas (see also Townsend 2013; Kitchin 2015a; Luque-Ayala and Marvin 2015; Willis and Aurigi 2018). The chapters that follow seek to do both and we encourage readers to move outside their comfort zones, to engage with the ideas presented and to be reflexive, challenging their own thinking and praxis, in order to consider the ways in which they might productively reimagine, reframe and remake smart cities.

Notes

1 http://progcity.maynoothuniversity.ie/
2 Compiled from Giffinger et al. (2007); Hollands (2008); Cohen (2012); Townsend (2013).
3 Compiled from Cerrudo (2015); Datta (2015); Dodge and Kitchin (2005); Elwood and Leszczynski (2011); Graham (2005); Greenfield (2013); Hill (2013); Kitchin (2014); Kitchin and Dodge (2011); Kitchin (2015b); Mattern (2013); Morozov (2013); Shelton et al. (2015); Townsend (2013); Vanolo (2014).

Acknowledgements

The research for this paper was funded by a European Research Council Advanced Investigator grant, The Programmable City (ERC-2012-AdG-323636).

References

Cardullo, P. and Kitchin, R. 2018. "Being a 'citizen' in the smart city: Up and down the scaffold of smart citizen participation in Dublin, Ireland." *GeoJournal*. doi:10.1007/s10708–10018–9845–9848.

Cerrudo, C. 2015. "An emerging US (and world) threat: Cities wide open to cyber attacks." Securing Smart Cities, securingsmartcities.org/wp-content/uploads/2015/05/CitiesWideOpen ToCyberAttacks.pdf (last accessed 12 October 2015).

Cohen, B. 2012. "What exactly is a smart city?" *Fast Co.Exist*, 19 September, www.fa stcoexist.com/1680538/what-exactly-is-a-smart-city (last accessed 28 April 2015).

Collier, S.J., Mizes, J.C. and von Schnitzler, A. 2016. "Public infrastructures/Infrastructural publics." *Limn* 7, http://limn.it/preface-public-infrastructures-infrastructural-publics/.

Datta, A. 2015. "New urban utopias of postcolonial India: 'Entrepreneurial urbanization' in Dholera smart city, Gujarat." *Dialogues in Human Geography* 5(1): 3–22.

Dodge, M. and Kitchin, R. 2005. "Codes of life: Identification codes and the machine-readable world." *Environment and Planning D: Society and Space* 23(6): 851–881.

Dutton, W.H., Blumler, J.G. and Kraemer, K.L. 1987. *Wired Cities: Shaping Future Communication.* New York: Macmillan.

Elwood, S. and Leszczynski, A. 2011. "Privacy reconsidered: New representations, data practices, and the geoweb." *Geoforum* 42: 6–15.

Gabrys, J. 2014. "Programming environments: Environmentality and citizen sensing in the smart city." *Environment and Planning D: Society and Space* 32(1): 30–48

Giffinger, R., Fertner, C., Kramar, H., Kalasek, R., Pichler-Milanović, N. and Meijers, E. 2007. *Smart cities: Ranking of European medium-sized cities.* Centre of Regional Science, Vienna UT. www.smart-cities.eu/download/smart_cities_final_report.pdf (last accessed 12 October 2015).

Graham, S. 2005. "Software-sorted geographies." *Progress in Human Geography* 29(5): 562–580.

Graham, S. and Marvin, S. 1999. "Planning cybercities: Integrating telecommunications into urban planning." *Town Planning Review* 70(1): 89–114.

Graham, S. and Marvin, S. 2001. *Splintering Urbanism: Networked Infrastructures, Technological Mobilities and the Urban Condition.* London: Routledge.

Greenfield, A. 2013. *Against the Smart City.* New York: Do Publications.

Halpern, O., LeCavalier, J., Calvillo, N. and Pietsch, W. 2013. "Test-Bed Urbanism." *Public Culture* 25(2): 272–306.

Hanley, R. ed. 2004. *Moving People, Goods, and Information in the 21st Century: The Cutting-Edge Infrastructures of Networked Cities.* London: Routledge.

Hill, D. 2013. "On the smart city: Or, a 'manifesto' for smart citizens instead." *City of Sound*, 1 February.www.cityofsound.com/blog/2013/02/on-the-smart-city-a-callfor-smart-citizens-instead.html (last accessed 5 February 2013).

Hollands, R.G. 2008. "Will the real smart city please stand up?" *City* 12(3): 303–320.

Ishida, T. and Isbister, K. 2000. *Digital Cities: Technologies, Experiences, and Future Perspectives.* Berlin: Springer.

Kitchin, R. 2014. "The real-time city? Big data and smart urbanism." *GeoJournal* 79(1): 1–14.

Kitchin, R. 2015a. "Making sense of smart cities: addressing present shortcomings." *Cambridge Journal of Regions, Economy and Society* 8(1): 131–136.

Kitchin, R. 2015b. "The promise and peril of smart cities." *Journal of the UK Society of Computers and Law.* http://www.scl.org/site.aspx?i=ed42789, June.

Kitchin, R. 2016. *Getting smarter about smart cities: Improving data privacy and data security.* Data Protection Unit, Department of the Taoiseach, Dublin, Ireland. http://www.taoiseach.gov.ie/eng/Publications/Publications_2016/Smart_Cities_Report_January_2016.pdf

Kitchin, R., Coletta, C., Evans, L., Heaphy, L. and MacDonncha, D. 2017. "Smart cities, urban technocrats, epistemic communities, advocacy coalitions and the 'last mile' problem." *it – Information Technology* 59(6): 275–284.

Kitchin, R. and Dodge, M. 2011. *Code/Space: Software and Everyday Life.* Cambridge, MA: MIT Press.

Komninos, N. 2002. *Intelligent Cities: Innovation, Knowledge Systems and Digital Spaces.* London: Routledge.

Luque-Ayala, A. and Marvin, S. 2015. "Developing a critical understanding of smart urbanism?" *Urban Studies* 52(12): 2105–2116.

Mattern, S. 2013. "Methodolatry and the art of measure: The new wave of urban data science." *Design Observer: Places.* 5 November. http://designobserver.com/places/feature/0/38174/ (last accessed 15 November 2013).

Morozov, E. 2013. *To Save Everything, Click Here: Technology, Solutionism, and the Urge to Fix Problems That Don't Exist.* New York: Allen Lane.

Shelton, T., Zook, M. and Wiig, A. 2015. "The 'actually existing smart city'." *Cambridge Journal of Regions, Economy and Society* 8: 13–25.

Shepard, M. 2011. *Sentient City: Ubiquitous Computing, Architecture, and the Future of Urban Space*. Cambridge, MA: MIT Press.

Townsend, A. 2013. *Smart Cities: Big Data, Civic Hackers, and the Quest for a New Utopia*. New York: W.W. Norton & Co.

Vanolo, A. 2014. "Smartmentality: The smart city as disciplinary strategy." *Urban Studies* 51(5): 883–898.

Willis, K. and Aurigi, A. 2018. *Digital and Smart Cities*. London: Routledge.

PART I

The political economy of smart cities

2

A DIGITAL DEAL FOR THE SMART CITY

Participation, protection, progress

Jathan Sadowski

Introduction

Most models and visions of the smart city—whether emanating from academia or media, government or business—tend to revolve around an arsenal of smart technologies. The smart city becomes, essentially, synonymous with data-driven, (semi-)automated, networked technologies; the city is just a place to install and implement these systems. There are sensor arrays to monitor the city, massive databases containing insights about the city, algorithms that help sort out the city, control rooms for real-time management of the city, and plenty of other smart systems that already exist or soon will. Undoubtedly these technologies are exciting. They grant powerful capabilities and valuable information to city governments and tech companies. Not long ago, such smart systems would have only existed in the hopes and fears of speculative stories.

But focusing on the smart city as only, or even primarily, a collection of technologies is a mistake. We easily become distracted by technology, whether celebrating its potential or criticizing its pitfalls. While these systems and devices are certainly consequential, they are also an effective red herring. Our attention is redirected away from what is really at stake with the smart city movement: The transformation of how cities are governed. As a growing body of scholarship argues, critically analysing the features and effects of smart technologies is crucial, however, they should be understood as parts of governance regimes[1] (Bulkeley et al. 2016; Cardullo et al. 2018; Ho 2017; Leszczynski 2016; Morozov and Bria 2018; Pollio 2016; Sadowski and Pasquale 2015).

To put it differently, the smart city is not just a band of geeks hacking the city. Nor is it only a branded image, empty of substance other than expos and pamphlets. Proponents of smart urbanism are surely focused on integrating technology into the city and our lives, but they are also concerned with how cities are managed, the goals that motivate cities, and what urban society looks like. If we only look at the technology, then we miss out on the ways in which smart initiatives can reflect the ideologies and reinforce the interests of city elites and global corporations (Alizadeh 2017; Hollands 2015; McNeill 2015; Söderström et al. 2014; Wiig 2015). Indeed, we do not have to look far to see corporations like IBM and Alphabet attempting to change existing physical and political landscapes so they fit these visions of smart urbanism.

In this chapter, then, I direct attention to the techno-politics of smart governance. First, I describe two primary drivers of smart governance: austerity and accumulation. I focus, in particular, on the highly capitalized and corporatized version of the smart city vision, which is in the process of colonizing urban environments and capturing political imaginations of elite decision-makers. Smart governance is more than just managerial policy. It is also a project that involves framing the future, constraining the imagination, and enrolling us into one vision of how to develop and administer cities (Greenfield 2013; Hollands 2015; Kitchin 2014; Luque-Ayala and Marvin 2016; Sadowski and Bendor 2018; White 2016). Exploring alternative arrangements requires that we recognize this determinism and clear new pathways. Second, I sketch a framework that could serve as the foundation of social, political, and legal interventions for building a more just smart city. I loosely model this framework on the social democratic New Deal programme enacted in the US during the 1930s. I call my programme the Digital Deal and base it on three pillars: Participation, Protection, and Progress.

Smart governance: Austerity and accumulation

To be clear, "governance" is not "govern-ish," or a lesser form of governing. It is rather, as Wendy Brown (2015: 123) writes, a hybrid concept that is

> often used interchangeably with both "governing" and "managing" ... This interchangeability and promiscuity suggest that governance comprises and indexes an important fusion of political and business practices, both at the level of administration and at the level of providing goods and services.

The concept is useful for understanding how society and individuals are governed in ways that do not (necessarily) mean *by the State* or *by governments*. Governance is the "primary administrative form" or "political modality" through which projects like smart urbanism become real—by structuring society, influencing behaviour, and materializing ideology (Brown 2015). In other words, by combining aspects of political governing and corporate management, governance offers a powerful way of creating and maintaining smartness.

Proponents of the smart city tend to assert that cities must establish new models of governance that are updated for the 21st century. Stephen Goldsmith, a Harvard professor and former mayor, exemplifies this neoliberal boosterism. Along with his co-authors, Goldsmith tells cities they must use smart technology to become "more agile," "unleash innovation," and even "act more like Amazon" (Goldsmith and Crawford 2014; Goldsmith and Kleiman 2018). If cities want to survive "the fight for investment," then they will have to embrace tech-fuelled entrepreneurialism and growth (Hodgkinson 2011). Cities will have to be governed by strong leaders who are not afraid to take risks on lofty visions and (untested) technologies. They will, according to Cisco, have to adopt and "promote a digital master plan that spans the entire city" (Clark 2013: 16). They will have to view the city as a platform, while the mayor acts like a CEO who runs the city like a business (McNeil 2017). Otherwise the city will be just another loser in the cutthroat competition between cities for resources and capital.

While the discourse of smart governance is based on radical disruption, revolutionary change, and catalysing the future, the underlying values and goals are all too familiar. The corporate public-private model of smart governance, which continues to spread and thrive (Hollands 2015), is largely driven by austerity and accumulation. These drivers are behind many smart initiatives, influencing the problems they solve, the methods they use, the values they represent, and the goals they achieve. More often than not, smart urbanism reproduces neoliberal modes of governance based on entrepreneurialism, efficiency, and extraction—but now with data, networks, and algorithms (Levenda et al. 2015; Morozov and Bria 2018; Sadowski and Pasquale 2015; Wiig 2017). Understanding these defining features of smart urbanism is important. Yet, at the same time, there is a need for work that tries to pose alternatives to neoliberal smart cities, even if it is just outlines of something different (McFarlane and Söderström 2017). The remainder of this section will provide a brief overview of how austerity and accumulation drive smart urbanism. Based on this analysis, the next section will then sketch a framework for progressive smart urbanisms based on three pillars: participation, protection, and progress.

Austerity

Even as they are gripped by tight budgets and austerity measures, cities around the world feel the pressure to constantly grow and attract capital, while also providing services and maintaining infrastructure for a rising population. These compounding crises open the way for models of smart urbanism that promise to mitigate and manage the problems facing cities (White 2016). As if the effects are not palpable to city leaders, the companies that sell smart systems and services often begin their pitches by describing the consequences cities will suffer if they do not innovate their way out of crises. For example, Cisco says that, "fragilities in the global financial system threaten to stall, if not reverse, years of economic progress" (Evans 2012: 1). IBM adds that the financial crash in 2008 "ushered in a systemic and prolonged economic adjustment that has severely crippled the ability of governments to deliver expected services to citizens, let alone push for innovative, new services" (IBM 2012: 1). Governments thus have no choice but to embrace new "models of economic efficiency and fiscal sustainability" because "*doing more with less*" is now "the new normal in government" (IBM 2012: 1).

The *raison d'être* of these smart systems is "economic vitality." This is IBM's term for a catchall economization of the city. Vitality means more than growth. It means brokering partnerships, or "collaborations," at all levels of the private-public sector. Discovering new sources of "value creation" from urban data. Establishing entrepreneurial principles at the core of city governance. Embracing competition as the normal condition of society. Using "emerging and disruptive technologies" to create "business and social environments that are connected and open, simple and intelligent, fast and scalable, innovative and reimagined" (Fleming et al. 2015: 3). Economic vitality, according to IBM, is necessary to survive, let alone to thrive:

> With global competition intensifying, and the disruption to global value chains increasing, the time to address the economic vitality challenge for the 21st century is now. "Opting out" is not an option. Turning the transformative potential of new technologies and changing demographics into economic and societal value should be viewed as a tremendous opportunity for improving our cities, regions and countries in the years to come. To realize this opportunity, public sector organizations must challenge and change their traditional organizational mindset, make the right connections and drive forward to become the standout success story in the data-driven global economy.
>
> *(Fleming et al. 2015)*

This relationship between austerity and vitality is key to understanding the corporate smart city. Economic vitality speaks to those who are hit hard by austerity, who face pressure from citizens and competitors, and who want to move up in the global rankings. Many mayors, such as NYC's Michael Bloomberg and Philadelphia's Michael Nutter, are quite conscious of their image as innovators, leading their city into the future. For them, smart urbanism is integral to cultivating that image (Wiig 2015). Many others, though, just want the easiest or cheapest or most reliable way to ramp up economic activity. If becoming a smart city means gaining efficiency, saving dollars, attracting investment, and beating competitors, then city leaders are happy to hop on the train to smartness. However, this train is often fuelled by "empty rhetoric" and leads to unfulfilled promises (Alizadeh 2017; Wiig 2015), while also smuggling on board a host of trade-offs related to issues like expansive surveillance and technocratic governance.

By exploiting austerity, smart tech companies are able to create new markets for their products and new positions for themselves in urban governance. As I have argued elsewhere, "this model of creating our urban future is also an insidious way of handing more control—over people, places, policies—to profit-driven, power-hungry corporations" (Sadowski 2017). Consider, for example, a 2016 *Guardian* exposé about Sidewalk Labs titled, "Secretive Alphabet division aims to fix public transit in US by shifting control to Google" (Harris 2016). In an age of austerity, these are the types of stories we should get used to seeing as tech and finance firms—sometimes working together—continue to take over cities.[2] Until, that is, the stories become so standard that such initiatives and agendas are not even worth reporting on.

Accumulation

The collection, exchange, and use of data have become a central element of increasingly more sectors of contemporary political economy (Fourcade and Healy 2017; Sadowski 2018). Data is both valuable and value-creating. Just as we expect corporations to be profit-driven, we should now expect organizations to be data-driven. In other words, the drive to accumulate data now has a strong influence over decisions about business practices, political governance, and technology development. Smart urbanism is both a manifestation and intensification of data accumulation (Kitchin 2014). In short, this logic of accumulation—what Fourcade and Healy (2017) call the "data imperative"—demands the extraction of all data, from all sources, by any means possible. Fulfilling the data imperative involves more than just passively collecting data; it is an active creation of everything as data. This entails the (total) datafication and surveillance of people, places, processes, things, and relationships among them (van Dijck 2014; Sadowski and Pasquale 2015).

Consider, for instance, a project in Chicago called the "Array of Things," which describes itself as a "fitness tracker" for the city. According to the project's description, the array uses "a network of interactive, modular sensor boxes that will be installed around Chicago to collect real-time data on the city's environment, infrastructure, and activity for research and public use."[3] Through public-private initiatives like the Array of Things, Chicago is working to become a leader in data-driven urbanism. According to the Chicago Council of Global Affairs (2014: 5), many of the city's public sectors—like transportation, education, and policing—have been retooled to fit with Mayor Rahm Emanuel's "comprehensive plan for employing technology to improve the local economy and the quality of city services." Chicago is but one example of how smart urban governance opens up all parts of the city—its environment, citizens, planning, policy, economy—to the imperatives of data accumulation.

The data imperative can also be seen in the proliferation of urban dashboards, control rooms, and benchmarking practices that transform governance into a process of collecting, crunching, and comparing numbers. These technologies of governance are not only meant to be objective representations of *the city*, they also result in decision-makers establishing "an aspirational and competitive agenda for areas/cities in terms of their relative performance to other locales and thus can be used to motivate policy changes deemed necessary to alter their relative rating/ ranking" (Kitchin et al. 2015: 9). Moreover, under a data-driven regime the role of citizens, and their relationship to governance, is changed (Gabrys 2014). Their rights and obligations are modified so they adapt better to the demands of accumulation. As Rolien Hoyng (2016: 402) explains, in the context of a Turkish case study,

> "pro-active" citizens merely generated data that were fed into apparatuses of service by the state, which enjoyed exclusive data ownership and informational overview. Often citizens' behaviour was simply registered by sensors and cameras embedded in the urban landscape, conscious involvement and awareness of these processes were considered unneeded.

Scholars have recently analysed this data-driven regime in terms of "surveillance capitalism" (Zuboff 2015) and "platform capitalism" (Srnicek 2016). Yet, recognition of this changing political economy is not limited to critical academics; the business world is embracing the new systems of accumulation. According to a 2016 report by Oracle, one of the largest software companies in the world, and the magazine *MIT Technology Review*, "Data is now a form of capital, on the same level as financial capital in terms of generating new digital products and services" (Oracle and MIT Technology Review 2016). Smart urbanism is, arguably, the apotheosis of a project that is driven by the logic of financial capital and data capital. The smart city requires both kinds of capital to operate, while also constantly creating and collecting capital. It is the ultimate suite of "digital products and services" applied to the ultimate space of power and profit.

Wall Street has long argued that the accumulation and circulation of financial capital should be unimpeded; the so-called "technology evangelists" now draw the same conclusions about data capital. The connection between data accumulation and economic prosperity is now regularly asserted by governments and companies (Bildt 2015). Any restrictions on the flow of data—like laws about privacy, security, or democratic rights—are said to hinder economic growth and technological innovation. Just as financialization has been a major driver in how cities are developed (Fields 2017; Halbert and Attuyer 2016), datafication is now a major driver in how cities are governed.

A programme for alternative smart urbanism

Like other political projects, the smart city is a battle for our imagination. We should think of this model of smart urbanism—with its initiatives and ideologies, texts and technologies—as a campaign to direct and delimit what we can imagine as possible. The advocates and purveyors of this idea of the smart city do not set out a suite of scenarios that represent radically different visions and politics. There are variations to the services they offer, but rarely do they deviate from the technocratic and neoliberal precepts that underlie this vision of the smart urbanism. The aim is to establish their version of smartness as *the* future—the only one available or possible. By capturing the imagination of city leaders and decision-makers all other techno-political arrangements are effectively closed off.

Rather than allowing smart cities to reproduce austerity and accumulation, we should have higher expectations for how our cities—and our lives within them—are planned and managed. We need alternative forms of smart governance that are based on different values and goals. In this section, I sketch a framework that could inform social, political, and legal interventions for building a more just smart city. The following framework is more about guiding principles and places to focus our attention. There is much worth debating in what I propose, but rather than just describing all the ways it is insufficient or wrong, I challenge readers to refine this framework or offer counter-proposals. Roberto Unger rightfully observed that, "In the present climate, around the world, almost everything that can be proposed as an alternative will appear to be either utopian or trivial. Thus, our programmatic thinking is paralyzed" (quoted in Srnicek and Williams 2015: 69). My goal here is to kick-start more of the positive, programmatic work needed to reframe, reimagine, and remake the smart city.

When thinking about alternative frameworks, there is no need to start from scratch or try to reinvent the wheel. It might very well be unproductive and impractical to do so. It is, instead, useful to look at past policies and programmes that shared similar values and goals. These antecedents can serve as models of what to do, foundations to build on, and inspiration for new interventions. In what follows, I offer a framework called the "Digital Deal" that is loosely based on the New Deal, a programme of social democratic policies enacted in the US from 1933 to 1938. The programme instituted some of the most well-known policies in the US dealing with social services, labour regulations, financial oversight, and public works.[4]

The Digital Deal is outlined via what I call a *snapshot* of the near future written in the form of a brief about a new political platform. This snapshot is not a prediction, nor is it a fully fleshed out scenario, rather it is a glimpse of a plausible pathway for the future. Future-oriented exercises like this one can be useful conceptual tools that help us with the tough task of envisioning alternatives.

Snapshot: The Digital Deal

"A New Deal for the 21st Century." That is the slogan of the *Digital Deal*, a political platform spearheaded by a generation of leaders who grew up at the turn of the Millennium. They were born into a strange nexus of global events: the rapid rise of digital ICT, the aftermath of multiple financial crashes, the violence of neoliberal social policy, the spread of social justice movements. The outcomes and lessons of those events are imbued in the politics of people who knew no other world. The Digital Deal is, in many ways, a response to those events. It is the type of political project that many who grew up in this generation—savvy on technological issues, supporters of progressive causes, sceptical of corporate overreach—wanted to see decades earlier.

Like its predecessor from a century ago, the New Deal—which was modelled after three 'R's of Relief, Recovery, and Reform[5]—the Digital Deal advances a framework based on three 'P's of *Participation, Protection,* and *Progress.* Both of these platforms emerge from times of unequal societies and uneven power, where many, if not most, people feel left behind and jerked around. They are called "deals" because they are meant to be a pact between the government and the people. That is, a promise to shield people—especially those who are marginalized and under-privileged—from the excesses of cutthroat capitalism and set society on a path towards justice and prosperity. At the heart of the Digital Deal are three principles.

First, enhancing citizen *participation* and service provision through the use of smart government systems that can make radical, responsive democracy a reality. For example, rapid polling online is used to take the pulse of the population(s) on public issues; shared data portals provide citizens with up-to-date information and user-friendly interfaces; and social services are managed by cognitive computation systems, which ensure individuals quickly and effectively benefit from the assistance they have a right to receive. Once agencies migrated over to a singular governance platform, the operations of government became much more efficient and accessible. Not just accessible as in the platform is easy to use or easy to understand, but accessible in terms of citizens actually having access to the government. Through the participatory platform, government's ability to meaningfully collate and use public input has greatly improved. These policies and initiatives start with the recognition that democratic participation requires public engagement, public access, and public assistance. Otherwise participation becomes a privilege, not a right.

Second, instituting *protections* that recognize the realities of people living in a networked, datafied world. We are constantly interacting with spies, sprites, and sniffers that are accumulating and circulating data about people. Our analogue and digital environments are now full of them. New safeguards cannot operate on a dualism of online and offline, nor can they discount the effects of actions that happen on digital platforms. Rules for collecting, storing, sharing, and using data must provide strict oversight of data systems and accountability of their owners. In the past, such protections were typically categorized in terms of privacy vs. security. Now we see these issues are not just about shielding individuals and stopping hackers. They are technopolitical issues of power and design—whose values, who's included, who benefits. Moreover, long-needed updates to labour laws now grant people stronger rights in our digital, datafied world. By accounting for new forms of exploitation and extraction, strict limitations are put on the ability of companies to profit from the digital labour and personal data of users without proper compensation and meaningful consent. When data is a form of capital, then appropriating data from others is theft.

Third, steering technology towards social *progress* by promoting projects that contribute to making the world a more just, equitable, prosperous place—instead of reflecting the desires of privileged groups and imperatives of profit. Ignoring technology is not an option; nor is surrendering its design and implementation to the interests of elites. We must create new innovations which embody different ideals of social and political life, and in ways that are informed by participatory input and iterative feedback. Achieving this goal involves an ensemble of initiatives, such as: incentives via R&D funding for the private sector to develop and deploy different technologies; standards and support for engaging with socio-political concerns and integrating ethical values into the R&D process; and audits used to analyse transformative technologies, ensure any hidden values/biases are made explicit, and issue advice for redesigning the technology. These initiatives are a form of soft governance. They do not restrict the design, deployment, and adoption of technologies. Rather, through guidance and resources, they exert pressures that promote the development of progressive technologies.

Information technologies have gone through many waves. The Digital Deal offers a framework for building the next wave and ensuring it provides everybody with the social support and political resources needed to fully participate in a truly smart society.

Conclusion

I have argued that smart urban governance—especially the corporatized model that has become dominant—is largely driven by two logics: austerity and accumulation. Recognizing the motivations and goals of smart governance is a crucial step towards understanding this increasingly influential model of urbanism. However, while my analysis helps us to explain and interpret the smart city, it is not enough to know more clearly how the techno-politics operate.

We need to challenge and change the smart city. In doing so, we have to challenge ourselves to think seriously about alternative arrangements. We need frameworks and initiatives that address inequality and exclusion, while also doing more than just alleviating these harms. We need processes and services that empower people who feel repressed by their cities, rather than embraced by them. We need to appropriate and innovate smart city technologies that are encoded with different values. "We need to create a particular kind of smart city that has a set of ethical principles and values at its heart" (Kitchin 2016: 60). None of this is easy—as any radical thinker who has tried to be critical *and* positive can attest—but it is necessary.

I have attempted to provide a possible path for developing these interventions by sketching a platform, the Digital Deal, which could serve as the foundation for new policies. The point is not to create an airtight or exhaustive framework. We will not get anywhere if that is the bar we set. Instead, the point is to be imaginative and generative, to offer alternative ideas that challenge dominant models of neoliberal smart urbanism. Only then will we be able to go beyond understanding the smart city, and begin redesigning it according to our own specifications.

Notes

1 The term "regime" is intentional and, as Langdon Winner argues, appropriate to use here: "For once they have been designed, built and put in operation, sociotechnical systems comprise regimes with features that can be described in a political way. It makes perfect sense to talk about freedom or its absence, equality or inequality, justice or injustice, authoritarianism or democracy, and the kinds of power relationships contained in technological instruments and systems" (Winner 1991: 20).

2 Indeed, as I was editing this chapter Sidewalk Labs and the city of Toronto announced a new project together. Sidewalk Labs will be developing a waterfront district, which will serve as a test-bed for it to experiment with new smart systems and urban planning techniques (Bozikovic 2017).

3 Array of Things. Accessed February 8, 2016: https://arrayofthings.github.io/

4 For the purposes of this chapter, there is no need (or space) to go into detail about the history and politics of the New Deal. For more on the development, details, and impact of the New Deal see Leuchtenburg (2009).

5 The three 'R's referred to the general goals of *relief* for the poor, *recovery* of the economy, and *reform* of the financial sector.

References

Alizadeh, T. 2017. "An Investigation of IBM's Smarter Cities Challenge: What Do Participating Cities Want?" *Cities* 63 (March): 70–80.

Bildt, C. 2015. "EU Should Resist Urge to Rig the Rules of Cyber Space." *Financial Times.* Accessed 9 October 2017: https://www.ft.com/content/5d626a4e-f182-11e4-88b0-00144feab7de.

Bozikovic, A. 2017. "Google's Sidewalk Labs Signs Deal for 'Smart City' Makeover of Toronto's Waterfront." *The Globe and Mail*, 17 October. Accessed 30 October 2017: https://beta.theglobeandmail.com/news/toronto/google-sidewalk-toronto-waterfront/article36612387/.

Brown, W. 2015. *Undoing the Demos: Neoliberalism's Stealth Revolution.* Cambridge, MA: MIT Press.

Bulkeley, H., McGuirk, P.M. and Dowling, R. 2016. "Making a Smart City for the Smart Grid? The Urban Material Politics of Actualising Smart Electricity Networks." *Environment and Planning A* 48(9): 1709–1726.

Cardullo, P., Kitchin, R. and Feliciantonio, C.D. 2018. "Living Labs and Vacancy in the Neoliberal City." *Cities* 73 (March): 44–50.

Chicago Council of Global Affairs. 2014. *The Emerging Power of Big Data: The Chicago Experience.* Accessed 30 October 2017: http://www.thechicagocouncil.org/publication/emerging-power-big-data-chicago-experience.

Clark, R.Y. 2013. "Smart Cities and the Internet of Everything: The Foundation for Delivering Next-Generation Citizen Services." IDC Government Insights (sponsored by Cisco). https://smartcitiescouncil.com/resources/smart-cities-and-internet-everything-foundation-delivering-next-generation-citizen-services.

Evans, D. 2012. "The Internet of Everything: How More Relevant and Valuable Connections Will Change the World." Cisco Internet Business Solutions Group. https://www.cisco.com/c/dam/global/vi_vn/assets/ciscoinnovate/pdfs/IoE.pdf.

Fields, D. 2017. "Urban Struggles with Financialization." *Geography Compass.* doi:10.1111/gec3.12334.

Fleming, M., Dencik, J., and Forcke, A.-R. 2015. "Economic Vitality: Prosperity and Public Engagement in the Data-Driven Economy." IBM Public Sector. Accessed 9 August 2018: http://aspheramedia.com/wp-content/uploads/2015/12/GVW03052USEN.pdf.

Fourcade, M. and Healy, K. 2017. "Seeing Like a Market." *Socio-Economic Review* 15(1): 9–29.

Gabrys, J. 2014. "Programming Environments: Environmentality and Citizen Sensing in the Smart City." *Environment and Planning D: Society and Space* 32(1): 30–48.

Goldsmith, S. and Crawford, S. 2014. *The Responsive City: Engaging Communities Through Data-Smart Governance.* San Francisco: Jossey-Bass.

Goldsmith, S. and Kleiman, N. 2018. "Cities Should Act More Like Amazon to Better Serve Their Citizens." *Next City*, 23 January. Accessed 5 April 2018: https://nextcity.org/daily/entry/cities-should-act-more-like-amazon-to-better-serve-their-citizens.

Greenfield, A. 2013. *Against the Smart City.* New York: Do Projects.

Halbert, L. and Attuyer, K. 2016. "Introduction: The Financialisation of Urban Production: Conditions, Mediations and Transformations." *Urban Studies* 53(7): 1347–1361.

Harris, M. 2016. "Secretive Alphabet Division Funded by Google Aims to Fix Public Transit in US." *The Guardian*, 27 June. Accessed 30 October 2017: https://www.theguardian.com/technology/2016/jun/27/google-flow-sidewalk-labs-columbus-ohio-parking-transit.

Ho, E. 2017. "Smart Subjects for a Smart Nation? Governing (Smart)mentalities in Singapore." *Urban Studies* 54(13): 3101–3118.

Hodgkinson, S. 2011. "Is Your City Smart Enough? Digitally Enabled Cities and Societies Will Enhance Economic, Social, and Environmental Sustainability in the Urban Century." A report by Ovum (sponsored by Cisco). Accessed 9 August 2018: https://www.cisco.com/c/dam/en_us/solutions/industries/docs/Is_your_city_smart_enough-Ovum_Analyst_Insights.pdf.

Hollands, R.G. 2015. "Critical Interventions into the Corporate Smart City." *Cambridge Journal of Regions, Economy and Society* 8: 61–77.

Hoyng, R. 2016. "From Infrastructural Breakdown to Data Vandalism: Repoliticizing the Smart City?" *Television & New Media* 17(5): 397–415.

IBM. 2012. "The Foundations of Efficiency: Learning to do More with Less is the New Normal in Government." IBM Smarter Government.

Kitchin, R. 2014. "The Real-Time City? Big Data and Smart Urbanism." *GeoJournal* 79: 1–14.

Kitchin, R. 2016. *Getting Smarter About Smart Cities: Improving Data Privacy and Data Security.* Dublin, Ireland: Data Protection Unit, Department of the Taoiseach.

Kitchin, R., Lauriault, T.P. and McArdle, G. 2015. "Knowing and Governing Cities Through Urban Indicators, City Benchmarking and Real-Time Dashboards." *Regional Studies, Regional Science* 2(1): 6–28.

Leszczynski, A. 2016. "Speculative Futures: Cities, Data, and Governance Beyond Smart Urbanism." *Environment and Planning A* 48(9): 1691–1708.

Leuchtenburg, W.E. 2009. *Franklin D. Roosevelt and the New Deal: 1932–1940.* New York: Harper Perennial.

Levenda, A.M., Mahmoudi, D. and Sussman, G. 2015. "The Neoliberal Politics of 'Smart': Electricity Consumption, Household Monitoring, and the Enterprise Form." *Canadian Journal of Communication* 40: 615–636.

Luque-Ayala, A. and Marvin, S. 2016. "The Maintenance of Urban Circulation." *Environment and Planning D: Society and Space* 34(2): 191–208.

McFarlane, C. and Söderström, O. 2017. "On Alternative Smart Cities: From a Technology-Intensive to a Knowledge-Intensive Smart Urbanism." *City* 21(3–4): 312–328.

McNeill, D. 2015. "Global Firms and Smart Technologies: IBM and the Reduction of Cities." *Transactions of the Institute of British Geographers* 40(4): 562–574.

McNeil, D. 2017. "Start-Ups and the Entrepreneurial City." *City* 21(2): 232–239.

Morozov, E. and Bria, F. 2018. *Rethinking the Smart City: Democratizing Urban Technology.* New York: Rosa Luxemburg Stiftung.

Oracle and MIT Technology Review. 2016. *The Rise of Data Capital.* Accessed 9 October 2017: http://files.technologyreview.com/whitepapers/MIT_Oracle+Report- The_Rise_of_Data_Capital.pdf.

Pollio, A. 2016. "Technologies of Austerity Urbanism: The 'Smart City' Agenda in Italy (2011–2013)." *Urban Geography* 37(4): 514–534.

Sadowski, J. 2017. "Google Wants to Run Cities Without Being Elected. Don't Let It." *The Guardian*, 24 October. Accessed 5 April 2018: https://www.theguardian.com/commentisfree/2017/oct/24/google-alphabet-sidewalk-labs-toronto.

Sadowski, J. 2018. "When Data is Capital: Datafication, Accumulation, Appropriation." Unpublished Manuscript (on file with author).

Sadowski, J. and Bendor, R. 2018. "Selling Smartness: Corporate Narratives and the Smart City as a Sociotechnical Imaginary." Unpublished Manuscript (on file with author).

Sadowski, J. and Pasquale, F. 2015. "The Spectrum of Control: A Social Theory of the Smart City." *First Monday* 20(7). Available at: http://firstmonday.org/article/view/5903/4660.

Söderström, O., Paasche, T. and Klauser, F. 2014. "Smart Cities as Corporate Storytelling." *City* 18(3): 307–320.

Srnicek, N. 2016. *Platform Capitalism*. Cambridge: Polity Press.

Srnicek, N. and Williams, A. 2015. *Inventing the Future: Postcapitalism and a World Without Work*. London: Verso.

van Dijck, José. 2014. "Datafication, Dataism and Dataveillance: Big Data Between Scientific Paradigm and Ideology." *Surveillance & Society* 12(2): 197–208.

White, J.M. 2016. "Anticipatory Logics of the Smart City's Global Imaginary." *Urban Geography* 37(4): 572–589.

Wiig, A. 2015. "The Empty Rhetoric of the Smart City: From Digital Inclusion to Economic Promotion in Philadelphia." *Urban Geography* 37(4): 535–553.

Wiig, A. 2017. "Secure the City, Revitalize the Zone: Smart Urbanization in Camden, New Jersey." *Environment and Planning C: Politics and Space*. doi:10.1177/2399654417743767.

Winner, L. 1991. "Artifact/Ideas and Political Culture." *Whole Earth Review* (Winter): 18–24.

Zuboff, S. 2015. "Big Other: Surveillance Capitalism and the Prospects of an Information Civilization." *Journal of Information Technology* 30: 75–89.

3

POLITICISING SMART CITY STANDARDS

James Merricks White

Introduction

Critical literature on smart cities has been taken to task for being ahistorical (Kitchin 2015) and for failing to engage with "actually existing" smart city policies and technologies (Shelton, Zook, and Wiig 2015). Somewhat at odds to this, the present collection attempts to redress the scarcity of positive, normative or speculative statements on what another smart city might involve. In this chapter, I aim to politicise the smart city not by playing out an alternate vision for its future, but by excavating the contingent and contested history of ideas which underlie one of its present technologies. My subtext is a different but related challenge: how to create smart cities without abandoning a post-structural framework. I attempt to achieve this by reinforcing existing but minority arguments in order to broaden the political spectrum of smart city standards.

The paper is structured in three parts. I begin by introducing smart city standards through an engagement with a strategy document of the International Organization of Standardization (ISO). Two questions guide my analysis: what do smart city standards attempt to standardise? and, what do they hope to achieve by doing so? In the second section, I trace three orders which grant meaning to smart city standards—systems theory, neoliberal rationality and urban governance—and give an example of a standard which adheres to them. Supposing that these together comprise a field of possibilities, in the final section I expose three extant arguments which challenge the most prominent assumptions and logics on this field. In doing this, my desire is to open up space for another smart city.

What do smart city standards standardise and why?

Smart city standards are an emerging phenomenon. In February 2014, the Technical Management Board of ISO established a strategic advisory group (SAG) to investigate opportunities for the international standardisation of smart cities (International Organization for Standardization 2014b, resolution 36). The group was made up of representatives from major national standards bodies (including the British, American and Chinese) and was chaired by an experienced quality management auditor, Graham Colclough. In September 2015, after more than a year of lively debate, the final SAG report was submitted to the Technical Management Board (International Organization for Standardization 2015). The report has since been used to help co-ordinate standardisation efforts within ISO, and to guide the organisation's collaboration with the International Electrotechnical Committee and the International Telecommunications Union.

The report identifies a need for smart city standards to function less as technical specifications, and more as leadership guides and management frameworks. Concise, well-written guides are needed to impress upon city leaders the benefits of smart cities and promote best practices in their implementation. Management frameworks are necessary for co-ordinating change by facilitating communication between government departments. During my interview with SAG Chair, Graham Colclough, he stressed the importance of high-level standards in facilitating management across the city as a whole.

> So, if you like, we've managed the domains, the verticals of cities through cutting budgets over the last decade or more (and so they are reasonably efficient, there is … a lot to go still), but what we haven't done is actually deal with what is going across the city. So, therefore the management framework layer provides an organising framework, a means by which the manager of the social services and the manager of place and parking and roads can have a structured dialogue, whereby they actually look at the same picture and recognise the interdependencies.
>
> (Graham Colclough, November 11, 2015)

Thus, technical standards address issues of infrastructural and departmental specialisation, management frameworks operate horizontally across the city as a whole, and leadership guides present decision makers with tools to drive systemic organisational change. In stressing the latter two types of standards, it is clear that the report seeks to advance the standardisation of governance practices rather than information technologies.

According to the SAG, smart city standards ought not standardise cities or the technologies of which they are composed. Instead, their aim should be to promote certain kinds of behaviour amongst city leaders and administrators. The justification for this is connected to the group's overall aims.

The report concludes by identifying a mismatch between supply and demand in the market for city services and technologies. Cities are held to be too numerous, too modestly sized, and too individualistic to act as consistent and stable consumers. This has led to market fragmentation. The report positions smart city standards as a way in which this might be addressed. As a third party, ISO has an opportunity to act as a trusted mediator, supporting "open choice for city buyers and an attractive market for suppliers" (International Organization for Standardization 2015, 38). To this end, the document recommends that ISO expand into areas deemed attractive to cities (such as financing, business models, performance assessment, strategic roadmaps, management frameworks and leadership guides) and that it be more proactive in promoting its standards at international smart city events.

By steering ISO towards leadership guides and management frameworks, the SAG hope to mediate the relationship between supply and demand in the market for city services and technologies. The logic proceeds in two steps. The first is to promote management tools for small and medium sized city governments. Rather than rely upon the personalised services of market research and assurance firms, cities will be able to turn to affordable, reliable and flexible documents developed by leading global experts. The goal is to harmonise and regularise city governance internationally. This leads on to the second step. By bringing city leaders and managers into alignment with best practice, ISO will help generate more consistent and stable consumer demand, thereby reducing marketplace fragmentation. The smart cities market will thus be nurtured into a more active and mature form.

Orders of meaning and action

Having teased out a general statement on what smart city standards are and hope to achieve, I want to now describe some of their conditioning apparatuses. Consistent with Barad's (2007) agential realism, I conceive of meaningful actions and utterances as emergent from a field of possibilities. This field is not static, regular and boundless. Rather, its terrain is uneven and in flux, continually worked and reworked by heterogeneous ensembles of things, people, institutions and their productive relations. In order to map out the field of possibilities, it is necessary to identify and describe the orders of meaning which give it shape. Three such orders, or apparatuses, will be the focus of this section: systems theory, neoliberal rationality and urban governance. I will briefly trace their origins, state their main aims and assumptions, and offer an illustrative example of their productive capacity in a published smart city standard.

Systems theory

Systems theory is a catch-all term for a variety of complex, ongoing and often conflicting domains of engineering and scientific knowledge production. While its origins can be traced to late nineteenth century physics, systems theory really established itself in the post-war US research funding climate (Mirowski 1997; Heyck 2015). It consists of three core traditions: the management practices of systems engineering, operations research and systems analysis (Fortun and Schweber 1993; Hughes 1998; Hughes and Hughes 2000); the ecological mind-set of general systems theory (Hammond 2002, 2003); and the information and communication theories of cybernetics (Richardson 1991; Heims 1993). These sciences all take as their primary ontological unit an open or closed system whose function emerges from the interaction of its parts. Early system scientists attempted to identify the specific feedback mechanisms through which the homeostasis of a system was maintained (Hayles 1999). The concept of control was used to describe both the achievement and the manipulation of the steady-state operation of any system. Analytically, systems theory prioritises function over form; its mode of analysis endeavours to be explanatory rather than descriptive. It tends to be a teleological and at times even deterministic world view.

The infiltration of systems theory into urban thinking follows a number of trajectories. Its influence can be identified in geography's quantitative revolution (Barnes and Farish 2006), to which Berry's (1964) paper "Cities as systems within systems of cities" made a seminal contribution. From there it crept into urban planning (Wilson 1968), where it dovetailed with the sociological tradition of structural functionalism (Scott and Roweis 1977; Gregory 1980). It is an important precursor to Forrester's (1961, 1969) system dynamics, in which the city was modelled as a dynamical system using metaphors of stocks and flows, and mechanisms of internal feedback loops and time delays. The spirit of this work persists in ongoing efforts to develop a rigorous science of cities using quantitative and mathematical techniques (Batty 2013; Bettencourt 2013). Additionally, aspects of systems theory were an important inspiration to the formative works of urban design, especially Jacobs (1961) and Alexander (1964, 1965). In architecture, it found expression in a paper by Pask (1969) and then through the work of Negroponte (1970, 1975). In urban government and policy its influence has long been recognised (Hoos 1972; Lilienfeld 1978) and given appropriate historical treatment (Light 2003, 2008).

Drawing on the organic metaphor of the city as a body, the foundational standard of the City Protocol Society (CPS) strives to establish "a common language" for discussing, evaluating and transforming cities (City Protocol Society 2015). The city is understood as "a system of systems" (a body and its organs) separated into structures and society (see Figure 3.1). Structures include nature (positioned strictly outside the city and as a concentration of resources), infrastructures (circulatory systems supportive of urban life), and the built environment (a set of scalar relations between dwellings, buildings, blocks, neighbourhoods and so on). Society encompasses citizens and the government, and the various institutions they form. At the intersection of these two material layers lie a set of interactions: the economy, culture, functions (such as living, working, shopping, healthcare and education) and information (that is, the city indicators and operating system that CPS hope to develop in the future). These are declared to be the essential elements which make up any and every city. By using the standard and by speaking across urban systems and scales, all city stakeholders are empowered to: "connect and/or break city silos" (City Protocol Society 2015, ii), develop projects collaboratively and share knowledge on effective solutions. In its epistemological focus on city systems and their function, and in its normative desire for systemic communication and integration, the City Anatomy reveals its debt to systems theory.

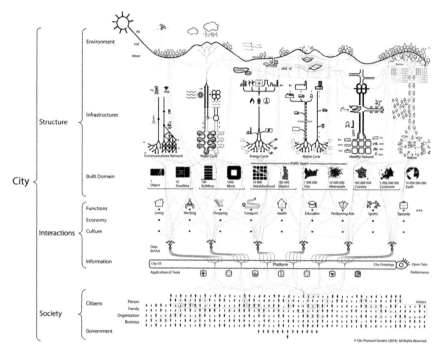

FIGURE 3.1 Visualisation of the City Anatomy, used with permission of CPS

Neoliberal rationality

Neoliberalism is often used as a broad pejorative for free market capitalism. Following a recent body of scholarship (usefully summarised by Davies 2014), I reject this use in favour of an engagement with intellectual origins, assumptions, logics and ethics. Neoliberal thought has been reinterpreted in the context of its continuity and dislocation with classical liberalism, its internal contingencies and inconsistencies (i.e., its differential expression by Austrian, Freiburg, Chicago and Virginia schools), and the think tanks responsible for devising and popularising neoliberal policies (Foucault 2008; Mirowski and Plehwe 2009; Peck 2010; Burgin 2012; Jones 2012; Gane 2013; Davies 2017).

Two broad phases of thought can be identified. Early neoliberal thinker Hayek (1944, 1945) argued that the economy is an ordered system composed of so many interconnected variables that it lies beyond the comprehension of any individual planner or centralised authority. Rather than act to distribute goods and services, the state should steward the market economy, ensuring its proper structure and correcting against market failure (such as monopoly formation and negative externalities). Later neoliberal thinkers, Coase (1960) and Stigler (1971), critiqued the legitimacy of the state to make judicial and regulatory decisions in the interest of preserving competition. Both authors argued that microeconomic assumptions and calculations rather than classical liberal values ought to be used to assess the necessity of intervention. This had two effects. The first was to limit the frequency with which the state acted on the market. The second was to displace a political logic by an economic one.

Putting the two phases together, I understand neoliberalisation to involve the withdrawal of the state from the (re)distribution of goods and services, a curbing of its role in the correction of market failure, and an increase in the use of micro-economic logics, assumptions and models in the organisation of political institutions. Liberalisation and marketisation are an important aspect of neoliberal reform, but they do not capture what makes it distinct from neoclassical economics (Jones 2012). That lies in the reconfiguration of social and political life as a domain of economic analysis (Foucault 2008; Brown 2015). Examples of neoliberalism at work include the explicit use of incentive structures within government organisations to steer behaviour towards the rational ideal of *homo economicus* (Ferlie et al. 1996), as well as the nudging, prodding and prompting that increasingly occurs when behaviour deviates from that ideal (Davies 2015).

British standard PAS 181 can be understood as a tool for deepening the neoliberalisation of city government. It presents itself as a leadership guide, offering "practical, 'how-to' advice, reflecting current good practice as identified by a broad range of public, private and voluntary sector practitioners" (British Standards Institution 2014, 2). These practices express a neoliberal logic however. PAS 181 positions cities as being burdened by their vertically-integrated, functionally-specialised substructures. In response, it envisages a number of "agile, cross-city, virtual franchise businesses ... that sit within the existing delivery structures of the city" (British Standards Institution 2014, 8). Narrowly-focused teams act across the system of systems with a project-based remit (see Figure 3.2). Here, the matrix management practices of large corporations are proposed as a solution to the functional problem of cities. More than this however, the standard also encourages the marketisation of city services. Throughout the document, cities are normalised as "best practice retailers" (British Standards Institution 2014, 32); rather than public service *providers*, local councils become public service *commissioners*. Conceived as such, the role of government is to encourage a marketplace of options from which users (that is, the voting public) can choose whatever solution best fits their particular needs and buying power.

Urban governance

Governance is more a concept than an explicit tradition of academic thought. While it is often used as a synonym for government, I want to emphasise a different and more specific meaning. Since the 1990s, governance has also been used to refer to decentred and distributed forms of governing (Jessop 1995; Rhodes 1996; Stoker 1998). The management and co-ordination of society is no longer understood to be the sole responsibility of a cohesive political core, but the result of action amongst a dispersed network of government, industry and civil society actors. This has not occurred by accident, but in response to the perceived complexities of the contemporary world (Walters 2004) and the shortcomings of earlier (neoliberal) efforts to respond to them by limiting the role of the state (Bevir 2010). Put succinctly, markets are out and networks are in. The public sector has

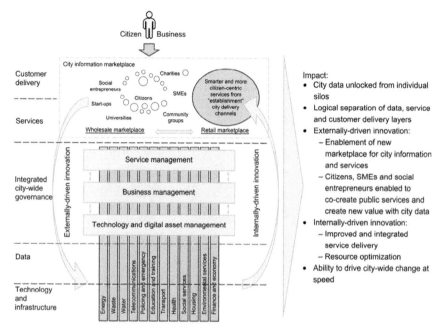

Customer delivery

City information marketplace

Social entrepreneurs   Charities

Start-ups   Citizens   SMEs

Universities   Community groups

Smarter and more citizen-centric services from "establishment" city delivery channels

Services

Wholesale marketplace   Retail marketplace

Integrated city-wide governance

Externally-driven innovation

Service management

Business management

Technology and digital asset management

Internally-driven innovation

Data

Energy   Waste   Water   Telecommunications   Policing and emergency   Education and training   Transport   Health   Social services   Housing   Environmental services   Finance and economy

Technology and infrastructure

Impact:
- City data unlocked from individual silos
- Logical separation of data, service and customer delivery layers
- Externally-driven innovation:
  - Enablement of new marketplace for city information and services
  - Citizens, SMEs and social entrepreneurs enabled to co-create public services and create new value with city data
- Internally-driven innovation:
  - Improved and integrated service delivery
  - Resource optimization
- Ability to drive city-wide change at speed

FIGURE 3.2 Vision of an integrated operating model for smart cities. Reproduced from British Standards Institution (2014, 15).

been rearranged to involve "'less government' (or less rowing) but 'more governance' (or more steering)" (Rhodes 1996, 655). In Jessop's view, its role has become one of metagovernance, "coordinating different forms of governance and ensuring a minimal coherence among them" (Jessop 1997, 574).

The concept of governance is used slightly differently by different academic disciplines and policy areas: urban studies favour urban governance; international relations, global governance; the World Bank, good governance; and finance and management, corporate governance (Walters 2004). In his genealogy of the term, Bevir (2010) locates its origins in rational choice theory, the new institutionalism, systems theory and regulation theory. While their particular concerns and perspectives differ, these approaches all share a recognition of the complexity and rapid change brought on by global finance and information technologies, an understanding that contemporary power is diffuse (rather than centralised or sovereign), and a preference for self-organising networks (as opposed to the state or unfettered market) as a model for social organisation.

ISO 37120 is a set of 100 performance indicators for measuring, benchmarking and evaluating the sustainability of cities globally (International Organization for Standardization 2014a). Initially developed under a World Bank funded research project, the standard was fast-tracked through ISO and published in 2014. The document sets out definitions for each of the indicators, describes the data needed to meet them and offers suggestions as to how those data might be sourced. ISO 37120's indicators are broken into 17 themes (intended to reflect the critical infrastructure and services of cities) and two types (core, encompassing all those data points which cities should to be able to collect, and supplementary, which are anticipated to pose more of a difficulty). Certification is achieved through an independent process conducted by the World Council on City Data (n.d.; WCCD), a non-profit spin-off from the University of Toronto. Cities are audited to assure the veracity and provenance of their submitted data, and are awarded a certification level contingent on the number of data points they are able to provide (see Figure 3.3).

ISO 37120	ISO 37120	ISO 37120	ISO 37120	ISO 37120
WORLD COUNCIL ON CITY DATA	WORLD COUNCIL ON CITY DATA	WORLD COUNCIL ON CITY DATA	WORLD COUNCIL ON CITY DATA	WORLD COUNCIL ON CITY DATA
Aspirational	**Bronze**	**Silver**	**Gold**	**Platinum**
30-45	**46-59**	**60-75**	**76-90**	**91-100**
Core indicator	Indicators (46 Core + 0-13 Supporting)	Indicators (46 Core + 14-29 Supporting)	Indicators (46 Core + 30-44 Supporting)	Indicators (46 Core + 45-54 Supporting)

FIGURE 3.3 ISO 37120 certification levels. Reproduced from World Council on City Data (n.d.).

The president and CEO of WCCD, Patricia McCarney, participated in the governance debates within development studies during the early 2000s (McCarney 2000, 2003). With ISO 37120, she is putting theory into practice. This is evident in its extra-governmental origins, in its global aspirations, and in its promotion of urban bench-marking and knowledge exchange. There is a well-established literature exploring the connection between international standards and the rise of governance practices (Brunsson and Jacobsson 2000; Higgins and Larner 2010; Ponte, Gibbon, and Vester-gaard 2011). What ISO 37120 reveals is the degree to which this is presently occurring at the level of local and urban government.

Each of the three conditioning apparatuses of systems theory, neoliberal rationality and urban governance grant form and meaning to smart city standards. As a body of unfolding material and discursive practices, they adhere to specific logics and assumptions without being perfectly consistent or consequential. When brought together, they sometimes reinforce one another and at other times produce tensions and outright conflicts. The result is an apparent mess of meanings, contradictions and possible positions. But my conceptualisation of the field of possibilities for smart city standards also presents opportunities for political engagement and intervention. It is to this that I now turn.

Reconfiguring the field of possibilities

Rather than impose upon those involved in smart city standards my opinions or recommendations as a somehow external, somehow disinterested expert, in this section I call attention to existing but minority positions in order to broaden the extent of the field's politics. In pursuing this strategy I take my lead from feminist scholars (such as Hayles 1996; Kember 2003) who, in the context of the mid-1990s dispute between natural science and cultural studies, attempted to engage ethically and politically with their research topic without abandoning a poststructuralist epistemology. It is worth developing what this means in the case of smart city standards.

I recognise that the field of possibilities from which voluntary standards emerge is uneven, its surface marred by contradiction and conflict. In the previous section, I interpreted three smart city standards as an expression of a *particular* apparatus or order of meaning—systems theory for City Protocol Anatomy, neoliberal rationality for BSI PAS 181 and urban governance for ISO 37120—wherein assumptions and logics are adhered to in order to maintain internal coherence and consistency. Nevertheless, aspects of *all* of these orders (and more besides) are identifiable within each of the published standards. Standards making is an intensely political act, during which ideas about how the world is, and how the world ought to be, inevitably come to affect the final artefact. But the politics of a standard do not cease with its publication. Through circulation and implementation, a standard both relies upon and reinforces its conditioning apparatuses, reworking their terms in subtle but nonetheless significant ways. As such, I consider smart city standards to be open, in that their meanings and materialisations are malleable through judgement and critique. I also consider them to be a site of important political engagement. Not only have standards the potential to affect how the smart cities phenomenon plays out, but through their constant repetition they allow for interventions within the field of possibilities. Thus, instead of making statements based upon an entirely foreign set of values and assumptions, I will press upon extant positions in an attempt to fashion alliances between myself and my interlocutors. My immediate aim is to expand the metaphysics, ethics and politics of standards development.

The remainder of the section describes three arguments that were encountered during my interviews. These are: an invitation to think with non-linear rather than linear systems; a suspicion of the logic of silo busting; and a priority for local indicators rather than global benchmarking. Each of these arguments queries a core supposition of one (or more) of the material-discursive apparatuses.

The more teleological and deterministic areas of systems theory are linked to a tendency to treat the system not as a prop to think about the world, but as an essence that transcends and precedes worldly manifestation. Hayles (1999) conceives this as a shift from the Platonic backhand to the Platonic forehand. With the Platonic backhand, data are drawn upon to infer simplified abstractions. In the case of the City Anatomy, observations about the form and function of urban infrastructure are used to develop a model for thinking about cities in general. All theorising necessarily involves this movement. The problem occurs when the abstraction is treated as an authentic and inceptive form, such that "complexity appears as a 'fuzzing up' of an essential reality rather than as a manifestation of the world's holistic nature" (Hayles 1999, 12). As such, "system" is no longer a metaphor for thinking about the city, but the city is actually treated as an expression of an essential system (or system of systems). When this shift occurs, the model becomes a real simulation of how things unfold. The city is granted purpose and its state becomes predictable.

Rather than attempt to undo this logic by exposing it to metaphysical critique, a more effective move is to call attention to a counter-trend within systems theory: namely, complexity theory (Gleick 1987; Waldrop 1992). Here, the system is conceived as open rather than closed (such that it exists within an environment with which it exchanges matter, energy and information) and the dynamics are understood to be non-linear rather than linear (such that a model's variables do not change at an even rate with respect to one another). Bringing complexity theory to thinking on urban systems does not undermine the Platonic forehand, but it does work against its effects. When the city is conceived as open rather than closed, it is understood to have an active and interactive relationship with its immediate environment. Mutual exchange rather than self-sufficiency is prioritised. When the model of the city is based on non-linear dynamics, it becomes highly dependent upon initial conditions. Slight changes in input values will, with time, produce wildly different outputs. This undermines the determinacy of systems theory and significantly alters what can be said about its purpose.

One of the pivotal members of City Protocol Society thinks about systems in this way. For this person, the dynamics of cities are inherently non-linear and therefore predictable only over a short period of time. But this does not mean that it is useless to model them.

> I thought if a city is a non-linear system (a highly non-linear system of systems and interactions), then there should be strange attractors, which in a city will not be like something that you have to imagine in a multi-dimensional space as a vector, but something that physically exists. Then you realise that strange attractors in cities are their public spaces.... [S]quares, parks, recreational areas, where people meet and ... develop a sense of community by interaction.
>
> *(Acting Chair of the Board of the City Protocol Society, September 14, 2016)*

Rather than use the model to determine how the city will behave and thus how it can be controlled, my interlocutor is suggesting that modelling can be used to inform planning for the use of public spaces. When complexity is introduced to the application of systems theory to cities, the result is a more modest appreciation of the kinds of outcomes that can be achieved.

The imperative to bust departmental silos in favour of a holistic and integrated approach is common to all three examples of smart city standards. There are however differences in how the broader apparatuses engage with the problem. Systems theory undermines the Cartesian apprehension of discrete, preformed objects in space by foregrounding functional coordination. When everything is a system, bureaucratic specialisation is perceived as a suboptimal way to organise and control activities. A more effective response would be in keeping with the order and purpose of the city as a dynamic, interactive whole. Neoliberalism is largely ambivalent about what form a government takes, focusing instead on how it can proliferate and improve competition. On the one hand, this confers a suspicion of publicly run utilities and a preference for their liberalisation. For the neoliberal, city silos engaged in the provision of services should be broken up and replaced by a marketplace of private providers. On the other hand, the neoliberal is also inclined to impress the logic of the market onto the public sector. Thus, corporate management tools can be used to decrease costs within and between government departments (either by creating incentive structures in keeping with economically rational behaviour, or by decreasing the amount of time spent on deciding what to do and how to do it). Finally, the frame of governance perceives the silo as an outdated organisational form that is unable to deal with the complexity of the contemporary world. Here, the inefficiency is not functional or economic, but managerial. By creating divisions within a city government, knowledge becomes specialised at the expense of the cohesion and responsiveness of the city as a whole. A diffuse network of state and non-state actors is a far better way to respond to complex problems.

In questioning the assumed logic of silo busting, my purpose is not to impede the capacity of a city to organise its services or respond to threats. Rather, I see this argument as tied to efforts to deliberately undermine trust in the ability of government employees to serve the public interest. I do not take it for granted that competition is always the best way to organise distribution. Nor do I consider dispersed, loosely coordinated action the only way to solve dynamic, multifaceted problems. As such, my resistance to the argument of silo busting is a resistance to the automatic deferral to markets and networks—which, I believe, typically represent fewer people and are less accountable than a democratically elected government.

Two suspicions of silo busting arose in my interviews. The first took the form of an appeal to evidence-based policy. Rather than assume that a holistic approach would be more efficient than bureaucratic specialisation, one smart cities professional urged for caution and for the development of quantitative evaluation mechanisms.

> Frankly speaking, no one knows if these famous integrated projects (or integrated approach) that we always say that a smart city project should have, that if this approach works or delivers something, or what exactly does it deliver … We really don't know, I think, or we don't have yet a proven way to measure or prove or evaluate … what an integrated project means and what does it deliver.
>
> (EUROCITIES smart cities project co-ordinator, May 24, 2017)

Put differently, integration is only warranted if and when there is a solid case for it, based on the best available data. I interpret this scepticism as a form of scientific empiricism that is broader than, but in keeping with, systems theory. The second suspicion was presented to me by the technical author of BSI PAS 181. While related to the first, it is more pragmatic, assuming that the structure of a city government serves a rational purpose.

> The problem is not silos or organisational structures … You've got a sort of functional organisational structure and that provides people with a career structure to work within and decision making structures and all of that. And whenever we've on a consulting basis worked with a city or whatever we almost never recommend organisational restructuring as being part of what you need to do. You need an organisational structure. You've got one. Fine.
>
> *(BSI PAS 181 technical author, March 18, 2016)*

Here, resistance to silo busting is not based on a need for evidence but on the belief that specialisation is often the result of functional and organisational optimisation. I interpret this as a Coasian approach, in which government is understood as a way of reducing transaction costs by internalising (social and economic) relations. Rather than decry state bureaucracy as an exception to the free market, later neo-liberals such as Coase and Stigler considered it as an actor within the economy, and applied microeconomic logics to an assessment of its forms, processes and outcomes. Perceived opportunities or threats need not be addressed by restructuring or downsizing, but by subtler, more sophisticated management techniques. It is thus that my interlocutor recommended that cities "work within [their] existing organisational structure, but embed within that a new virtual business structure which is based around user needs rather than organisational constructs" (BSI PAS 181 technical author, March 18, 2016).

The final argument finds me once more shifting my allegiance, this time to argue against a technique of governance by drawing on the values of scientific empiricism. Benchmarking is a management process used to continually improve the performance of a firm or agency. It involves measuring products, services and practices, and comparing them against those of competitors in order to identify and adopt best practices (Camp 1989). While initially used within companies, benchmarking is now also performed by third-party analysts, and is applied to the public and non-profit sectors. Benchmarking is an attractive tool for those sympathetic to principles of governance. It recognises that problems are not unique, but are encountered over and over again by different actors. By benchmarking, firms can diagnose areas where they are weak and learn from (and potentially collaborate with) others in order to improve. Rather than being centralised, management is thus exercised through a web of interrelated actors held together by common data points. This is especially true when benchmarking is applied to the public sector by a third-party in an open manner, as is the case for ISO 37120.

Performance assessment and benchmarking have been criticised for standardising a narrow band of acceptable practices—such as profit-driven self-interest (Brown 2015) or metric-based medicine (Adams 2016)—at the expense of local ways of perceiving, knowing and caring. I encountered a similar criticism of ISO 37120 in my interviews. An epidemiologist I spoke with cautioned against the validity of international comparison based on the indicators "number of in-patient hospital beds per 100,000 population" and "number of physicians per 100,000 population".

> Okay, yes, that is nice, it might be a handy thing just to have off on the side. Is it a measure of how we are doing health wise? I don't think so. Health is about something else. It is not about the number of doctors you have got. It can impact in a negative way if you only have one doctor in the whole city of Toronto, but there are so many other things that are much heavier hitters. Maybe we should be looking at … the slum lord and those kinds of things. That's impacting on health. What are those kind of things that help us to know that we are doing better, what gives context maybe to some of these numbers or slightly different health related ones?
>
> *(Canadian epidemiologist, January 28, 2016)*

The interviewee's position is that the chosen metrics are unable to account for social determinants of health (such as economic status, living conditions, health insurance costs, and so on). While this individual might agree that international benchmarking overrides local knowledge, they would not want to do away with metrics altogether. They would prefer that health indicators be tuned to the specific problems encountered within well-defined geographic limits. Put differently, the opposition is to global benchmarking, not performance assessment. In this way, the interviewee is seeking to align evidence-based medicine with a more sophisticated understanding of the distribution of morbidity and mortality.

Opting to argue with complexity theory, scientific empiricism and Coasian neoliberalism on specific issues is not the same thing as agreeing with them. Rather, my aim is to reconfigure the field of possibilities such that minority positions can become more powerful and effective, perhaps even opening up the space for alternative orders of meaning. Had I encountered radical feminist, postcolonial, queer or anti-capitalist voices during my research, I would consider adding my own voice to theirs. At present however, I do not believe that it would be particularly effective to try to develop my own approach to smart city standards, nor do I believe that to do so would be in keeping with my poststucturalist interpretative framework.

I have attempted, in this paper, to politicise smart city standards by first identifying and describing their conditioning apparatuses, and then by using the dissonances between them to expose potential points of political engagement. There is a normative dimension to this work—that a more democratic smart city would be better than a less democratic one—but I have resisted arguing from first principles in order to remain consistent with an interpretive and epistemologically-focused analysis. As such, the smart city being created does not involve a proposal of an ideal urban form, function or practice, but an opening up of possibilities through the agitation of political dissensus. Put differently, my hope has been to unstandardise smart city standards.

Acknowledgements

The research for this paper was provided by a European Research Council Advanced Investigator Award, "The Programmable City" (ERC-2012-AdG-323636).

References

Adams, Vicanne, ed. 2016. *Metrics: What Counts in Global Health?* Durham, NC: Duke University Press.

Alexander, Christopher. 1964. *Notes on the Synthesis of Form.* Cambridge, MA: Harvard University Press.

Alexander, Christopher. 1965. "A City is not a Tree." *Architectural Forum* 122(1): 58–62.

Barad, Karen. 2007. *Meeting the Universe Halfway: Quantum Physics and the Entanglement of Matter and Meaning.* Durham, NC: Duke University Press.

Barnes, Trevor J. and Matthew Farish. 2006. "Between Regions: Science, Militarism, and American Geography from World War to Cold War." *Annals of the Association of American Geographers* 96(4): 807–826.

Batty, Michael. 2013. *The New Science of Cities.* Cambridge, MA: MIT Press.

Berry, Brian J. L. 1964. "Cities as Systems Within Systems of Cities." *Papers in Regional Science* 13(1): 147–163.

Bettencourt, Luís. M. A. 2013. "The Origins of Scaling in Cities." *Science* 340: 1438–1441.

Bevir, Mark. 2010. *Democratic Governance.* Princeton, NJ: Princeton University Press.

British Standards Institution. 2014. *PAS 181: Smart City Framework – Guide to establishing strategies for smart cities and communities.* London: BSI Standards Limited.

Brown, Wendy. 2015. *Undoing the Demos: Neoliberalism's Stealth Revolution.* New York: Zone Books.

Brunsson, Nils, and Bengt Jacobsson, eds. 2000. *A World of Standards.* Oxford: Oxford University Press.

Burgin, Angus. 2012. *The Great Persuasion: Reinventing Free Markets since the Depression.* Cambridge, MA: Harvard University Press.

Camp, Robert C. 1989. *Benchmarking: The Search for Industry Best Practices That Lead to Superior Performance.* Milwaukee, WI: ASQC Quality Press.

City Protocol Society. 2015. "City Anatomy: A Framework to support City Governance, Evaluation and Transformation." City Protocol Society. Accessed April 5, 2018. https://cpsociety.sharepoint.com/sites/cptf/CPTSC/Private%20Documents/Publications/CPA-I_001-v2_City_Anatomy.pdf

Coase, Ronald H. 1960. "The Problem of Social Cost." *The Journal of Law & Economics* 3: 1–44.

Davies, William. 2014. "Neoliberalism: A Bibliographic Review." *Theory, Culture & Society* 31(7/8): 309–317.

Davies, William. 2015. *The Happiness Industry: How the Government and Big Business Sold Us Well-Being.* London and New York: Verso.

Davies, William. 2017. *The Limits of Neoliberalism: Authority, Sovereignty and the Logic of Competition.* Revised ed. Los Angeles: Sage.

Ferlie, Ewan, Lynn Ashburner, Louise Fitzgerald, and Andrew Pettigrew. 1996. *The New Public Management in Action.* Oxford and New York: Oxford University Press.

Forrester, Jay W. 1961. *Industrial Dynamics.* Waltham, MA: Pegasus Communications.

Forrester, Jay W. 1969. *Urban Dynamics.* Waltham, MA: Pegasus Communications.

Fortun, Michael, and Silvan S. Schweber. 1993. "Scientists and the Legacy of World War II: The Case of Operations Research (OR)." *Social Studies of Science* 23(4): 595–642.

Foucault, Michel. 2008. *The Birth of Biopolitics: Lectures at the Collège de France, 1978–79*, edited by Michel Senellart. Basingstoke and New York: Palgrave Macmillan.

Gane, Nicholas. 2013. "The Emergence of Neoliberalism: Thinking Through and Beyond Michel Foucault's Lectures on Biopolitics." *Theory, Culture & Society* 31(4): 3–27.

Gleick, James. 1987. *Chaos: Making a New Science*. New York: Viking.

Gregory, Derek. 1980. "The Ideology of Control: Systems Theory and Geography." *Tijdschrift voor Economische en Sociale Geografie* 71(6): 327–342.

Hammond, Debora. 2002. "Exploring the Genealogy of Systems Thinking." *Systems Research and Behavioral Science* 19(5): 429–439.

Hammond, Debora. 2003. *Science of Synthesis: Exploring the Social Implications of General Systems Theory*. Boulder, CO: University Press of Colorado.

Hayek, Friedrich A. 1944. *The Road to Serfdom*. London and New York: Routledge.

Hayek, Friedrich A. 1945. "The Use of Knowledge in Society." *The American Economic Review* 35(4): 519–530.

Hayles, N. Katherine. 1996. "Consolidating the Canon." In *Science Wars*, edited by Andrew Ross, 226–237. Durham, NC: Duke University Press.

Hayles, N. Katherine. 1999. *How We Became Posthuman: Virtual Bodies in Cybernetics, Literature and Informatics*. Chicago and London: University of Chicago Press.

Heims, Steve J. 1993. *Constructing a Social Science for Postwar America: The Cybernetics Group, 1946–1953*. Cambridge, MA: MIT Press.

Heyck, Hunter. 2015. *Age of System: Understanding the Development of Modern Social Science*. Baltimore, MD: Johns Hopkins University Press.

Higgins, Vaughan, and Wendy Larner, eds. 2010. *Calculating the Social: Standards and the Reconfiguration of Governing*. Basingstoke: Palgrave Macmillan.

Hoos, Ida R. 1972. *Systems Analysis in Public Policy: A Critique*. Revised ed. Berkeley, CA: University of California Press.

Hughes, Agatha C. and Thomas P. Hughes, eds. 2000. *Systems, Experts and Computers: The Systems Approach in Management and Engineering, World War II and After*. Cambridge, MA: MIT Press.

Hughes, Thomas P. 1998. *Rescuing Prometheus: Four Monumental Projects That Changed Our World*. New York: Pantheon Books.

International Organization for Standardization. 2014a. *ISO 37120: Sustainable Development of Communities — Indicators for City Services and Quality of Life*. Geneva: ISO copyright office.

International Organization for Standardization. 2014b. "Resolutions adopted by the Technical Management Board in 2014." ISO Technical Management Board. Accessed April 5, 2018. http://isotc.iso.org/livelink/livelink/fetch/-15620806/15620808/15623592/15768654/TMB_resolutions_-_2014_%28Resolution_1-128%29.pdf?nodeid=16383402&vernum=-2

International Organization forStandardization. 2015. *ISO/TMB Smart Cities Strategic Advisory Group Final Report*. Geneva: ISO Technical Management Board.

Jacobs, Jane. 1961. *The Death and Life of Great American Cities*. New York: Vintage Books.

Jessop, Bob. 1995. "The regulation approach, governance and post-Fordism: alternative perspectives on economic and political change?" *Economy and Sociology* 24(3): 307–333.

Jessop, Bob. 1997. "Capitalism and its future: remarks on regulation, government and governance." *Review of International Political Economy* 4(3): 561–581.

Jones, Daniel S. 2012. *Masters of the Universe: Hayek, Friedman, and the Birth of Neoliberal Politics*. Princeton, NJ: Princeton University Press.

Kember, Sarah. 2003. *Cyberfeminism and Artificial Life*. London and New York: Routledge.

Kitchin, Rob. 2015. "Making sense of smart cities: Addressing present shortcomings." *Cambridge Journal of Regions, Economy and Society* 8(1): 131–136.

Light, Jennifer S. 2003. *From Warfare to Welfare: Defense Intellectuals and Urban Problems in Cold War America*. Baltimore, MD: The Johns Hopkins University Press.

Light, Jennifer. 2008. "Taking Games Seriously." *Technology and Culture* 49(2): 347–375.

Lilienfeld, Robert. 1978. *The Rise of Systems Theory: An Ideological Analysis*. New York: John Wiley & Sons.

McCarney, Patricia L. 2000. "Thinking about Governance in Global and Local Perspective: Considerations on Resonance and Dissonance between Two Discourses." *Urban Forum* 11(1): 1–29.

McCarney, Patricia L. 2003. "Confronting Critical Disjunctures in the Governance of Cities." In *Governance on the Ground: Innovations and Discontinuities in the Cities of the Developing World*, edited by Patricia L. McCarney and Richard E. Stren, 31–55. Washington, DC: Woodrow Wilson Center Press.

Mirowski, Philip. 1997. "Machine Dreams: Economic Agents as Cyborgs." *History of Political Economy* 29(S1): 13–40.

Mirowski, Philip, and Dieter Plehwe, eds. 2009. *The Road from Mont Pèlerin: The Making of the Neoliberal Thought Collective*. Cambridge, MA: Harvard University Press.

Negroponte, Nicholas. 1970. *The Architecture Machine: Toward a More Human Environment*. Cambridge, MA: MIT Press.

Negroponte, Nicholas. 1975. *Soft Architecture Machines*. Cambridge, MA: MIT Press.

Pask, Gordon. 1969. "The Architectural Relevance of Cybernetics." *Architectural Design*, Sep.: 494–496.

Peck, Jamie. 2010. *Constructions of Neoliberal Reason*. Oxford and New York: Oxford University Press.

Ponte, Stefano, Peter Gibbon, and Jakob Vestergaard, eds. 2011. *Governing through Standards: Origins, Drivers and Limitations*. Basingstoke and New York: Palgrave Macmillan.

Rhodes, Roderick A. W. 1996. "The New Governance: Governing Without Government." *Political Studies* 44: 652–667.

Richardson, George P. 1991. *Feedback Thought in Social Science and Systems Theory*. Philadelphia, PA: University of Pennsylvania Press.

Scott, Allen J. and Shoukry T. Roweis. 1977. "Urban Planning in Theory and Practice: A Reappraisal." *Environment and Planning A* 9(10): 1097–1119.

Shelton, Taylor, Matthew Zook, and Alan Wiig. 2015. "The 'Actually Existing Smart City'." *Cambridge Journal of Regions, Economy and Society* 8(1): 13–25.

Stigler, George J. 1971. "The Theory of Economic Regulation." *Bell Journal of Economics and Management Services* 2(1): 3–21.

Stoker, Gerry. 1998. "Governance as Theory: Five Propositions." *International Social Science Journal* 50(155): 17–28.

Waldrop, M.Mitchell. 1992. *Complexity: The Emerging Science at the Edge of Order and Chaos*. New York: Touchstone.

Walters, William. 2004. "Some Critical Notes on 'Governance'." *Studies in Political Economy* 73(1): 27–46.

Wilson, Alan G. 1968. "Models in Urban Planning: A Synoptic Review of Recent Literature." *Urban Studies* 5(3): 249–276.

World Council on City Data. (n.d.) "What is the WCCD?" World Council on City Data. Accessed April 5, 2018. http://www.dataforcities.org/wccd/

4

URBAN REVITALIZATION THROUGH AUTOMATED POLICING AND "SMART" SURVEILLANCE IN CAMDEN, NEW JERSEY

Alan Wiig

Introduction: From industrial collapse to economic revitalization

In October 2015, then-United States President Barack Obama spoke at the Annual Meeting of the International Association of Chiefs of Police, where he highlighted efforts Camden, New Jersey made in data-driven policing (Obama 2015). Camden was cast as prototype for innovative community policing, reliant on multi-instrument, automated, digital surveillance. The logic was that securing the city from drug dealing and criminal gangs, and lowering crime in general—and murders specifically—necessitated outfitting the city with new, algorithmic systems of cybernetic control (Krivý 2016) to augment police officers on foot and in patrol cars. A month before Obama's speech, on Camden's formerly-industrial, then vacant waterfront, the Governor of New Jersey joined local politicians and corporate leaders in announcing an $800 million waterfront redevelopment project as the cornerstone of nearly $2 billion in public and private investment in Camden (City of Camden 2015a; Sheridan 2016). The governor's announcement intended to signal Camden's economic resurgence after decades of decline, and was predicated in part on changing perceptions of the city's safety through the transformed, automated policing strategy. A fuller discussion of the economic development can be found in Wiig (2018), but it bears noting that New Jersey's approach to economic growth and urban revitalization followed established, neoliberal free market-driven strategies that assumed when large, multi-national corporations located or re-located into Camden, there would be attendant job creation within the city. Neither local job creation nor workforce education measures were part of the economic development agenda, even though both were desired in the city (LAEDA 2016).

Camden's decline mirrored that of many industrial-era cities in the United States, with anchor companies abandoning the city as the economy shifted manufacturing to cheaper, non-union regions (Cowie 2001), disinvestment and white flight to the suburbs following riots in 1971, and the resulting emptying of the city's tax base leading to significant cuts to civic services including education, infrastructure, and policing. In reaction to the hollowing out of its tax base and resulting structural deficit, Camden's city government was forced to operate under severe fiscal constraints enforced by state control of the budget beginning in the early 1980s (Gilette 2006). The racialized poverty of Camden is most potently manifest in the divide between the city and its surrounding county, of which the city is part. As of the last US Census, Camden city, with 76,000 residents, was 48% African American and 17% white, with 8% holding a bachelor's degree or higher, and with a median household income of $26,201 and 39% poverty rate (US Census 2015a). Camden County, with 511,000 residents (including the city's 76,000), was nearly 70% white and 21% African American, with 29% attaining a bachelor's degree or higher, a median household income of $61,842—over twice that of Camden city—and a poverty rate of 13% (US Census 2015b). These census facts briefly encapsulate the high degree of disparity in Camden today, a divide manifest in capital investment, or the failure of investment, leading to neighborhood decline citywide (Gilette 2006).

Ensuring the success of revitalization through the renovation of dilapidated areas, surveillance, and enforcement of conduct has been a core component of urban regeneration efforts since the 1980s (Raco 2003). These processes of securing a city worked to "ensur[e] that new urban spaces are safe and *are seen to be safe*" (Raco 2003, 1870, italics in the original). The need for a city to be perceived as safe is noteworthy and reflects the Camden case, where the installation of surveillance networks established real estate development and attracted new business before crime levels dropped. In Camden, securing the city was a key element of drawing corporate enterprise to invest in the city. It should be noted that this corporate investment was spatially bounded into specific zones like the waterfront the governor stood on to announce the revitalized city: residential neighborhoods proximate to the new economy felt displacement pressures due to new construction (Lake 2018) and neighborhoods further away continued to struggle with long-standing economic and environmental concerns not limited to crime. Specifically, the director of a local community economic development organization lamented that given the low-lying nature of the city, many neighborhoods experienced significant flooding even during minor rainstorms, leading to raw sewage in the streets and subsequent difficulties navigating automobiles around large puddles of standing sewage-water (LAEDA 2016). While the corporate districts have renovated municipal infrastructures, this investment has been much slower to spread citywide.

This chapter argues that Camden's application of a city-wide, militarized surveillance and policing system was exceptional in vision and execution, and points to new avenues of digitally-driven municipal governance agendas underpinning ambitions for economic growth. As a means of securing the terrain for outside investment, Camden employed data-driven, automated policing, where officers on the street operated in tandem with a control room monitoring the city. Many of these policing technologies and tactics mirrored those used in the United States

Military's counterinsurgency efforts in Iraq and Afghanistan (Petraeus 2006), part of the ongoing militarization of cities worldwide (Graham 2010). Deploying a city-wide surveillance network was intended to shift perception of Camden away from what *Rolling Stone* magazine called "Apocalypse, New Jersey" (Tabbi 2013) to a safe, secure, and promising place to invest capital and locate large corporate enterprise; this effort was considered *the* primary factor in setting the stage for the city's current, if highly uneven, economic transformation (Director of Communications 2016). While the surveillance systems functioned as expected, they did not immediately reduce citywide crime as anticipated.

The role of surveillance networks and automated, algorithmic authority is central to "smart" visions, "anchoring" the "spectrum of control" through interlinking, adaptable technologies that are constantly "tracking bodies as they move through space; surveilling the types of faces on the street; sending police to remove unwanted people; moving traffic along the roads; and more" (Sadowski and Pasquale 2015, 9). Theorizing this societal control through "smart city" systems focuses on the digitization of urban surveillance and policing as an "apparatus" of power (Foucault 1980, 194), and more specifically on the role contemporary forms of surveillance play in controlling an urban population (Deleuze 1992). This "management at a distance" through "automated" systems (Klauser et al. 2014, 870, 871) intensifies the ability to control a city as "interconnected and continuous", trackable spaces (Martinez 2011, 201). Even without the immediate presence of a police officer to note a crime, the systems can record and document an incident for later analysis, a radical shift in surveilling a city. Theorizing Camden's surveillance networks and policing tactics as an apparatus of security (Agamben 2009, 14; Foucault 1980, 194), this chapter extends understandings of the smart city as a disciplinary tactic relying on law, digital infrastructure, and a particular vision of a city as a stage for orderly and planned economic development. Considering the digital infrastructure, community policing tactics, data analytics, police officers, and their more traditional policing devices such as patrol cars as a security apparatus is a means of weaving together these linked systems, bodies, and devices as they prepared Camden for spatially-targeted urban transformation. The apparatus became inseparable from the city's governance.

The evolution of policing practices

The transformation of policing in Camden began with the dissolution of their longstanding city police force and the installation of a county police force in May 2013 (Zernike 2014), but was only the latest stage in the city's structural inability to fund and manage its police force, which was first an issue in 1986 and continued into the 2000s, forcing the city to rely on the state to provide financial support (Rogovin 2006, 7; Zernike 2012). In implementing a county-controlled police force, Camden reduced costs by laying off unionized police officers and eliminating a variety of pay-bonuses associated with patrolling in the city. The impetus to revamp the police force was longstanding. As laid out in a 2006 report by the state's Attorney General's office, "the absence of community-engagement [was seen] as central to the failings of the police to provide adequate services to the city's residents" (Rogovin 2006, 7–8).

The need to reform a police force largely operating outside of the city's control was highlighted by a 2004 designation that Camden was the most unsafe city in the United States (Rogovin 2006, 1). A full discussion of the politics of county control is beyond the scope of this chapter, but it should be noted that largely suburban Camden County has had a contentious relationship with the politically more liberal and minority-majority population city of Camden (Gilette 2006, 191–243). Shifting management of the police force allowed the county, and its "wealthier and whiter" residents to dictate how the city was policed (Tabbi 2013). In relinquishing control of its police force, Camden County took over fiscal management of policing. While the county police force could be organized to patrol any and all cities in the county if a city agreed to dissolve their locally-controlled force, Camden city was the only one to sign up for the new police force (Zernike 2012).

With the transition to a county force, policing in Camden took two parallel tracks: integrating digital surveillance into policing efforts and implementing community policing by placing more officers more of the time on the streets in an effort to regain the trust of Camden's residents. Because community policing is the public and visible face of the new force, it will be discussed first, before shifting to discuss the underlying monitoring systems that form the digital backend to Camden's security apparatus. The initial turn to community policing and the militarization of police forces in the US began in response to the civil rights protests of the 1960s (Williams 2011). While community policing has been purposely defined vaguely in order to be inclusive of nearly any policing strategy, in general it has succeeded in improving a city's opinion of its police force, but has not definitively contributed to the general decline in crime over the same period. Scholars recognize that it is difficult to effectively evaluate community policing because what community policing actually entails is ambiguous and, nationwide, its implementation has been concurrent with other major changes to policing strategies such as the implementation of new technologies (Gordner 2014).

In disenfranchised cities like Camden, the expectation that community policing would involve a neighborhood-based community is flawed due to the lack of existing communitarian social relations that the police and residents could draw on: there has to be a functioning, neighborhood-based sense of community for this style of policing to work (Herbert 2014), something Camden largely lacked (Wheeler 2016). Recommendations for implementing a community policing strategy in Camden specified, in addition to internal organizational changes, training officers in problem-solving techniques, ensuring district commanders have completed sensitivity and cultural training, and holding officers accountable to their city (Rogovin 2006, 11–12). Community policing, as its name suggests, necessitates knowing the neighborhoods and their residents; this is one area where, in recent history, the strategy has achieved success (Gordner 2014). The Camden County force implemented community policing strategies as a means of moving "from reactive to pro-active policing" (CCPD 2011, 1), notably installing a "Neighborhood

Resources Officer" in each district to "work on addressing long term, systemic problems" and organizing "collaborative efforts between community members and the police" (CCPD 2011, 7). Camden's community policing strategy quickly realized significant crime reduction, and positive local and national media attention as a result. In a 2014 article, the *New York Times* published a relatively positive tribute to the city, acknowledging that in the two years since the county police took over, homicides were down significantly, shootings were down 43% and violent crime down 22%. Average response time was down to under five minutes from over sixty minutes previously. The police also held "meet-the-officer events at parks and churches", and sent a soft-serve ice cream truck into the neighborhoods to give free ice cream to children (Zernike 2014). At the same time, while dishing out ice cream or interacting with the city and its residents, the officers on the street are in constant contact with the operations center and its networked systems monitoring action throughout the city (Ercolani 2014).

Securing the city through automated surveillance

As mentioned above, the militarized, digital surveillance network, and the attendant makeover of Camden's police force, were seen as necessary factors to both lower crime in the city and to challenge widespread and longstanding perceptions that Camden's residents and economy were beyond investment (Gilette 2006; Tabbi 2013; Vice 2015). In Camden, creating the conditions for successful revitalization necessitated state-backed initiatives to attract enterprise but, more importantly, that the city be perceived safe (Director of Communications 2016). Facilitating these changed perceptions involved both the community policing script put forward by the Camden County Police force discussed above, as well as the multi-faceted, digital security apparatus operating both horizontally and vertically throughout the city, through cameras mounted above the streets, within police vehicles, and fixed on the bodies of officers.

Driving or walking through Camden, the surveillance network was unobtrusive but could be found without difficulty. Seen in Figure 4.1, cameras are the most visible element, mounted on utility poles, light posts, and stoplights, often at busy intersections. As is typical of digital infrastructure, the presence of these networked devices does not change the material fabric of the city so much as actively transform the experience of the place through the potential-and-very-likely monitoring from above. The elements of the surveillance network are discussed below.

The technological heart of the effort is the Camden County-operated *urban control room*, utilizing "Cutting Edge Crime Fighting Technology" (State of New Jersey 2014). This "Real-Time Tactical Operations and Information Center" (RT-TOIC) located in the central police station in downtown Camden, opened in 2011 at a cost of $4.5 million (Tabbi 2013). When the county police force took over in 2013, it employed 120 civilian operators (Zernike 2014), 28 working at any one time (Bereznak 2015) working in the space, and as the county policing plan states,

FIGURE 4.1 At Marlton Pike and Federal Street in east Camden, a surveillance camera is mounted on a lightpole, providing surveillance capabilities at a busy intersection

"maintain[ing] a real-time awareness of conditions with the operating environment [...] and monitor[ing] the tactical deployment of all assets in the field" (CCPD 2011, 5). The control room has adopted an aesthetic of control rooms elsewhere (Luque-Ayala and Marvin 2016), with a wall of large computer monitors above the analysts' desks. The control room used algorithms for automatic processing of big data from the citywide monitoring systems. Police cruisers were tracked by global positioning system (GPS) in order to alert officers to nearby issues identified through the camera network (Laday 2013; Tabbi 2013; Zernike 2014). 911 emergency services and police dispatch also are managed through the control room, as was a Strategic Analysis Unit that evaluated crime data and policing data and conducted predictive planning for crime fighting efforts (CCPD 2011, 5).

As part of a nationwide effort to produce "21st century policing" such as practiced in Camden, the Police Data Initiative was launched by President Obama in the city in May 2015. Noting Camden's early success harnessing surveillance technology and data analytics to lower crime, the initiative's goal was to use open data to foster "increased transparency" and trust-building between city residents and their police. Fifty-three policing jurisdictions covering 40 million people joined the initiative in its first year (Wardell and Ross 2016), but many of those jurisdictions did not release their data, including Camden (Police Foundation 2015). As is often the case with smart city initiatives, the potential of the project often overshadows the successful, long-term achievement of the stated goals of the project (Shelton et al. 2015).

The *Eye in the Sky* camera network went online alongside the urban control room in 2011 with 131 cameras at a cost of $1.8 million (Associated Press 2011). In 2015, the network expanded to 221 cameras citywide, with an additional cost of $2.3 million (City of Camden 2015b). The camera network "gives the ability to 'virtually patrol the community'" according to Camden's mayor (Fiedler 2011), to augment the eyes of police in the neighborhoods and to record what could become visual evidence of crimes committed. These cameras provide the core of Camden's "smart" policing abilities both through catching criminal events in the moment, but also through the ability to recall events after the fact, for instance tracking a car through the city both before and after its passengers committed a crime.

In tandem with the camera network, Camden installed the privately-owned *ShotSpotter* system, with thirty-five microphones placed in areas known for crime, microphones that triangulate the location of gunshots down to a few feet (State of New Jersey 2014). These microphones could also automatically direct nearby Eye in the Sky cameras to train their lenses toward a location of a gunshot (Bereznak 2015). Between the first and second year of use, total shootings within Shot-spotter's covered range fell from 704 in 2013 to 366 in 2014 (CCPD 2015b). The apparent success in lowering gunshots in the city led Camden to invest further in the system to cover more of the city (Bereznak 2015).

The *Interactive Community Alert Network* (abbreviated *iCan*) is a social media-styled, anonymous, online neighborhood crime watch where vetted city residents can, after passing a background check, view live Eye in the Sky video feeds from near to their home and/or work, and directly report activity deemed suspicious back to the urban control room downtown, where a technician can send a police officer out to the area (Tsiaras 2015). The system was justified by its private developer because it enabled residents to interact with police without having to be seen on the street doing so, which can be an issue in cities like Camden, with long histories of mistrust of the police. As the developer writes in promotional materials, "iCan adds an important element that helps transform the 'If You See Something, Say Something' campaign into 'If You See Something, Show Us... Instantly'" (CCPD 2015a; Packettalk 2011). Since its launch in 2014, the network has had over seventy residents or community groups sign up (Tsiaras 2015).

With *automated license plate readers*, the ability to track people who live in, work in, or just pass through the city was significant and not without concern due to the privacy implications (Farivar 2015). As the Electronic Frontier Foundation argued, at issue was that, with the long-term storage of vehicle data, personal information about city residents was acquired and a data breach could reveal significant, other-wise private information (Quintin and Maass 2015). Regardless of the ability to monitor cars driving into Camden to, for instance, purchase drugs, or to track stolen vehicles in the city, the system was also inherently tracking all residents as they make their daily journeys. Every patrol car has the automated license plate readers installed and constantly running, logging the license plate numbers of passing vehicles, comparing the plate to a record of earlier crimes, and using GPS to mark where the vehicle was at that time. Maintaining this database allows the police to follow past journeys long after they occurred (Bereznak 2015). Camden's data is officially kept for five years (Camden Police Department 2011, 9).

Camden piloted a *body-worn camera program* for officers in early 2016, purchasing 325 cameras at a cost of $800 each (Bereznak 2015; CCPD 2016). The installation of these cameras was touted as a means of offering accountability to the community, that the use of body worn cameras would

> hold civilians and officers accountable to act responsibly and lawfully, increase officer and civilian safety, foster a sense of trust and transparency between citizens and the CCPD, reduce the number of false allegations of police assaults, and encourage prompt resolution of citizen complaints and internal investigations.
>
> *(CCPD 2016, 3)*

In bringing the security apparatus onto the bodies of officers, the body-worn cameras finalize in a sense the process of adding a layer of digital mediation to community policing in Camden. Even the face-to-face interaction of officers and residents relied on the digital, networked back-end of real-time, automated information gathering and algorithmic analysis facilitated through the surveillance network and the control room staff.

Conclusion: Who benefits from the surveilling of Camden?

Presentations of Camden's decline in national media have persisted over time, reflecting and distorting (Gilette 2013) the depths of poverty, crime, and despair present in the city. While *Rolling Stone* magazine (Tabbi 2013) as well as *Vice Magazine*'s HBO show (Vice 2015) sensationalized both the crime and the militaristic surveillance measures taken to combat crime, critics of this reportage do not deny the presence of longstanding problems, most notably "violent crime and [a] murder rate [...] so high that on a per capita basis, it 'put [Camden] somewhere between Honduras and Somalia,'" as the police chief told *Rolling Stone*'s reporter (Tabbi 2013).

Automating the surveilling and policing of undesirable activity was a foundational step in prototyping Camden's near-future economic revival. How Camden policed the city became crucial for signaling that Camden had crime under control, even as crime rates were not actually declining, as will be discussed below. The security apparatus had to be in place before businesses would come: urban transformation was predicated on this. Early on, the security apparatus appeared to have succeeded at its purpose. Crime was down 42% between 2013 and 2014, with homicides dropping 42% and violent crime down 21% (CCPD 2015b). Camden used these statistics to highlight their success in creating a safer city in promotional materials that touted improvements in safety, measured through reductions in violent and nonviolent crime and extolled as a marker of "unprecedented progress" (City of Camden 2015c, 4–7). As the mayor put it, "Our improved policing model and increased public safety has an impact that can be seen in the neighborhoods, where children play on the streets, in the civic sphere, and in changed perceptions of Camden" (Cooper's Ferry Partnership 2015, 2). The city and its residents were themselves a backdrop to the narrative of transformative change.

While the American Civil Liberties Union-New Jersey praised a drastic, 93% reduction in police response times in Camden, they also raise attention to the vast increase in summonses for a variety of minor nuisance matters, such as riding a bicycle without a bell, driving with tinted windows, and inadequate lights on an automobile. A part of the expanded policing that went unmentioned in the promotional materials discussed above was an escalation in arrests and citations for trivial matters, with "the potential to [then] create a climate of fear" (ACLU-NJ 2015). The surveillance apparatus nourished a narrative of change, and it remains unclear if and when the narrative will align with progress toward a safer city. After two years of declining crime, 2016 brought a 150% uptick in murders. Forty-seven murders were committed in 2016, compared to thirty-two in 2015 (Walsh 2017). However, 2017 brought a significant decline in homicides, down to twenty-three for the year, and a general reduction in both violent crime and property crime (Everett 2018). High-technology efforts at community policing still require trained, skilled police officers, and Camden's force initially had both high attrition rates and was not able to reach its full staffing level of 400 officers until the end of 2016 (Walsh 2017; Zalot 2016). The increase in violence in 2016 led some to question whether the surveillance network and the focus on community policing had achieved substantive change, or if the city had descended into the same public safety crisis that precipitated transforming the police force in 2011 (Adomaitis 2016). Data-driven, automated policing and cameras in crime-plagued neighborhoods were not the same as safe neighborhoods. Progress toward a safer city has been made, with open air drug markets significantly lessened and over 600 vacant buildings tied to drug crime torn down (Everett 2018).

No simple fix has emerged for Camden's economy nor the safety of its neighborhoods, especially not one that relies so heavily on investment in "smart city" technologies that are solely used for surveillance and economic development into targeted areas with little incentive to spread into residential neighborhoods. Recent statements from Camden's police chief and county-level politicians acknowledge this, and recognize that education and economic investment are also necessary. The security apparatus in Camden could not and did not reduce crime rates on its own. Achieving a safe city where revitalization takes hold citywide necessitates more than a technological fix. However, as of writing in spring 2018, the latter two elements have yet to receive the attention and investment that automated policing has received (LAEDA 2016). Harnessing the surveillance apparatus to address ongoing civic and municipal matters beyond policing could be a starting point to a community conversation where city residents could articulate their desires for actualizing the city's digitized, "smart" future. These desires would in all likelihood align with expanding on the educational and economic opportunity city and county politicians and officials speak of. As of writing, five years after the updated police force began patrolling the streets, this has not yet taken place.

Acknowledgements

Thanks to Renee Tapp, Jonathan Silver, Daniel Silver, Rob Kitchin, Martin Dodge and Joseph Brown for their feedback and support. The author acknowledges the University of Massachusetts, Boston Joseph P. Healey Research Grant's support. This chapter draws heavily on the author's 2018 paper: "Secure the city, revitalize the zone: Smart urbanization in Camden, New Jersey". *Environment and Planning C: Politics and Space*. 36(3): 403–422.

References

ACLU-NJ (American Civil Liberties Union-New Jersey). 2015. Policing in Camden has improved, but concerns remain. May 18. https://www.aclu.org/news/policing-camden-has-improved-concerns-remain (accessed: 7 July 2016).

Adomaitis, Greg. 2016. 2016 Camden homicide count climbs even as number of other violent crimes decline. *NJ.com*, December 31. http://www.nj.com/camden/index.ssf/2016/12/camden_homicides_2016.html?utm_source=dlvr.it&utm_medium=twitter (accessed: 10 February 2017).

Agamben, Giorgio. 2009. *What is an Apparatus? and Other Essays*. Stanford, CA: Stanford University Press.

Associated Press. 2011. Crime-plagued Camden to receive Nntwork of security cameras. *NJ.com*, January 30. http://www.nj.com/news/index.ssf/2011/01/crime-plagued_camden_will_be_g.html (accessed: 5 July 2016).

Bereznak, Alyssa. 2015. High-tech policing: Do cities need Big Brother to lower crime? *Yahoo News*. August 19. http://news.yahoo.com/the-effects-of-a-high-tech-police-force-in-one-of-america-s-most-dangerous-cities-152325047.html (accessed: 10 July 2015).

Camden Police Department. 2011. Automatic License Plate Reader policy, April 22. https://www.aclu.org/files/FilesPDFs/ALPR/new-jersey/16470-16483%20Camden%20OPRA%20Response%2007.pdf. (accessed: 2 July 2016).

CCPD (Camden County Police Department). 2011. Proposed Draft Plan, September 26. http://camdencountypd.org/wp-content/themes/ccpd/pdf/Timoney-Draft-Plan-dated-9-26-11.pdf (accessed: 6 July 2016).

CCPD (Camden County Police Department). 2015a. Interactive community alert network (iCan). http://camdencountypd.org/ican/ (accessed: 6 July 2016).

CCPD (Camden County Police Department). 2015b. Camden shows 48 percent drop in gunfire. http://www.camdencountypd.org/camden-shows-48-percent-drop-in-gunfire/ (accessed: 27 June 2016).

CCPD (Camden County Police Department). 2016. Public feedback on the CCPD's body worn camera policy: Report on the comments received and the CCPD's response. Prepared with the assistance of the Policing Project at NYU School of Law. https://policingproject.org/wp-content/uploads/2016/05/Report_Public-Feedback-on-the-CCPDs-Body-Worn-Camera-Policy.pdf (accessed: 6 July 2016).

City of Camden. 2015a. City of Camden, business & community leaders announce that Liberty Property Trust will lead development of 'The Camden Waterfront.' Camden, NJ, September 24. https://www.libertyproperty.com/pdfs/The_Camden_Waterfront_Press_Kit.pdf (accessed: 14 July 2016).

City of Camden. 2015b. City of Camden prepares to bolster 'Eye in the Sky' camera system. City of Camden, July 8. http://www.ci.camden.nj.us/releases/city-of-camden-prepares-to-bolster-eye-in-the-sky-camera-system/ (accessed: 17 June 2017).

City of Camden. 2015c. Economic development resources: Moving Camden Forward! American Images Publishing. http://www.nxtbook.com/aip/Camden/Camden2015/index.php#/0 (accessed 20 June 2016).

Cooper's Ferry Partnership. 2015. Coming together for Camden: 2015 Annual Report, Camden NJ. http://www.coopersferry.com/files/reports/CFP_PrintReleaseFinal.pdf (accessed: 6 July 2016).

Cowie, Jefferson. 2001. *Capital Moves: RCA's Seventy-Year Quest for Cheap Labor*. New York City: The New Press.

Deleuze, Gilles. 1992. Postscript on the societies of control. *October* 59, 3–7.

Director of Communications. 2016. Interview of Camden County Director of Communications with author. November 18, Camden, New Jersey.

Ercolani, Steve. 2014. Minority Report Meets the Wire: How New Jersey Police use military technology to fight crime. *The Guardian*, June 13. Source: https://www.theguardian.com/world/video/2014/jun/13/new-jersey-police-crime-video (accessed: 15 July 2016).

Everett, Rebecca. 2018. Camden's 2017 murder rate was the lowest in decades. Will the trend continue? *NJ.com*. http://www.nj.com/camden/index.ssf/2018/01/camdens_2017_murder_rate_was_the_lowest_in_decades.html. (accessed: 18 April 2018).

Farivar, Cyrus. 2015. We know where you've been: Ars acquires 4.6M license plate scans from the cops. *Ars Technica*, March 24. http://arstechnica.com/tech-policy/2015/03/we-know-where-youve-been-ars-acquires-4-6m-license-plate-scans-from-the-cops/ (accessed: 3 July 2016).

Fiedler, Elizabeth. 2011. 'Eye in the Sky' is watching over Camden. Newsworks.org, July 11. Source: http://www.newsworks.org/index.php/local/south-jersey/22911-eye-in-the-sky-is-watching-over-camden (accessed: 8 July 2016).

Foucault, Michel. 1980. *Power/Knowledge: Selected Interviews and Other Writings, 1972–1977*. Ed. G. Gordon. New York: Pantheon Books.

Gilette, Howard. 2006. *Camden After the Fall: Decline and Renewal in a Post-Industrial City*. Philadelphia: University of Pennsylvania Press.

Gilette, Howard. 2013. Rolling Stone's Camden profile just more 'urban porn'?http://www.newsworks.org/index.php/essay-works/item/63048-rolling-stones-camden-profile-just-more-urban-porn?linktype=featured_articlepage (accessed: 7 July 2016).

Gordner, Gary. 2014. Community Policing. *The Oxford Handbook of Police and Policing*. Edited by Reisig, Michael and Robert Kane. New York: Oxford University Press.

Graham, Stephen. 2010. *Cities Under Siege: The New Military Urbanism*. New York: Verso.

Herbert, Steve. 2014. *Citizens, Cops, and Power*. Chicago: University of Chicago Press.

Klauser, Francisco, Till Paasche, and Ola Söderström. 2014. Michel Foucault and the smart city: power dynamics inherent in contemporary governing through code. *Environment & Planning D* 32(5): 869–885.

Krivý, Maroš. 2016. Towards a critique of cybernetic urbanism: The smart city and the society of control. *Planning Theory* 17(1): 8–30.

Laday, Jason. 2013. Camden County Metro Division boasts $4.5 million in surveillance equipment and other technologies. *NJ.com*, May 15. http://www.nj.com/camden/index.ssf/2013/05/camden_county_metro_division_b.html (accessed: 6 July 2016).

LAEDA (Latin American Economic Development Association). 2016. Interview with director by author. Camden, New Jersey. May 12.

Lake, Robert. 2018Locating the social in social justice. *Annals of the American Association of Geographers* 108(2): 337–345.

Luque-Ayala, Andrés, and Simon Marvin. 2016. The maintenance of urban circulation: An operational logic of infrastructural control. *Environment and Planning D: Society and Space* 34(2): 191–208.

Martinez, Daniel. 2011. Beyond disciplinary enclosures: Management control in the society of control. *Critical Perspectives on Accounting* 22(2): 200–211.

Obama, Barack. 2015. POTUS at the Annual Meeting of the International Association of Chiefs of Police 2015. Chicago, Illinois. https://www.youtube.com/watch?v=Kcps W1iVBww. October 27 (accessed: 5 July 2016).

Packettalk. 2011. iCan. http://www.packetalk.net/ican.php (accessed: 7 July 2016).

Petraeus, David. (2006) *The U.S. Army and Marine Corps Counterinsurgency Field Manual.* Washington DC: Department of the Army.

Police Foundation. 2015. All Data. Public Safety Open Data Portal. http://publicsafetydatap ortal.org/all-data/ (accessed 7 July 2016).

Quintin, Cooper and Dave Maass. (2015) License plate readers exposed! How public safety agencies responded to major vulnerabilities in vehicle surveillance tech. Electronic Fron- tier Foundation, October 28. Source: https://www.eff.org/deeplinks/2015/10/license- plate-readers-exposed-how-public-safety-agencies-responded-massive (accessed 18 June 2017).

Raco, Mike. 2003. Remaking place and securitising space: Urban regeneration and the strategies, tactics and practices of policing in the UK. *Urban Studies* 40(9): 1869–1887.

Rogovin, Charles. 2006. *Final Report: Attorney General's Advisory Commission on Public Safety.* Trenton: New Jersey Office of the Attorney General.

Sadowski, Jathan, and Frank Pasquale. 2015. The spectrum of control: A social theory of the smart city. *First Monday* 20(7).

Shelton, Taylor, Matt Zook, and Alan Wiig. 2015. The "actually existing smart city." *Cambridge Journal of Regions, Economy and Society* 8(1): 13–25.

Sheridan, Mike. 2016. Camden's comeback. Urban Land Institute. April 11. Source: http:// urbanland.uli.org/development-business/camdens-comeback/ (accessed: 8 May 2016).

State of New Jersey. 2014. Coming together for Camden. http://www.nj.gov/governor/ news/news/552014/pdf/20140924b.pdf (accessed: 6 July 2016).

Tabbi, Matt. 2013. Apocalypse, New Jersey: A dispatch from America's most desperate town. *Rolling Stone*, December 19, 2013–January 2, 2014 issue. http://www.rollingstone. com/culture/news/apocalypse-new-jersey-a-dispatch-from-americas-most-desperate- town-20131211?page=5 (accessed 14 October 2015).

Tsiaras, Anna. 2015. Technology advances contribute to civilian safety. *Rutgers Camden Report.* April 3. https://report.camden.rutgers.edu/2015/04/technology-advances-contribute- to-civilian-safety/ (accessed: 7 July 2016).

US Census. 2015a. Camden City, New Jersey population estimates. //www.census.gov/ quickfacts/table/PST045215/3410000 (accessed: 12 July 2016).

US Census. 2015b. Camden County, New Jersey population estimates. //www.census.gov/ quickfacts/table/PST045215/34007 (accessed: 14 July 2016).

Vice. 2015. Surveillance City and the Forgotten War. Vice on HBO (Season 2, Episode 12). https://www.youtube.com/watch?v=fVDvJCeCe54 (accessed: 1 June 2016).

Walsh, Jim. 2017. Homicides up in Camden, across region. *Courier-Post* (online). January 23. http://www.courierpostonline.com/story/news/crime/2017/01/23/camden-crime-statis tics-increase/96954166/ (accessed: 10 February 2017).

Wardell, Clarence, and Denice Ross. 2016. The police data initiative year of progress: How we're building on the President's call to leverage open data to increase trust between police and citizens. The White House, April 22. https://medium.com/the-white-house/the-police-data-initiative-year-of-progress-how-we-re-building-on-the-president-s-call-to-leverage-3ac86053e1a9#.cs9pbp7xt (accessed: 7 July 2016).

Wheeler, Christopher. 2016. Barriers to community development in distressed cities: A case study of Camden, New Jersey. *Community Development* 47(4): 496–513.

Wiig, Alan. 2018. Secure the city, revitalize the zone: Smart urbanization in Camden, New Jersey. *Environment and Planning C: Politics and Space* 36(3): 403–422.

Williams, Kristian. 2011. The other side of the COIN: Counterinsurgency and community policing. *Interface* 3(1): 81–117.

Zalot, Morgan. 2016. Camden's homicide count reaches grim milestone as city murders more than double last year's. *NBC 10 Philadelphia*. May 31. http://www.nbcphiladelphia.com/news/local/Camden-Homicide-Count-Murder-Rate-Shooting-Police-Terron-Phillips-381430161.html (accessed: 25 June 2016).

Zernike, Kate. 2012. Overrun by crime, Camden trades in its police force. *The New York Times*. September 28. http://www.nytimes.com/2012/09/29/nyregion/overrun-by-crime-camden-trades-in-its-police-force.html?action=click&contentCollection=N.Y.%20%2F%20Region&module=RelatedCoverage&region=EndOfArticle&pgtype=article&_r=0 (accessed: 7 July 2016).

Zernike, Kate. 2014. Camden turns around with new police force. *New York Times*, August 31. http://www.nytimes.com/2014/09/01/nyregion/camden-turns-around-with-new-police-force.html?_r=0 (accessed: 7 July 2016).

5

CAN URBAN "MIRACLES" BE ENGINEERED IN LABORATORIES?

Turning Medellín into a model city for the Global South

Félix Talvard

Introduction

"How did the 'Medellín miracle' happen? And what can it teach other cities?", a 2014 article from *The Economist* began by asking.[1] Mayors, planners and consultants around the world are preoccupied by these two questions ("how did other cities solve certain issues and what can be learnt from it?") and they have learned to seek the benefits of a "model city" status. Medellín did not become an example by accident, nor through the long historic sedimentation that made other cities paragons of urban governance or innovation: positioning Medellín as an international exemplar is an ongoing, experimental project that fits into a "smart" city agenda. This chapter seeks to make sense of growing discourses about urban exemplars and the best practices of "smart" urbanism, specifically in the context of so-called developing countries. The literature on "smart" cities tends to be polarized between superlative discourses anticipating a technologically optimized democratic panacea and critical research that sometimes assumes cities have little agency, falling prey to the corporate interests of the digital economy (Hollands 2015). The goal of this chapter is to enrich our collective critical understanding of smart urbanism by analysing a case that requires rethinking those critical poles. As cities all over the world appropriate the discourses and practices of "smart" urban innovation, questions arise such as: How do smart urbanism projects fit into development narratives and adjust to places in the Global South? Does it mean standardization or diversity? How is the tension between universalist smart programmes and local idiosyncrasies managed in order to position Medellín as an "urban laboratory for the Global South"?

Colombia's second largest city makes for an interesting site to investigate these issues, for at least three reasons. First, it positions itself explicitly as a "developing" city – its GDP is an order of magnitude below that of other "smart cities" that have been studied, but it definitely qualifies as an "actually existing smart city" (Shelton,

Zook, and Wiig 2015), as opposed to planned or greenfield sites destined to showcase urban innovation. Public issues remain centred on eliminating poverty and violence, guaranteeing access to basic public services and maintaining functioning infrastructures covering the whole territory. Second, in Medellín, cutting-edge ICT and data-oriented "solutions" for urban planning are not being implemented to the extent they are in wealthier cities. In many cases, the initiatives I describe here care less about collecting data and building information systems than about managing a largely informal economy, emphasizing "good governance" inside local government, providing capacity-building tools for residents and modernizing public procurement. This reflects the interpretative flexibility of "smart" urbanism; innovation here is expected to solve problems that are explicitly linked to political participation and governance rather than focusing on technical efficiency. Third, the development economics and geography literature portray Medellín as an example of a "post-Washington consensus approach to local economic development in Latin America", the city's authorities having supposedly moved away from neoliberalism for more "leftist-oriented" approaches (Bateman, Duran Ortiz, and Maclean 2011), which echoes Medellín's branding operations as an "inclusive smart city". However, as is often the case with the intricacies of all things urban, this story is one of unclear borders (between "public" and "private" or "local" and "global") and uneasy categories (such as "neoliberal" or "development-oriented").

I focus on Medellín as an empirical case to explore how it has been and is being made into a model, an exemplar that travels across borders, and what consequences it had for city life. To do so I connect different sites and actors through the city, aiming not at exhaustiveness (this is not a monography of Medellín) but intending to show how heterogeneous actors work to turn the city into an "urban laboratory for the Global South". This chapter is based on fieldwork conducted in Colombia in November 2016. In addition to documentary sources (including planning documents, urban strategic plans, promotional leaflets, institutional websites, municipal meetings' minutes and newspaper articles), data was collected through a dozen formal interviews and more informal encounters with people working with local government, corporations, unions, non-governmental organizations and academia. Ethnographic observation was used to investigate workplaces, meetings and interactions between residents and local government and provided insight on the city's infrastructure and built environment.

The city of Medellín has deployed considerable efforts in the last decades to position itself as a regional and international model for innovative urban planning. It can count on an engaging narrative, widely chronicled by the media and some scholars as the "Medellín miracle" (Brand 2013; Brand and Dávila 2011; Maclean 2015). This narrative can be summed up as follows: once home to some of the deadliest drug cartels of South America, including the one led by the infamous Pablo Escobar, Medellín has gone from one of the most violent to one of the most vibrant and innovative cities in the world thanks to visionary planning policies that emphasized urban innovation for social inclusiveness. After undergoing a dramatic transformation in the early 2000s, the city of 3 million people received several awards[2] and worldwide attention for spectacular megaprojects, such as the *metroc-ables*, gondola systems installed in 2004 and 2008 to connect Medellín's poor *comunas* (districts) clinging to the valley's steep slopes to the city centre; or the *Biblioteca España*, a monumental public library located in one of the poorest *comunas*, designed as a place of education for residents and as a statement of social inclusion, bringing spectacular architecture (and attracting visitors) to disenfranchised districts. Those initiatives were undertaken under the banner of "social urbanism" (*urbanismo social*), a notion theorized by mayor Sergio Fajardo (2004–2007). Subsequent administrations claimed to carry on the doctrine, while in effect policies shifted to pursue competitiveness and growth-related projects as well as local development goals. In recent years, city strategic plans became increasingly geared towards a "smart city" imaginary, relying on innovation for local development and aspiring to turn the city into a regional and national exemplar – the "Silicon Valley of Latin America". Representatives from Medellín can regularly be found emphasizing the "social" aspects of the smart city in international conferences, such as the Cities for Life summit.[3] Backed by the financial power of a large municipal utility company, a new entity devoted to leading the transition towards a regional investment and innovation hub was created in 2010: Ruta N, which is the main protagonist of this chapter. Ruta N now acts as a landing pad for international businesses, an advisor to modernize public action (e.g. rationalizing public procurement by issuing challenges and testing solutions beforehand) and a platform for citizen engagement. Central to its work is an "innovation district" called *Medellinnovation*, which delineates a portion of the city as experimental grounds where tests and demonstrations of new technologies and practices could take place.

This chapter is organized in three sections. In the first one, I briefly discuss the literature on urban experiments and how it can inform our understanding of model cities. In the second section, I outline the empirical material the chapter is based on – pertaining for the most part to Ruta N Corporation, its parent company EPM and the innovation district they manage. A last section deals with what can be learned from studying Medellín's innovation strategy: framing it first as a local development project that assembles inward- and outward-oriented goals, which then raises questions about heterogeneous, public/private interventions in urban development. I contend that positioning Medellín as a national and regional exemplar on the one hand and pursuing local development goals on the other (what I call outward- and inward-oriented projects) cannot be dissociated, for the "global" characteristics of cities (e.g. being part of a "smart" urbanism movement) are rooted in local features and networks. For urban policymakers, articulating the two aspects of Medellín's innovation strategy and turning it into a "smart city" requires translating the requirements of international capitalism into local practices, infrastructures and economic or institutional arrangements; but it also implies maintaining transnational networks of exchange, cooperation and competition where Medellín could thrive as a model city. I argue that such operations of translation depend on the government's and non-public organizations' ability to do two things: representing the concerns and behaviours of residents on the one hand; and managing the tension between universalist "smart" imaginaries and local idiosyncrasies on the other.

From entrepreneurial to experimental cities: Urban exemplars and innovation in the social sciences

The idea of promoting model cities that could become sources of inspiration for others, successful practices being possibly replicated in other urban sites, is linked to the emergence of "entrepreneurial cities", which have been widely studied (Harvey 2007; Hall and Hubbard 1998; Jessop 1997; Ward 2003). Cities fitting that category are supposed to act as urban entrepreneurs, conducting emblematic projects and nurturing innovation capacities in order to foster competitive advantages to attract jobs, know-how and capital (in the form of grants or investments) in inter-urban competition. This trend has been made possible by the proliferation of actors and spaces dedicated to communication and exchange between cities, allowing the circulation of knowledge, best practices and technologies, and establishing metropolises as privileged geopolitical actors of global transformations, from conflict resolution to climate change (Béal 2014). An important point is that cities do not stay idle in this process: they actively take part in urban competition, devise strategies for marketing territories or urban features and eagerly promote themselves as regional or national exemplars. "Smart" city projects and discourses can be read as strategic moves in a global, inter-urban competitive environment (Hodson and Marvin 2007).

In this chapter, I make use of the term "smart" as a shortcut to refer to the transformations the metropolitan area of Medellín is attempting to accomplish. I use it primarily because it is the vocabulary employed by city officials I met during fieldwork, whose stated goal is to turn Medellín into an "inclusive and competitive smart city".[4] Critics of the smart city movement have pointed out the technocratic features of its agenda, looking to deploy industry-pushed, one-size-fits-all "solutions" that were sometimes lacking a problem – as well as specific governmentalities and conceptions of civic engagement – to *any* urban area, marginalizing local communities and institutions (Luque-Ayala and Marvin 2015). Others have simply remarked that, in some cases, the discourse of social inclusiveness, digital empowerment and quality of life improvement was but an empty rhetoric masking growth- and competitiveness-related goals. As I will show below using the example of Medellín's innovation district, the case I develop here shows a different picture. Looking from afar, the public-private partnerships and international experts' interventions I describe appear like clear cases of forcibly importing conceptions of city life and government, effectively marginalizing local knowledge and ways of life. Local critics of the "Medellín miracle" have for instance pointed out the rising inequalities in public service provision between districts, which threaten the very existence of the poorest neighbourhoods (Velásquez 2010). What I show in this chapter, however, is that administration officials in Medellín tend to share a lot of the concerns related to imported knowledge and the rationalization of public action. This makes Medellín an interesting case to discuss what an "actually existing smart city" might look like in a "developing country"[5] and how reflexive innovators handle such criticism. Many authors also point out that institutions such as innovation districts or technological parks can be described in terms of privatization of public space and city services (Kitchin 2015; Hollands 2015). The cases I develop in this contribution are less clear-cut: rather, they are better described in terms of "partnered government" (Larner and Butler 2007; McGuirk and Dowling 2009), showing institutional creativity beyond the public-private divide.

The actors in charge of Medellín's urban innovation strategy appropriate the lexicon of the "urban laboratory", a metaphor widely used in "smart" urbanism (Evans and Karvonen 2014). The term carries the promise of both knowledge and controlled transformation (Evans 2011); it also evokes flexibility and "lightweight" government, as experimentation is supposed to produce ad-hoc, adjustable policies, and comes with public-private partnerships (Evans et al. 2016). Experimental discourse has gained considerable rhetorical force as cities are increasingly budget- and time-constrained, as a way to optimize public resource use and collaboratively design problems and solutions: Amin and Thrift (2002: 77) see urban experimentation as "the ordering of uncertainty", an "ecology of circumstance" moving away from long-term planning. It is worth mentioning here that the term "laboratory" is used in a very loose sense by urban actors: cities are far from controlled environments where quantifiable modifications could be carefully introduced and their effects measured. The "experimental cities" literature (Evans et al. 2016), however, does not account for the coproduction of fact-making and political-economic ordering that experiments entail, as Science and Technology Studies (STS) have shown (Shapin and Schaffer 2011). Urban experiments, I argue, produce site-specific knowledge about technologies, but are also used to conceive economic and regulatory frameworks that are intended as being replicable elsewhere. A tension then arises between the city as a place of uniqueness and as a place where assemblages and economic arrangements can emerge to be replicated in other urban sites. This tension has been identified by Gieryn (2006) in a paper analysing the work of the Chicago School social scientists, who used the city as a "truth-spot", both as an authoritative space for generalizable knowledge production and as a place for inquiry into site-specific issues. These epistemological displacements between the city as a field site and the city as a laboratory are used by urban experimenters in Medellín to establish it as a travelling exemplar of urban regeneration and governance, while at the same time mobilizing experiments to transform its urban political economy and the political identities of social groups.

Innovation as an "engine for development"

There is a surprisingly long list of cities on the South-American continent that have expressed their intention to become "the Silicon Valley of Latin America": recent examples include Santiago de Chile, São Paulo in Brazil, or Guadalajara in

Mexico.[6] Specific features, however, set Medellín apart as a would-be innovation landmark. Medellín has cultivated a unique relationship with a local utility company called *Empresas Públicas de Medellín* (Public Enterprises of Medellín or EPM). Founded in 1955 as a joint venture of several firms providing public services (electricity generation and distribution, natural gas and water distribution, telecommunications) in an attempt to thwart corruption, EPM is owned by the municipality. EPM is now a successful multinational, and the second largest Colombian corporation: it made six billion US dollars in revenue in 2016, conducting business from Chile to Mexico, mainly in renewable energy and power distribution. It owns dams, solar farms, offshore wind turbines, complete sewage systems and power networks and recently became one of the largest waste collection and management companies in Colombia. What makes it an interesting and unique case is that EPM allocates a third of its revenue to the city's budget, in effect financing much of Medellín's urban development projects.

EPM has had a role in the functioning and continuity of the local government far beyond the services it provides and the products it sells. As the director of its Innovation Department proudly explains to me, the company is listed in the Dow Jones Sustainability Index, has "a credit rating even better than the country's" and manages its international operations like any large transnational corporation from its imposing and modernistic headquarters in Medellín's administrative centre, dubbed the *edificio inteligente* ("smart building"), a building located near city hall and noticeably much taller. The statutes of the company stipulate that 30% of its revenue goes to municipal coffers, which represents more than 40% of Medellín's annual budget and has allowed the city to finance ambitious infrastructures and redevelopment projects, including the gondolas, libraries and parks of "social urbanism" fame.

> We want to make money and we love making money – it's our mission as public servants ... We are [the city's] cash cow – not even the province has this kind of money. The city of Medellín earns more than the whole province: That's how you get a very developed city in the middle of sub-Saharan Africa living standards.
>
> *(EPM, Gerencia Desarollo e Innovación Director, November 17, 2016)*

EPM not only plays a financial role in Medellín's urban development, it also ensures consistency in city policies. Whereas in other Colombian cities, Bogotá in particular, urban (re)development projects have a life span of roughly four years because of difficult transitions between administrations, city officials I interviewed in Medellín praised the stability and cohesion of planning initiatives there. EPM, acting as an unelected second administration (the Mayor has a seat on the board of administrators which appoints the bulk of the top management), smooths out transitions and ensures that major undertakings see completion. As a strange hybrid between multinational corporation and local government, EPM raises questions about public-private relationships in Medellín's politics and about corporate conceptions of the common good. It is reminiscent of the rich historical tradition of "ad-hoc governance" Mariana Valverde (2016) describes in the UK and the USA, "entities that combine public powers such as expropriation with the financial flexibility of private corporations".

In 2008, following EPM's idea, Medellín's administration began integrating "Science, Technology and Innovation" plans (often abbreviated "CT+i") to the strategic plans mayors publish when they take office. In 2010, a project to "put innovation at the heart of competitiveness and development"[7] was voted by the city council: it ratified the creation of *Corporación Ruta N*, a private entity funded by EPM, with a mission to "develop the knowledge economy [and] turn Medellín into a leader city in innovation in Latin America through the implementation of public-private partnerships".[8] The name Ruta N means "North route" and refers to the location of its imposing, LEED-certified headquarters. Ruta N, referred to as "EPM's brainchild", lives on public funds but exists to attract and care for private capital. This organization is important for at least three reasons: it institutionalizes urban innovation and experiments while incorporating local development goals; it is in charge of bringing businesses and government to work together; and it organizes the circulation of knowledge, practices and technologies between Medellín and other cities, promoting its brand of "inclusive" smart urbanism around the world. Central to Ruta N's work is an experimental district created in 2013, called "Medellinnovation". As in Barcelona, Boston, Seattle and many other cities, a portion of urban space has been marked as a testbed site for urban innovation. If Medellin intends to become a model city, it also has its models: the innovation district 22@Barcelona and its American counterpart in Boston provided inspiration for Medellín's own district, which was designed by MIT architect Carlo Ratti. This 172-hectare neighbourhood has been chosen for different reasons: a number of research institutions and universities (including the biggest hospital and the largest university in Colombia) are located inside the district, and it is well connected to various infrastructures, such as optic fibre cables and public transportation. As with other urban spaces with "laboratory" status, setting up the district required thorough mapping and detailed surveys to produce reporting indicators. The feature that most distinguishes it from its Barcelona or Seattle counterparts, however, is the demographics: the district is located in a relatively poor and populated area. Indeed, the stated goal of the *Medellinnovation* district, in the words of Ruta N's "CT+i" Director, is to "turn innovation into a development engine for the city".

Assembling economic performance and social inclusiveness through urban experiments

The objective of Ruta N's innovation district can first be analysed as an inward-oriented, local development project. It is an experimental site the purpose of which is to enrol public and private actors in a city strategy and to build consensus on how the conurbation should be organized politically and economically using tests, modelling and demonstrations. One of the functions of the *Medellinnovation* district is to attract transnational investment. This aspect is visible in a programme called "Landing", which offers a variety of services to companies looking to operate in Medellín: it rents working spaces for tech companies (complete with bean bags, ping-pong tables, 3D printers and Steve Jobs quotes on the walls) and acts as a facilitator for funding and regulatory procedures so that, in a programme manager's words: "companies can grow and bring their knowledge to the city". The "value proposition" of the programme, according to the same interviewee, is not only the working space, but Ruta N's "innovation ecosystem". The Landing programme doesn't target early-stage companies, but rather large firms such as Hewlett-Packard, UPS or Huawei. Ruta N hopes that opening up an experimental space to such firms will generate positive externalities and benefit the local economy, but also sees it as a way to "connect the city to the world".

The district thus coordinates interventions from outside the city (foreign direct investments, international experts' contributions, replicated experiments) while also allowing local authorities to maintain control over what urban innovation does to Medellín. Unlike most innovation corridors or "urban laboratories", *Medellinnovation* is not a greenfield development and isn't set in a blighted or abandoned part of the city. There are universities, hospitals, shops, houses and street vendors everywhere. Its 100,000 residents are in the bottom half of income distribution[9] in a city where almost 40% the population lives under the UN's poverty threshold. Economic activity is mostly informal, with small car repair shops and food-related businesses representing the dominant sectors. But surveys were not undertaken to ensure that the district was a representative sample of the population. On the contrary, it was chosen to demonstrate what sustaining an innovation "ecosystem" could do for the city if it worked in a poor neighbourhood:

> The easy choice was to do it in El Poblado [Medellín's financial centre, prized by connected local elites, businesses and tourists], but if we can generate new development capacities here (…), attain a critical mass of successes inside the district, people will see that it's happening, that it's tangible, and the rest of the city will be easier [to transform].
>
> (Medellinnovation *project manager, November 15, 2016*)

Here, the district is thought of as a public demonstration to prove to residents and, to a certain extent, authorities, what "innovation" or "the knowledge economy" can do for companies and citizens, from opening up business opportunities to lifting people out of poverty. In its promotional documents and on the *Medellinnovation* website, Ruta N refers to the district as an "urban laboratory", a "living lab for challenges". However, if the rhetoric is similar to other similar projects, Ruta N officials wish to distinguish it clearly from them:

> This goes beyond a living lab, it is more than a technological park. What we want is to change the drivers of socioeconomic development. It's an urban

regeneration project that also aims at injecting innovation capabilities in the territory, finding how to have people connect more with each other.

(Ruta N, Director CT+i, November 15, 2016)

This notion of innovation as a social, relational process stemming from sometimes serendipitous encounters (another Ruta N official says: "innovation is a virus that is transmitted from one person to another") echoes a theory of the city as generating innovation and value through encounters, central to Silicon Valley's lore. At one point my main interlocutor at Ruta N explicitly refers to Edward's Glaeser's best-seller, *Triumph of the City* (Glaeser 2011) during an interview, explaining that the *Medellinnovation* district maximizes "collisionable hours" – business opportunities-generating times and places which, in Glaeser's theory, are the historical force driving the success of cities. Replicating foreign exemplars is also about circulating theories and books. Innovation-generating encounters support discourses of social inclusive-ness put forward by Ruta N, another distinction from other innovation districts:

> Other cities have done similar things, but always in a remote location, and it always failed because nobody wants to live there. … This district is different because it takes the community into account. The challenge for us is to make the community stay here and to prevent gentrification … it's not about changing only the lives of the wealthiest 10%.
>
> *(Ruta N, Director CT+i, November 15, 2016)*

In this view, surveys and mapping also take place to ensure that *Medellinnovation* doesn't exclude pre-existing communities but instead improves the skills and cap-abilities of its inhabitants, in turn improving their livelihood. This idea is illustrated by two examples. The first is a programme aimed at giving access to legal credit markets to the informal businesses that make for a third of the economic activity inside the district. Those unofficial businesses usually resort to "*cobradiarios*" to cover their cash needs: loan sharks often tied to drug trafficking that demand daily payments at 20% interest rates or more. Ruta N is currently experimenting with indicators that would allow banks – who usually rely on high levels of doc-umentation to evaluate credit risk – to estimate the financial health of informal businesses, in order to offer them competitive legal credit rates. For instance, in the absence of tax reports or income statements, banks might use utility or phone bills to evaluate credit worthiness. The idea of the programme is to transform both banks and local shops, giving the former tools to interpret new kinds of informa-tion about informal economic agents (such as software to anonymize tele-communications data) and teaching the latter some accounting basics. The challenge, as identified by the project's team, is to normalize economic activity in the district, but not up to the point where it would be too constraining for business owners, which would result in them leaving the neighbourhood. The second example is a project started in February 2017 to test electric (and possibly driverless) vehicles inside the district. Since roughly 18% of the economic activity in the neighbourhood is made of small, family-owned, informal repair shops (*talleres* or "workshops"), Ruta N plans to offer formations to *taller* owners to convert them to the maintenance and reparation of new vehicle technologies so they can adjust to and thrive in the "new economy" the district is trying to bring about. This way, experimentation not only means testing a new technology but also implies transforming professional identities as part of an attempt to elaborate a space where it could function (in this case enabling on-site maintenance).

Ruta N officials see it as their mission to manage the tension between importing innovative solutions and growing them in-house. Referring to the planned pilot for autonomous vehicles mentioned above, one Ruta N manager explains that "driverless cars, as they are tested in California or Singapore would never work here. The pedestrian model is just too different". Indeed, walking the streets of Medellín I realize that notions of a safe distance or motorcycle driving patterns, for instance, seem dramatically different to the more policed habits of San Francisco, overloaded with signage and synchronized traffic lights. Serious coding work (and potentially street-level ethnography, as Californian firms hired social scientists to do) would probably be needed to have driverless cars cruising in Medellín without constantly braking in emergency. The people I interviewed in the city's institutions in charge of urban innovation took the critique of smart imperialism seriously: they worked, they said, to put mechanisms in place in order to adapt best practices rather than copy them; to include existing populations and "help their skills adjust to the pace of innovation" rather than replace them with entrepreneurial elites or co-working spaces catering for the needs of digital nomads. Does that make *Medellinovation* residents "smart citizens" as, some authors argued, the real beneficiaries of a "smart" city (Hill 2013)?

On the one hand, Ruta N's work does take district residents into account (and quite literally so, as it involves counting them and getting them into accounting) and the project of "upgrading" skills is presented as a form of empowerment. On the other hand, it's obviously a rather paternalistic and market-oriented notion of "smartness",[10] one that involves the normalization of economic activity and paves the way to discipline or control procedures embedded in the built environment (Vanolo 2013; Gabrys 2014). Furthermore, it embodies an injunction to follow a very linear path of development, one that is tied to the interests of powerful commercial actors such as banks, car manufacturers and – especially in the case of electric mobility projects – utility companies like EPM. It is consequently tempting to read the *Medellinnovation* strategy as a case of corporate capture of the public interest masquerading as local development. We should, however, be cautious of misrepresenting the critical poles if this debate: Medellín officials acknowledge such criticism (some of the people I met at Ruta N and in City Hall agreed to that assessment to a certain extent) and the innovation district I presented here can be read as an intended response to the problem of "smart imperialism". In a way, Ruta N, the centrepiece of Medellín's smart city strategy, can be seen as a technology of coordination built to assemble two goals that seem to contradict each other: to bring about a "competitive smart city", embracing the "knowledge economy", while pursuing development-related projects geared toward social inclusiveness. Doing that requires forms of sensing and citizen representation produced through experiments like those conducted in the *Medellinnovation* district.

Conclusion

In the case of Medellín, EPM's and Ruta N's work is not interesting solely because it reshapes public and private identities. In reworking the public-private divide, the corporation and its subsidiaries most importantly coordinate the work of heterogeneous actors to produce a coherent – and exportable – city exemplar. This has historically been apparent in EPM's ability to "sit everyone around the table" and devise an economic strategy for the city. The contemporary "shift from a traditional economy to a knowledge economy", heralded by Ruta N's director at a conference in Paris in November 2016 echoes transformations that took place in the 1980s when Medellín transitioned from an economy based on agriculture and mining, to one relying on services, adjusting to the requirements of international capitalism. Local corporations and businessmen, drug cartels, old landlord families, right-wing paramilitary forces and communist militias all gathered around local government to make the city "pivot" toward new economic goals, aiming to position Medellín as a primary target in Latin America for large-scale transnational investment in industrial mining, power generation, wood, palm oil and urban transportation infrastructures (Hylton 2007). The fact that Ruta N is a publicly funded private corporation does not say much about what it does to the city. Rather, it is the specific ways it acts as a mediator between government and corporates that inform our understanding of the transformation of Medellín into an "urban laboratory for the Global South".

I have also argued that urban experimentation matters for the constitution of city exemplars, as I tried to show the connection between claims of making Medellín attentive to its residents, sensible to local idiosyncrasies (by conducting various kinds of surveys and experiments) and its emergence as a regional and international exemplar. Urban experiments allow specific city features to be made tractable and to circulate across borders as "best practices" to be replicated, positioning some cities as leaders in inter-urban competition. This is problematic in the case of Medellín, as I have shown how the conditions of possibility for Medellín's "miracle" are grounded in idiosyncratic features (the relationship between the city and EPM) and would make replication very uncertain if not impossible. Projects undertaken in the newly-created *Medellinnovation* district show that it is geared toward assembling economic performance and social inclusiveness in order to establish Medellín as an innovation hub adapted to the particular challenges of Latin America. "Smart" city experiments matter for inventing urban technologies and the economic, infrastructural and regulatory environments where they may function, but also for representing concerns and shaping social and political identities. Corporate interventions are critical to such processes as they often rely on what is described as public-private partnerships. However, in Medellín's case, the public/private divide risks masking both the institutional diversity of urban actors that drive the city's transformations and the fact that they share the same objective: to position Medellín's elite favourably in the "global knowledge economy".

The case of Medellín also allows us to look at cities as global actors: experiments matter beyond experimental sites, as they are critical in locating a city within transnational markets; as they highlight circulations of knowledge and capital and because they raise questions pertaining to the larger geopolitical significance of cities. This should not, however, obscure the fact that those transformations matter first and foremost for the inhabitants of Medellín and the Aburra valley who have seen their jobs, landscapes and modes of political expression transformed, sometimes drastically, in less than two decades. For some, Medellín's quest for the "knowledge economy" has meant so far better access to education, sanitation and income – for others, such as the workers of the poorest *comunas*' rich informal economy, it could mean the disappearance of entire livelihoods. As Anna Tsing (2011) argues, it is precisely this kind of friction that makes the smart city a global phenomenon, as it is being rolled out in cities of the South and elsewhere. Studying its misunderstandings, fragile adaptations and risky importations is an opportunity to improve our critical understanding of "smart" and experimental urbanism while rejecting claims of its easy and unproblematic roll-out around the world.

Notes

1   "Medellín's comeback. The trouble with miracles", *The Economist*, June 2014.
2   In 2013, Medellín was recognized as "Innovative city of the year" by the Urban Land Institute, Citigroup and the *Wall Street Journal*. It was awarded the Lee Kwan Yew World City Prize, the "Nobel of urbanism", by the eponymous institute in Singapore, in 2016.
3   Cities for Life is a network of mayors from around the world, created by Ruta N and the mayor of Medellín in 2014 and backed by the OECD, which organizes summit-like public events. The second edition took place in Paris on 21–22 November 2016. It promotes the "inclusive smart city". See: http://citiesforlife-latribune.paris/ (accessed 06/08/2017).
4   "*Medellín, laboratorio mundial sobre desarollo urbano*", World Bank Blog, June 2017. (http://www.bancomundial.org/es/news/feature/2017/06/09/medellin-laboratorio-mundial-sobre-desarrollo-urbano-colombia).
5   A label which fits Colombia according to the 2017 "World Economic Situation and Prospects Report" by the IMF and the United Nations.
6   "How Colombia went from murder capital to tech powerhouse", CNN Money, March 2015   (http://money.cnn.com/2015/03/13/investing/colombia-tech-silicon-valley/index.html); "El Silicon Valley mexicano está en Jalisco", *El Pais*, March 2017.
7   Medellín's Mayor's Office, Activity Report 2008–2011, pp. 54–55.
8   Medellín's Mayor's Office, Activity Report 2008–2011, pp. 54–55.
9   Colombian citizens are divided into *estratos* going from 1 to 6 according to their place of residence; it determines their taxation level and how much they are charged for some public services. People living inside district boundaries are 1 to 3 in this social stratification.
10 A critique that echoes that of other "smart" initiatives, such as the city-making and state-making projects in Singapore: see Ho 2017 for a critical reading of the Smart Nation programme and Laurent and Pontille this volume for a discussion of the role of experiments.

References

Amin, Ash, and Nigel Thrift. 2002. *Cities: Reimagining the Urban*. Cambridge: Polity Press.

Bateman, Milford, Juan Pablo Duran Ortiz, and Kate Maclean. 2011. 'A Post-Washington Consensus Approach to Local Economic Development in Latin America? An Example from Medellín, Colombia'. Available at SSRN: https://ssrn.com/abstract=2385197.

Béal, Vincent. 2014. 'Trendsetting Cities: Les modèles à l'heure des politiques urbaines néolibérales'. *Métropolitiques*. https://www.metropolitiques.eu/Trendsetting-cities-les-modeles-a.html.

Brand, Peter. 2013. 'Governing Inequality in the South Through the Barcelona Model: "Social Urbanism" in Medellin, Colombia'. Interrogating Urban Crisis: Governance, Contestation, Critique. De Montfort University, Leicester, United Kingdom.

Brand, Peter, and Julio D. Dávila. 2011. 'Mobility Innovation at the Urban Margins: Medellín's Metrocables'. *City* 15(6): 647–661.

Evans, James. 2011. 'Resilience, Ecology and Adaptation in the Experimental City'. *Transactions of the Institute of British Geographers* 36(2): 223–237.

Evans, James, and Andrew Karvonen. 2014. '"Give Me a Laboratory and I Will Lower Your Carbon Footprint!"—Urban Laboratories and the Governance of Low-Carbon Futures'. *International Journal of Urban and Regional Research* 38(2): 413–430.

Evans, James, Andrew Karvonen, and Rob Raven. 2016. *The Experimental City*. London: Routledge.

Gabrys, Jennifer. 2014. 'Programming Environments: Environmentality and Citizen Sensing in the Smart City'. *Environment and Planning D: Society and Space* 32(1): 30–48.

Gieryn, Thomas F. 2006. 'City as Truth-Spot Laboratories and Field-Sites in Urban Studies'. *Social Studies of Science* 36(1): 5–38.

Glaeser, Edward. 2011. *Triumph of the City: How Our Greatest Invention Makes Us Richer, Smarter, Greener, Healthier, and Happier*. New York: Penguin.

Hall, Tim, and Phil Hubbard. 1998. *The Entrepreneurial City: Geographies of Politics, Regime, and Representation*. Chichester: John Wiley & Sons.

Harvey, David. 2007. 'Neoliberalism and the City'. *Studies in Social Justice* 1(1): 2–13.

Hill, Dan. 2013. 'On the Smart City: Or, a "Manifesto" for Smart Citizens Instead'. *City of Sound*, February 1.

Ho, Ezra. 2017. 'Smart subjects for a Smart Nation? Governing (smart)mentalities in Singapore'. *Urban Studies* 54(13): 3101–3118.

Hodson, Mike, and Simon Marvin. 2007. 'Understanding the Role of the National Exemplar in Constructing "Strategic Glurbanization"'. *International Journal of Urban and Regional Research* 31(2): 303–325.

Hollands, Robert G. 2015. 'Critical Interventions into the Corporate Smart City'. *Cambridge Journal of Regions, Economy and Society* 8(1): 61–77.

Hylton, Forrest. 2007. 'Extreme Makeover: Medellín in the New Millennium'. In Mike Davis and Daniel Bertrand Monk (eds), *Evil Paradises: Dreamworlds of Neoliberalism*, 152–163. New York: New Press.

Jessop, Bob. 1997. 'The Entrepreneurial City: Re-Imaging Localities, Redesigning Economic Governance, or Restructuring Capital'. *Transforming Cities: Contested Governance and New Spatial Divisions* 46: 28–41.

Kitchin, Rob. 2015. 'Making Sense of Smart Cities: Addressing Present Shortcomings'. *Cambridge Journal of Regions, Economy and Society* 8(1): 131–136.

Larner, Wendy, and Maria Butler. 2007. 'The Places, People and Politics of Partnership: After Neoliberalism in Aotearoa New Zealand'. In Helga Leitner, Jamie Peck, and Eric Sheppard (eds), *Contesting Neoliberalism: Urban Frontiers*, 71–89. New York: Guilford.

Luque-Ayala, Andrés, and Simon Marvin. 2015. 'Developing a Critical Understanding of Smart Urbanism?' *Urban Studies* 52(12): 2105–2116.

Maclean, Kate. 2015. *Social Urbanism and the Politics of Violence: The Medellín Miracle*. Basingstoke: Palgrave Macmillan.

McGuirk, Pauline, and Robyn Dowling. 2009. 'Neoliberal Privatisation? Remapping the Public and the Private in Sydney's Masterplanned Residential Estates'. *Political Geography* 28(3): 174–185.

Shapin, Steven, and Simon Schaffer. 2011. *Leviathan and the Air-Pump: Hobbes, Boyle, and the Experimental Life*. Princeton: Princeton University Press.

Shelton, Taylor, Matthew Zook, and Alan Wiig. 2015. 'The "Actually Existing Smart City"'. *Cambridge Journal of Regions, Economy and Society* 8(1): 13–25.

Tsing, Anna Lowenhaupt. 2011. *Friction: An Ethnography of Global Connection*. Princeton: Princeton University Press.

Valverde, M. 2016. 'Ad Hoc Governance: Public Authorities and North American Local Infrastructure in Historical Perspective'. In Michelle Brady and Randy K. Lippert (eds), *Governing Practices: Neoliberalism, Governmentality and the Ethnographic Imaginary*, 199–217. Toronto: University of Toronto Press.

Vanolo, Alberto. 2013. 'Smartmentality: The Smart City as Disciplinary Strategy'. *Urban Studies* 51(5): 883–898, doi:0042098013494427.

Velásquez, Carlos. 2010. 'Medellín Desconectada… de La Dignidad'. *Observatorio K* 2(1): 103–109.

Ward, Kevin. 2003. 'Entrepreneurial Urbanism, State Restructuring and Civilizing "New" East Manchester'. *Area* 35(2): 116–127.

6

BUILDING SMART CITY PARTNERSHIPS IN THE "SILICON DOCKS"

Liam Heaphy and Réka Pétercsák

Introduction

As a maritime city bisected by a river, Dublin has long signalled its periods of prosperity and progress, relative or absolute, with new bridges across the river Liffey in accordance with increases in the flows of goods and people. The port has progressively moved east on reclaimed land with new berths for larger ships, creating new crossing points as obsolete shallow water docks were ceded to urban development. Dublin Port now occupies the eastern extremity of the Dublin Docklands, with the central part largely converted from industrial use and warehousing to office blocks, residential apartments, civic amenities, and commercial usage. The "Celtic Tiger" that preceded the banking and housing crash of 2007–2008 left behind unfinished projects and vacant lots and the intangible promise of further development on dockland parcels adjacent to both sides of the river. Ten years after the onset of an economic crisis that led to an international rescue package from the EU and IMF, the economy is once again growing, albeit under more cautious management to try and prevent a repeat of the trauma of the 2008–2015 period. However, the crisis resulted in a severe housing shortage in Dublin, Cork, and other Irish cities due to years of construction inactivity.

The Dublin Docklands is the most significant urban development in Ireland in recent decades, in terms of its strategic importance for economic development, its central location extending the city centre east along the Liffey, and its trialling of new ideas and technologies for urban living. As of 2018, it is the host area of the "Smart Docklands", an initiative led by Dublin City Council and a new organisational unit called Smart Dublin which is a joint venture of the four local authorities (Coletta, Heaphy, and Kitchin 2017). Smart Dublin has established various project partnerships with locally-based information and communication technologies (ICT) companies, many of which are resident in the Docklands. The area is home to forty of the major technology companies, including nine out of the ten largest ICT organisations and financial institutions globally. It is a commercially vibrant part of the city and its inhabitants comprise recently arrived high-skilled workers and longstanding poorer communities in areas such as the East Wall and Ringsend. Smart Dublin is supporting the rollout of testbeds and pilot projects for Internet of Things and sensor-based technologies in the docklands to create a new "smart district". Acting effectively as a boundary organisation between the public and the private sector (Guston 2001), Smart Dublin seeks to have strong relationships with both sectors in the interest of driving innovation-based job growth and supporting city services. Similar organisational units are emerging in all the major cities on the island of Ireland, from Cork and Limerick in the Republic of Ireland to Belfast and Derry in Northern Ireland.

As part of an engagement with Smart Dublin, a university research project was devised to better understand the key stakeholders' perceived challenges, needs and visions. This research is intended to feed back into an URBACT project called SmartIMPACT and inform the strategy-building process for the Smart Docklands. Our research consists of 30 approximately one-hour semi-structured interviews with 32 stakeholders, split evenly between the public and private sectors. Participants were either initially identified by Dublin City Council or nominated by stakeholders themselves during the interview process. Our sample includes those who have recently started conversations with the city council (such as some of the resident multinationals), those working in local government, enterprise initiatives and quangos, relevant national agencies, university researchers, infrastructure providers, and those who were unfamiliar with Smart Dublin (including community representatives).

The interviews covered roles and responsibilities, concepts of measuring success, value creation, business practices with the local authority, expectations and ways of learning, best practices, challenges, and defining the concepts of smartness and sustainability. We also attended and contributed to various smart city events including meetings, workshops and programme launches, which offered an insight into how stakeholders initiated partnerships and moved towards aligning their interests.

Drawing from this research, this chapter examines how the Docklands has become a symbolic site of importance as the heart of the new economy, driven by technology innovation. In relation to its designation as a "smart district" we note how a new configuration of partnerships has evolved from its unsure and idealistic start towards an established footing with a clear central responsibility given to Dublin City Council and its smart city programme shared with the other three local authorities. We argue that local government organisations such as Smart Dublin should not be seen solely as the key enablers of urban technological modernisation. They are also central learning and innovation units that, given their boundary work in the public and private sphere, experiment with novel collaborative organisational and managerial practices that will underpin the relationship between urban space and the ICT sector. Rhetorically, the smart city is cast as a means to prepare urban regions to combat increasing social and environmental pressures, yet it is also a strategically important conduit for technology companies based in Ireland to experiment with new products for wider markets. In this sense, the smart docklands is the latest iteration of experimental urbanism on the island, in which city administrations are seeking to validate the agency given to corporate interests with demonstrable benefits for the citizenry.

In the following section, we briefly outline the historical importance of the Dublin Docklands in the dominant narrative of the State and the latter's contested engagement with urbanism. We highlight the role of Dublin as a beacon of socio-economic transformation and the status of the docklands as a national signifier. We then trace the evolution of the stakeholder network in Dublin and the central place of the smart city team. Finally, we position the Smart Docklands initiative as an experimentation site for organisational transformation by drawing attention to the emergence of inter-organisational work practices that underpin the smart city ecosystem.

Selective modernity and urban decline

The urban form of Dublin, as well as that of other cities and towns throughout Ireland, has a complex relationship with its inhabitants old and new. Its Georgian and Edwardian architectural heritage is shared with England, Scotland, and Wales, and evidences the composite culture of Ireland. In contrast with Belfast, for a time the largest city on the island with the bulk of its heavy industrialisation and suburbanisation, Dublin at the start of the 20th century was still a rather compact city with a legacy of overpopulated tenements (O'Leary 2014: 69). However, when the Irish Free State (*Saorstát Éireann*) was established in 1922 following a guerrilla warfare-based campaign against the apparatus of the British State, its inner-city buildings and streetscapes were in dire need of reform and slum clearance.

The first forty years of the new State, particularly under the stewardship of Éamon de Valera, steered through the heady politics of the time with a selective embrace of modernity, and combined a vision of rural self-sufficiency with select large-scale industrial projects. This period is immortalised in Seán Keating's painting "Night's Candles are Burnt Out", depicting the interwar construction of the Ard na Croise hydroelectric dam on the Shannon (completed by Siemens) which could then power the whole country (Boyd and McLaughlin 2015). The State's ambivalence towards metropolitan culture reflected a popular zeal to restore life to a hinterland decimated through cycles of poor landlordism, endemic poverty, emigration, and famine (Thornley 1964). Nevertheless, Dublin Corporation (now Dublin City Council) undertook a number of small scale urban projects. These included the Thorncastle Street flats in the docklands (completed in 1936) influenced by De Stijl, an Art Deco building for the Department of Industry and Commerce on Kildare Street (in 1942), and Dublin Airport's modernist Terminal 1 (originally Collinstown Airport, also in 1942) (Kincaid 2006a).

For all the rhetoric of national renewal, emigration and underdevelopment continued to characterise the country until Ireland began a programme in the 1960s to industrialise and attract foreign direct investment (FDI), creating the Industrial Development Agency to handle and promote inward investment. The ambivalent relationship to heritage attracted further controversy as many of Dublin's Georgian buildings and heritage were allowed to fall into decline and were then demolished (McDonald 1989). The brutalist architectural style favoured by architects like Sam Stephenson arose over the old order in the form of the former Central Bank on Dame Street and the ESB headquarters on Fitzwilliam Street (Graham and Ashworth 2013; Kincaid 2006b). However, while Dublin had extended beyond its traditional boundaries delimited by the Grand and Royal canals, the inner city was in decline until the 1980s. This was particularly notable in the docklands where there was a residual dependent population following the mechanisation and containerisation of the port, including many elderly, unemployed, and educationally deprived (Doucet and Duignan 2012; Moore 1999, 138). Henceforth, inner city market-driven renewal programmes began to reverse that trend, at the same time as architecture took inspiration from influential contemporaries like Aldo Rossi and Peter Eisenmann (Hebbert 2006), seeking to develop a sense of place based on mixed-use, walkable neighbourhoods. These currents of thought, which rejected the functionalist form of planning in the British tradition, found their way to Dublin with the "Group 91" collective of designers and architects and their project "Making a Modern Street" (Group 91 1991). This collective would inform the 1990s development of Temple Bar as a cultural quarter (Lawton and Punch 2014).

The initial two phases of docklands redevelopment, from 1986 to 1997, were managed by the country's first Urban Development Corporation, and encompassed the Custom House and its immediate eastern environ. With its development tax breaks and exceptions, the Custom House Docks Development Authority (CHDDA) emulated the success of Shannon Airport's pioneering Free Trade Zone, repurposed towards urban development with tax incentives for potential tenants by means of the Urban Renewal Act in 1986 (O'Leary 2014, 162). This entrepreneurial approach to planning and development opened the way for private companies to take part in shaping and delivering urban policies and projects (MacLaran and Kelly 2014). The CHDDA oversaw the development of the International Financial Services Centre, while simultaneously seeking to appeal to an urbane and lucrative clientele through cultural attractors such as exhibition spaces and restaurants.

A third phase of development ensued when the Dublin Docklands Development Authority (DDDA) replaced the CHDDA in 1997 and implemented an Integrated Area Plan approach to regeneration that took more account of social needs and local participation (Bartley 2007). The DDDA covered 526 hectares of land, including well-established residential communities, who could voice their concerns and ideas through a Council of 25 members that oversaw the implementation of the masterplan and provided recommendations to the Executive.

The Dublin Docklands becomes a national signifier

The area is currently the largest urban development in the country, which in its post-2015 guise covers 96 hectares (69 ha of land) in a new iteration of a special purpose planning vehicle called a Strategic Development Zone (SDZ) (see Figure 6.1). This is a model for holistic planning with a fast-tracking process, as only the SDZ masterplan itself needs to be approved by An Bord Pleanála (the Planning Board). Individual developments are approved by the delivery body itself without recourse to planning appeals once the SDZ is approved. Unlike the DDDA, however, the delivery body is now Dublin City Council rather than an urban development corporation.

The North Lotts and Grand Canal Dock SDZ masterplan encloses only a small subset of the former wider Docklands area covered by the DDDA, selectively isolating the remaining undeveloped central plots controlled by a bad debts holding entity called the National Assets Management Agency (NAMA). This redrawing of the boundaries was critiqued and debated during a conference called "A Community for All" held before the SDZ was finalised (Clancy, Donnelly, and Olofsson 2013). Participants from the community sector have noted the loss of focus in local issues once subsumed within the plans for the wider city. The City Development Plan 2016–2022 (Dublin City Council 2016) envisages the city as a whole to be a compact, green, walkable city of varied neighbourhoods. It contains provision for the Docklands as a "Strategic Development and Regeneration Area" and details programmes to address concerns over continued social deprivation.

The Docklands SDZ has largely preserved the design guidelines and requirements that informed the DDDA before it, with building heights capped to conform to a relatively low-profile (seven storeys for residential and six for office in Dublin) and provision for cultural amenities and mixed-use developments, with retail units at the ground floor. In contrast, political outbursts from cabinet ministers have looked more towards examples from the Anglophone world and its former colonies. Former Minister of Finance, Michael Noonan, hoped that this strategically important area might "rival the likes of London's Canary W[h]arf, Boston's Seaport and Singapore's Marina Bay" (Byrne 2016, 9), while an early 1990s push from the former Progressive Democrats party assembled a medley of skyscrapers and pasted them onto a brochure envisioning a Manhattan on the Docks. These are a rather unlikely set of examples, given that aesthetically and conceptually, the development is more akin to other docklands projects in Europe such as the Oostelijke Haveneilanden in Amsterdam, and Hafencity in Hamburg. Where perhaps they relate more to American examples is through the role of US property companies such as Hines and Kennedy-Wilson, which have taken up distressed assets in Dublin for developing and managing long-term rental accommodation at the higher end of the market. In addition, following Google's acquisition of buildings in the area, many technology corporations have also purchased adjacent properties, thereby justifying the "Silicon Docks" moniker (Roberts, Worrall, and Burke 2015). It is this cultural fusion of American investment and

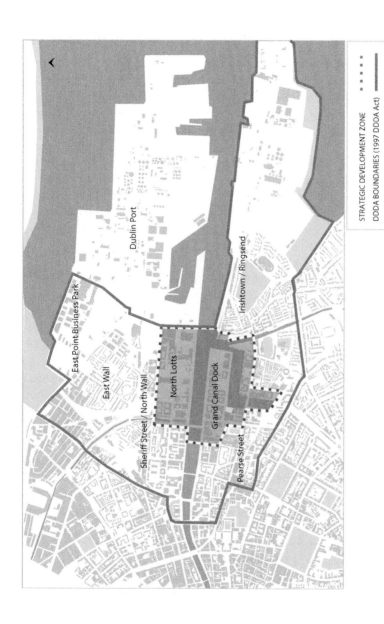

FIGURE 6.1 The 96-hectare SDZ as managed by Dublin City Council (dotted line) within the 526-hectare area (solid line) formerly managed by the DDDA (Dublin City Council, 2014)

Irish industry, together with property companies and a European-centred urbanist vision for the area that has made it an intriguing prospect for the fortunes of urban planning and architecture in Ireland.

Dublin's enrolment of the smart city into local innovation strategies

The *Build Ireland's Smart Economy* report was born out of the effort to prevail through the Irish chapter of the global financial crisis starting in 2008, reconceptualising Ireland as a platform for economic growth with city regions as its engines. Accordingly, it denotes a journey through five key action areas towards economic improvement marking the future direction for all ministries and departments. This framework, written in the aftermath of the crash, characterises the "continued success of Dublin" as "critical for the performance of the entire economy" (Department of the Taoiseach 2008, 99). The document redefines various geographic areas according to their capacity for innovation, an essential factor in determining urban competitiveness. This is also reflected in studies of the area, using the concept of *Ideopolis*, compressing the growing responsibility of cities "to drive growth in the wider city region" (Williams and Redmond 2006, 3) into a single, elegant term.

The Smart Strategy represented the Irish government's effort to enable "an exemplary research, innovation and commercialisation ecosystem so as to create 'The Innovation Island'" (Department of the Taoiseach 2008, 33). It envisages energy-efficient "management" of the environment calling for resource-awareness across sectors. To enable better governance, it also aims to strengthen the city's core authorities through more efficient management and accountability of performance and information sharing. This is imagined through the introduction of cross-departmental ICT in the hope of facilitating citizen and business initiatives in collaboration with the city authorities. Additionally, cities as the economic engines for their respective regions are to receive funds to create critical infrastructure and enable the better flow of people, goods, and information. And finally, pro-enterprise financial measures are introduced to boost economic development including corporate tax incentives and re-securing an active banking sector in Ireland. The first Smart Strategy thus demarcates the critical systems and institutions of economic growth and thereby reflects on the contemporary mind-set for addressing local and global crises through (urban) efficiency and innovation.

The impact of the programme was to be made visible through both the number of innovative outputs and Dublin's place in quality of life rankings. The Dublin Economic Action Plan of 2009 described this change in terms of improvements to the built environment, integrated transport and infrastructure planning. It highlighted that a "high quality of life within a compact urban environment is central to the promotion of a knowledge-based economy that attracts and retains highly talented people to the city region" (Dublin Regional Authority 2009, 18). Following a series of initiatives that included Creative Dublin and Digital Dublin, the creation of Smart Dublin in 2015 (officially launched at City Hall in March 2016) has remained both a symbolic and practical effort to bring about change in the way it manages its resources to enhance technology-driven innovation. The initiative has since then embodied the public sector's effort to bring about socio-economic change through taking the lead on the systemic integration of ICTs in the urban fabric to "attract mobile talent, FDI, and to stimulate innovation" (Department of Jobs, Enterprise and Innovation 2016, 74). It is in this context that the Smart Docklands project emerged as the newest focus of Smart Dublin and Dublin City Council.

Creating the Smart Docklands stakeholder network

Our stakeholder network is mapped out below using Gephi, indicating degrees of centrality and marginality, and spatialised using the ForceAtlas2 algorithm (Jacomy et al. 2014) with automated adjustments to ensure legibility of text (see Figure 6.2). The presence of actors with smaller nodes is contingent upon the numbers of interviews undertaken and the pre-selection made by the research team, as well as the snowballing strategy followed. Individual actors are represented as nodes, sized proportionally (ranked) according to the number of times they have been proposed as key stakeholders by other actors. The nodes are also colour-coded according to the sector in which they are based. The arrows (edges) connecting nodes are sized according to the frequency of times a stakeholder has been suggested by a participant and indicate the directionality of this based on our interviewees.

Dublin City Council (DCC), and the Smart Docklands and Smart Dublin by extension, are the central actors in the network. Interviewees stressed the coordinative functions of DCC, and the benefits of triple helix partnerships including local universities and national research networks. As the strategic development zone largely consists of land assets managed by NAMA, this and other planning bodies such as the national regulator, An Bord Pleanála, were given prominence among those involved in urban development and social care. There was also an emphasis on the central role played by ICT companies and agencies or consultants supporting innovation and economic development. In part, the emphasis on individual companies reflects a tendency to namecheck the most well-known and recognised companies in the Docklands as symbolic of the ICT sector.

As the Smart Dublin initiative advanced, the team began to create new connections with key stakeholders and re-establish old ones. For many of the potential partners, working with the city council as part of this initiative was uncharted territory that each approached with unique expectations. The challenge for the dedicated city council team was to make use of these relationships to advance the Smart City agenda and create mutually beneficial outcomes for the parties involved. Depending on each other for resources and expertise, stakeholders participated in various events to explore opportunities for aligning interests and finding common "use-cases". Here we could observe stakeholders, and experts in their respective areas "negotiating and combining ingredients from different contexts to achieve hybrid situations" (Engeström, Engeström, and Kärkkäinen 1995, 319).

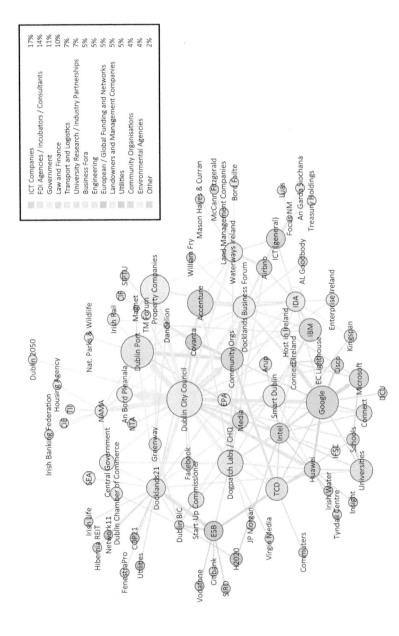

FIGURE 6.2 Stakeholder mapping based on social network analysis of suggested key stakeholders. A colour version is available at: http://progcity. maynoothuniversity.ie/wp-content/uploads/2018/09/Figure2.pdf

The legend contains:

ICT Companies	17%
FDI Agencies / Incubators / Consultants	14%
Government	11%
Law and Finance	10%
Transport and Logistics	7%
University Research / Industry Partnerships	7%
Business Fora	5%
Engineering	5%
European / Global Funding and Networks	5%
Landowners and Management Companies	5%
Utilities	5%
Community Organisations	4%
Environmental Agencies	4%
Other	2%

These events opened up the possibility for participants to experiment with work practices that are uniquely linked to the formation of stakeholder relationships. For example, we observed recurrent meetings between universities, technology companies and local government that have eventually led to the establishment of research centres, the designation of urban experimentation sites for new technologies, and the submission of joint grant proposals.

Meetings, workshops, and conversations functioned as experimentation sites for new organisational practices that over time resulted in successful projects. Occasionally, this also resulted in disappointed withdrawals from the network, such as where stakeholders became overwhelmed by the challenges of collaborative work and resolved to deliver projects through their own organisation. Indeed, hybrid work practices and new routines across professional disciplines took time to establish and brought about voices of frustration and questions of responsibility:

> I actually think that it is the city or the government's job to provide the plumbing for this [district-wide public Wi-Fi scheme], and then it is their job to get out of the way. In the same way that they provide roads, or they provide street lighting, or they provide other things which we all take for granted, they should be providing, in partnership with industry.
>
> *(Interview SDD03, local business and innovation promoter)*

Although relationships between organisations in smart cities are often conceptualised as constituting an ecosystem with multiple members, on the project-level, a relatively low number (2–8) of organisational actors start out co-developing a project. These individual-level processes underpin the development of inter-organisational work practices and impact on creating the inter-organisational capabilities (Orlikowski 2002) necessary to deliver city-wide strategies. While the development of organisational routines and capabilities in a single organisation is easier to account for, innovative capabilities that emerge from the complex interactions of multiple actors require deeper exploration. In many cases, these actors may not ever be formally bound to each other, or there may not be any protocols they can follow to deliver projects. We also noted another challenge in the docklands: those stakeholders who from their daily work had an insight into the reality of public service delivery were doubtful about the value of working on smart city initiatives. In contrast, for "networkers" in the innovation and business side, participation in smart city initiatives was easier to imagine. Being on familiar terrain in-between organisations, these stakeholders would envisage "work" materialising through "building collaborations", "finding use-cases" and "creating a new brand and storyline for the Docklands". In Figure 6.2 above, these include many of those within the Docklands Business Forum, such as local business leaders and consultants as well as governance and community leaders. It also includes Docklands21 and companies located towards the centre of the network.

Our interviews and observations document a difficult, often chaotic process where stakeholders struggle to make sense of their responsibilities (Weick 1995) in the face of "novel combinations of capital, tacit knowledge, and regimes of justification" (Jay 2013, 138). In 2016, the formal processes and legal and financial frameworks for supporting collaborative innovation across sectors were still missing, making stakeholders in the Docklands uneasy about the prospect of taking part in a public-private endeavour. Historic distrust between some of the public and private institutions also frequently dominated the interviews followed by the need for rebranding not only the Docklands, but also the inter-organisational effort itself. At this initial stage, engagement would not unfold naturally, due to the variety of professional contexts and the history of partnerships between stakeholders. The challenge for the Smart Cities initiative became not only to experiment with urban technologies, but to track the best ways in which to create interlocking mechanisms (Ciborra and Andreu 2001) between different organisational practices, thereby opening up pathways to collaborative innovation.

Examples of such experimental ways of working were visible during the preparatory phases of collaborative grant proposals, periods preceding the establishment of research centres, and the discussions before incorporating start-up projects in the smart city development process. The development of inter-organisational work practices and routines which underpin the capabilities of the Smart City ecosystem, then, were shaped during exploratory conversations, meetings, and workshops, where corporate, start-up, non-profit, and city council work practices are negotiated and merged. In other words, when we speak of engagement in the case of Smart City stakeholders we denote a frequently chaotic sequence of events that, taken separately, allow for the participants to establish a common experience and find opportunities to share and transfer knowledge, but seen conjointly, they amount to the "everyday" organisational reality of the Smart City. Over time, however, some of the interdisciplinary practices became standardised, the responsibilities of the remaining stakeholders became clearer and meetings started to follow a stable sequence that became organisational routines. The results of this process also manifested themselves at the level of individual organisations. For example, the local authority started to have more cross-departmental interactions and began to look for formal ways of including start-ups and other companies in their projects. In other words, the formative context of the local authority, and the work culture of the central organisation in the smart city ecosystem also began to change. Interdisciplinary practices emerging as a result of exploratory events slowly transformed into constituents of a critical infrastructure, associated with the production of the city.

Conclusion

The emerging smart city partnership in the Dublin Docklands is a means of building new partnerships between local government and innovation, trialling new technologies for urban management, and boosting economic development in sectors that are strategically important to the country. It is not yet clear to what extent this may reshape how city service provision is reconfigured, not least because many of the corporate actors are themselves engaged in a process of discovering what commitments they can make, what technologies might be utilised, and what gain might be acquired in what timeframe. Part of this emerging network is linked to a common cultural space between the US and Ireland, with many US firms well integrated into the Irish economy. This US FDI dependency is being enrolled into the formation of a stronger local innovation system. Smart Dublin supports this maturing innovation system while also recruiting the resultant pool of innovation to support government-led urban challenges.

The Docklands itself now occupies a middle ground between the ideals which underpin Silicon Valley and a more local push to ensure Dublin is competitive with other mid-sized European national or regional capitals. The early development during the DDDA phase had a strong social and community angle that distinguished it from its Anglophone peers and placed it in a more European mould of dense, yet low-profile, mixed-use urban space with social provision. Given the decidedly European focus of many of the research projects under way, an important part of future work in building partnerships will be to reconcile the ideals of urban and community-focussed place-making evident in the original work of the DDDA with sustainable economic development and increasing demands from a larger, more informed, and more mobile workforce.

The Smart Docklands brings together a unique network of stakeholders from various backgrounds with differing levels of engagement. In many instances, they themselves lead long-standing ecosystems or forums in the area and as such, have played their part in constructing the pre-history of the so-called Silicon Docks. Regardless of their roles, however, they all represent existing expertise in the Docklands, and possess knowledge to be linked, shared, and used in meaningful ways. This suggests that a further challenge for the Smart Docklands initiative will be to create a mutually beneficial, responsive platform for its stakeholders in an emergent, innovative context to help operationalise their hybrid knowledge with the aim of building a more sustainable, resilient environment.

Acknowledgements

The research for this paper was supported, in part, by a European Research Council Advanced Investigator award (ERC-2012-AdG-323636-SOFTCITY), the Programmable City, and in part by a Science Foundation Ireland grant 13/RC/2094 and co-funded under the European Regional Development Fund through the Southern & Eastern Regional Operational Programme to Lero – the Irish Software Research Centre (www.lero.ie).

References

Bartley, Brendan. 2007. "Planning in Ireland." In *Understanding Contemporary Ireland*, edited by Rob Kitchin and Brendan Bartley, 31–43. London: Pluto Press.

Boyd, Gary A., and John McLaughlin. 2015. *Infrastructure and the Architectures of Modernity in Ireland 1916–2016*. Farnham: Ashgate.

Byrne, Michael. 2016. "Entrepreneurial Urbanism After the Crisis: Ireland's 'Bad Bank' and the Redevelopment of Dublin's Docklands: Entrepreneurial Urbanism After the Crisis." *Antipode* 48(4): 899–918. doi:10.1111/anti.12231.

Ciborra, C., and Rafael Andreu. 2001. "Sharing Knowledge across Boundaries." *Journal of Information Technology* 16: 73–81. doi:10.1080/02683960110055103.

Clancy, Annette, Michael Donnelly, and Siobhán Olofsson. 2013. *A Community for All.* Dublin: Dublin Docklands Development Authority. http://www.dublincity.ie/sites/default/files/content//Planning/OtherDevelopmentPlans/LocalAreaPlans/Documents/DOCKLANDSFINAL2014.pdf.

Coletta, Claudio, Liam Heaphy, and Rob Kitchin. 2017. "From Accidental to Articulated Smart City: The Creation and Work of Smart Dublin." In *The Programmable City Working Paper 28.* socarxiv. https://osf.io/preprints/socarxiv/93ga5.

Department of Jobs, Enterprise and Innovation. 2016. *Action Plan for Jobs: Dublin 2016– 2018.* Rialtas na hÉireann. https://www.djei.ie/en/Publications/APJ-Dublin-2016-2018.html.

Department of the Taoiseach. 2008. *Building Ireland's Smart Economy: A Framework for Sustainable Economic Renewal.* Dublin: The Stationery Office.

Doucet, Brian, and Enda Duignan. 2012. "Experiencing Dublin's Docklands: Perceptions of Employment and Amenity Changes in the Sheriff Street Community." *Irish Geography* 45(1): 45–65. doi:10.1080/00750778.2012.698972.

Dublin City Council. 2014. North Lotts and Grand Canal Dock Planning Scheme 2014. http://www.dublincity.ie/main-menu-services-planning-urban-development-plans-local-area-plans/north-lotts-grand-canal-dock.

Dublin City Council. 2016. Dublin City Development Plan 2016–2022. Available at: http://dublincitydevelopmentplan.ie/.

Dublin Regional Authority. 2009. *Economic Development Action Plan for the Dublin City Region.* Dublin: DRA.

Engeström, Yrjö, Ritva Engeström, and Merja Kärkkäinen. 1995. "Polycontextuality and Boundary Crossing in Expert Cognition: Learning and Problem Solving in Complex Work Activities." *Learning and Instruction* 5(4): 319–336. doi:10.1016/0959-4752(95)00021-00026.

Graham, B. J., and Gregory Ashworth. 2013. "Heritage Conservation and Revisionist Nationalism in Ireland." In G.J. Ashworth and P.J. Larkham (eds), *Building a New Heritage: Tourism, Culture and Identity in the New Europe,* 135–158. London and New York: Routledge.

Group 91. 1991. *Making a Modern Street: An Urban Proposal: The Work of 8 Irish Architects.* Dublin: Gandon.

Guston, David H. 2001. "Boundary Organizations in Environmental Policy and Science: An Introduction." *Science, Technology & Human Values* 26(4): 399–408. doi:10.1177/016224390102600401.

Hebbert, Michael. 2006. "Town Planning versus Urbanismo." *Planning Perspectives* 21(3): 233–251. doi:10.1080/02665430600731153.

Jacomy, Mathieu, Tommaso Venturini, Sebastien Heymann, and Mathieu Bastian. 2014. "ForceAtlas2, a Continuous Graph Layout Algorithm for Handy Network Visualization Designed for the Gephi Software." Edited by Mark R. Muldoon. *PLoS ONE* 9(6): e98679. doi:10.1371/journal.pone.0098679.

Jay, Jason. 2013. "Navigating Paradox as a Mechanism of Change and Innovation in Hybrid Organizations." *Academy of Management Journal* 56(1): 137–159. doi:10.5465/amj.2010.0772.

Kincaid, Andrew. 2006a. *Postcolonial Dublin: Imperial Legacies and the Built Environment.* Minneapolis, MN: University of Minnesota Press.

Kincaid, Andrew. 2006b. "'They Stand for All the Things I Hate': Georgian Architecture and Cultural Memory in Contemporary Dublin." In Timothy Gibson and Mark Lowes (eds), *Urban Communication: Production, Text, Context*, 111. Lanham: Rowman and Littlefield.

Lawton, Philip, and Michael Punch. 2014. "Urban Governance and the 'European City': Ideals and Realities in Dublin, Ireland." *International Journal of Urban and Regional Research* 38(3): 864–885. doi:10.1111/1468-2427.12152.

MacLaran, Andrew, and Sinéad Kelly, eds. 2014. *Neoliberal Urban Policy and the Transformation of the City*. Basingstoke: Palgrave Macmillan.

McDonald, Frank. 1989. *Saving the City: How to Halt the Destruction of Dublin*. Dublin: Tomar Pub.

Moore, Niamh. 1999. "Rejuvenating Docklands: The Irish Context." *Irish Geography* 32(2): 135–149.

O'Leary, Sean. 2014. *Sense of Place: A History of Irish Planning*. Dublin: The History Press.

Orlikowski, Wanda J. 2002. "Knowing in Practice: Enacting a Collective Capability in Distributed Organizing." *Organization Science*, 13(3): 249–273.

Roberts, Joanna, J. J. Worrall, and Elaine Burke. 2015. *Silicon Docks: The Rise of Dublin as a Global Tech Hub*. Dublin: Liberties Press.

Thornley, David. 1964. "Ireland: The End of an Era?" *Studies: An Irish Quarterly Review* 53 (209): 1–17.

Weick, Karl E. 1995. *Sensemaking in Organizations*. Thousand Oaks, CA: Sage.

Williams, Brendan, and Declan Redmond. 2006. *Ideopolis: Knowledge City Region, Dublin Case Study*. Dublin: The Work Foundation.

7

TOWARDS A STUDY OF CITY EXPERIMENTS

Brice Laurent and David Pontille

Introduction

In 2016, Singapore National Research Foundation (NRF) announced the launch of a partnership with Dassault Systems in the development of 'Virtual Singapore', a 'dynamic three-dimensional (3D) city model and collaborative data platform'. This platform would 'enable users from different sectors to develop sophisticated tools and applications for test-bedding concepts and services, planning and decision-making, and research on technologies to solve emerging and complex challenges for Singapore.'[1]

The same year in San Francisco, the Municipal Transportation Authority (SFMTA) was testing the new features of its mobile application, called MuniMobile, in partnership with a non-profit organization, yet closely tied to investment funds City Innovate Foundation. These new features would allow it to optimize the gathering of data related to mobility practices in San Francisco, and possibly use them to introduce incentives designed to nudge people into using transportation systems in such a way that it would alleviate pervasive congestion problems.

These two examples can be seen as almost perfect illustrations of the current trend to try and create smart cities. These initiatives are based on the production, manipulation and circulation of large amounts of data. They are tied to new understanding of how to act on the city, by targeting urban issues, and providing solutions to challenges, such as pollution and waste management, ageing and health services, or public transportation and mobility practices. As they rely on close associations between public bodies and private entities, these initiatives might redefine not only the city's modes of governing, but also the urban political identities. Citizens in Singapore might be offered new ways to intervene in issues that matter to them, and San Francisco inhabitants might be turned into economic agents optimizing their choices according to the incentives that their transportation app provides them.

The 'smartness' of these examples is problematic though. Are these projects connected to concrete realizations or mere flagship announcements that serve window dressing objectives? In what ways are the data on which they rely being used in a 'smart' manner? As we encountered these cases in the context of a research project on urban innovation,[2] we gradually displaced the problematic 'smart' label in order to be able to ask other questions: How to analyze them, not as standalone innovative projects, but as components of a wider evolution in urban policies? How are these initiatives connected to the political and economic ordering of the city? What do they tell us about potential alternatives being left out in that process?

In this chapter, we argue that a way to approach these questions is to set aside, at least temporarily, the 'smart' label, and study cases such as Virtual Singapore or San Francisco's transportation app as 'city experiments'. We use the expression 'city experiments' to point to situations of urban life where experiments are conducted which directly engage the nature of the city itself. A growing literature has been focusing on 'urban experimentations' (Evans et al. 2016), and is an invitation to analyze the means through which experiments can be empirical and theoretical entry points for the study of contemporary urban transformations. The focus on city experiments, we argue, is a way of studying these transformations without taking the claim of novelty at face value, while also reflecting on the possibility for replication, extension, and possibly widespread deployment.

This chapter builds on the two case studies briefly introduced above to explore the analytical interest of the study of city experiments. We start by discussing why these two initiatives can be considered as 'city experiments', and what the analytical consequences of this notion are. We then break down the components of city experiments, again illustrating them with these two cases. Finally, we discuss the analytical value of studying city experiments.

Investigating city experiments

Two experimental situations

The vocabulary of experiments has become a pervasive trope in the contemporary urban discourse. The two examples briefly introduced above can be seen as illustrations of this trend. 'Virtual Singapore' is expected to provide a digital infrastructure through which 'concepts and services' can be 'test-bedded'. Singapore National Research Foundation states that this project offers possibilities for 'virtual experimentation' (e.g. exploring 4G coverage), and 'virtual test-bedding to validate the provision of services' (e.g. modelling crowd dispersion).[3] Here, the simulated environment can be used to test possible scenarios and/or explore in virtual ways the consequences of a particular situation. For instance, as the person in charge of Virtual Singapore showed us during an interview:

> the Dassault Systems' 3D Experience tool is meant to simulate a variety of situations such as a leak in the natural gas network supply and its spreading in a

building (meant to determine, by drawing on various behavioural models, the best evacuation plan that would be implemented depending on the profile of inhabitants in the area); a short-time sales operation in a mall (requiring testing the speed and direction of escalators); the positioning of rooftop solar panels (to find out their profitability according to their exposure to certain weather conditions).

(A.P., Dassault Systems, 15 February 2017)

In these virtual experiments, 3D visualization is key to envision a series of scenarios generated by the combination of various datasets. When we met the people in charge of Virtual Singapore at Dassault Systems, they also underlined another dimension of the test, namely that the platform itself, and its components, was experimented with in the process.

In San Francisco, the language of experiments is a recurrent part of the official discourse of public bodies like the SFMTA. The experimental dimension of the MuniMobile App was explicit in the initial testing phase, which was managed by a dedicated private company, and during which self-registered users tested a beta version and offered feedback to the SFMTA.[4] But the experiment extends far beyond the initial testing phase of the app. Once in place, the app offers a platform gathering data, which can be used to test various mechanisms related to pricing and incentives. As the person in charge of innovation at the SFMTA said to us during an interview:

We're experimenting with what the customers actually care about – what they care about is getting free things. We call that gamification. We don't have the money to pay for these things so we think the right approach is to partner with the private sector and have them do it.

(T.P., SFMTA Office of Innovation, 10 February 2016)

For all their differences, Virtual Singapore and Muni Mobile share a dual dimension of the experimental platform. On the one hand, they are meant to serve as infrastructures on which various tests can be conducted. On the other hand, they are also meant to be tested as platforms supposed to be designed to optimize urban interventions.

Experiments as an analytical category

In these two cases, the language of experiments is that of the actors involved. We see this pervasiveness as an invitation to theorize the notion of experiments, and use it as an analytical category. While this move can build on the recent literature of cities and urban innovation (Gieryn 2006; Halpern et al. 2013; Laurent and Tironi 2015; Tironi and Sànchez Criado 2015; Evans et al. 2016; Kitchin 2016), we take our inspiration here from a series of work in STS that has discussed the politics of experiments. Early works in the field considered experiments as operations that simultaneously act on the production of knowledge and social ordering. Shapin and Schaffer's seminal study of the nascent experimental physics in 17th century England (Shapin and Schaffer 1985) and detailed studies of practices of testing (Pinch 1993) have been followed by studies that have extended the discussion of experiments to situations where economists test, in vitro or in vivo, their theories or models thereby re-arranging the economy itself (Callon 2009; Mitchell 2005), protesters reinvent the forms of political activism (Barry 1999; Doubleday and Wynne 2011), experts test 'technologies of democracy' (Lezaun and Soneryd 2007; Laurent 2011), and users of mundane technologies make sustainable development a matter of personal experience (Marres 2012).

We do not want to provide a detailed review of the rich STS literature on experiments, but rather point to a few lessons that are directly useful for our study of cases, such as Virtual Singapore or San Francisco's MuniMobile. First, experiments associate a sociotechnical apparatus with demonstration practices, for the sake of a learning objective (Barry 1999; Rosental 2013). Crucial to this collective production of knowledge are the ways in which the heterogeneous components of the apparatus are specifically assembled and the demonstration practices are actually performed.

Second, experiments can be 'economic' in that they participate in the making of markets (Callon and Muniesa 2007), and 'political' in that they are components of democratic ordering processes (Laurent 2016). Virtual Singapore and MuniMobile can be seen as both 'economic' and 'political' experiments in that they engage both the elaboration of markets and the would-be appropriate mode of intervention of the city's public bodies.

Third, the study of experiments is neither 'micro' nor 'macro', but focuses on the association between the apparatus making the test possible and the spaces that are re-ordered to make its validation possible (Callon and Latour 1981; Latour 1983; Laurent 2016). Thus, understanding Virtual Singapore as an experiment requires that one connects the test conducted on the platform with the audiences they are expected to convince, including foreign companies that Singapore's government might hope to attract, or investors eager to fund potentially lucrative technological developments. Similarly, San Francisco's MuniMobile cannot be understood as an experiment without accounting for the ecology of actors involved in the design of the app, its successive tests, and the distinct audiences assembled.

City experiments

We use the important body of STS work devoted to experiments to see Virtual Singapore and San Francisco's MuniMobile as 'city experiments'. The expression points to the fact that these initiatives are urban-related projects intended to explicitly serve as tests, arranged to produce new knowledge that remains at least partly uncertain, and tied to public demonstrations.

In the course of these tests, the city itself (or part thereof) is experimented with: whether it is a virtual representation of the city expected to determine future urban organization (e.g. in designing emergency routes), or a transportation test eventually re-routing flows of passengers, any city experiment envisions, explicitly or not, a peculiar definition of the future, and a redesigned and reordered city (e.g. easily manageable, congestion free, etc.) at the core of the test itself.

Echoing the ways in which the Chicago School made Chicago a laboratory and a field-site (Park 1929; Gieryn 2006), these projects are entry points for us to develop an analysis of contemporary forms of urban organizations, in their political and economic dimensions. Such an approach comes with descriptive questions orienting the investigations: What is tested in practice? Who are the experimenters? In which site(s) and experimental conditions are the tests conducted? What are the audiences addressed by the public demonstrations? Who is expected to certify results?

The components of city experiments

Analyzing urban initiatives such as Virtual Singapore or MuniMobile as city experiments implies that we account for a series of components of these projects. In this section, we break down city experiments and discuss their components.

Experimenters

All experiments need experimenters, and city experiments are no exception. But the identity of these experimenters might be more distributed in the latter. In San Francisco, the tests developed with MuniMobile not only associate the SFMTA and the City Innovate Foundation, but also a wide range of private transportation providers such as Uber, Lyft and the local group rideshare company Chariot, and service companies as well (such as Waze or other apps). Virtual Singapore associates a private company, Dassault Systems, and a public body, the National Research Foundation, in the development of the platform. Who might then use it to test 'concepts and services' is still uncertain, but may comprise many different actors. Other examples in Singapore have shown that public bodies might be keen to call for diverse actors to use urban data to test technologies. For instance, the Jurong Lake District has been conceived of as a 'smart district' aimed to make data available for companies, start-ups, or individuals to develop technological 'solutions'.[5] The language of 'solutions' here points to problems that are not yet identified, but could be so thanks to the intervention of a wide range of actors having expertise related to housing, transportation, healthcare, etc.

For all the possibility of a diversity of experimenters to intervene, city experiments are also strongly dependent on the ability to restrain the perimeter of who is expected to act as experimenters. In Singapore, the circulation of data is problematic. During an interview, a scientist in charge of numerous data production and analysis projects at the Jurong Lake District spoke of an 'Asian point of view'[6] as he referred to the ways in which open data protocols were used in Singapore. He stressed that making urban data available was also counter-balanced by an active control of their circulation and use. Other kinds of tension are visible in San Francisco, as the tests conducted by the City Innovate Foundation are meant to use data provided by private companies eager to benefit from their economic value, and reluctant to make them widely available. While the political value of data is what makes their circulation problematic in Singapore, it is their economic value that makes it so in San Francisco – a tension that has been dealt with by introducing third party contracts to regulate data circulation.[7]

Experimental subjects and objects

Experiments operate on entities that are made experimental, possibly by cutting their ties, standardizing them, making them comparable with each other (Latour 1987). In city experiments, the entities that are experimented with might be technical systems of data acquisition, pricing mechanisms, or human behaviors. Thus, city experiments shape political objects, whether market objects (Callon et al. 2002) or objects of government (Lezaun 2006), such as testable scenarios and the virtual platform that Virtual Singapore relies on. In doing so, they also manufacture political subjects, such as citizens turned into economic agents expected to make real-time decisions in San Francisco (Laurent and Talvard 2017), or citizens framed as 'smart, efficient subjects' within the Smart Nation program in Singapore (Ho 2016).

Virtual Singapore can operate only if data are available, and this also involves participating inhabitants. Some data layers of the Virtual Singapore Platform have been completed by distributing 40,000 individual sensors to students. These sensors collected data about the students' geolocalized displacements, the noise they were exposed to, or the wifi coverage and connectivity they experienced from one place to another. Thus, Singapore's inhabitants become part of the experiments, as crucial components of the infrastructure required to make the laboratory work.

The MuniMobile app also calls for various kinds of data related to the use of public transport among the municipal network (subways, tramways, buses and trolleys), so that riders can plan their journeys, knowing the transit times of vehicles to a particular stop. To make such data available in real-time, for instance, the precise position of buses is detected with an algorithm calculating an estimation from previous rides on the same line and information remotely provided by the vehicle thanks to GPS tracking tools. Thus, each bus is not a mere transportation vehicle anymore, but also becomes a key data provider, and as such part of the experiment.

Laboratories

The 'laboratorization' of the world (Latour 1987; Callon 1989) is particularly well illustrated in the city, as parts of the urban space are turned into testing grounds (Karvonen and van Heur 2014; Evans et al. 2016) or entire cities are erected from scratch as test-beds (Halpern et al. 2013). Exploring the laboratories on which city experiments occur means that one is attentive to, at least, the following elements.

First, and contrary to scientific laboratories where secluded research is performed (Callon et al. 2009), the laboratories where city experiments are conducted are part of what is tested (Coletta 2017). Virtual Singapore and MuniMobile are less stable data systems serving as infrastructural background for future tests than socio-technical apparatus in the making, which might evolve significantly according to the outcomes of city experiments.

Second, analyzing the laboratories of city experiments requires an attention to the spatial organization of the city. In San Francisco, it helps point to an emerging understanding of city organization in terms of permanently evolving flows (of people, cars and other means of transportation) that are supposed to be managed in real-time. This 'real-time' reorganization construes the space of the city as a permanently revised outcome of optimization operations (Kitchin 2014). As such, it can be opposed to long-term planning, which sees the spatial organization of the city as a long-term intervention on costly material elements (Laurent and Talvard 2017). Virtual Singapore offers an illustration of the articulation between virtual and physical spaces. While the boundaries of the virtual laboratory seem neatly defined, as they separate the virtual world from the material one, the articulation between the two is crucial. Gathering data requires that a network of sensors is extended across the city, possibly through the help of inhabitants (see above). The virtual space is less a digital representation of a physical city than a reconstruction of another space, part virtual and part material, that is meant to be a laboratory.

Third, investigating the boundaries of city experiments' laboratories allows us to identify framing operations and subsequent overflowings (Callon 1998), and offer an analytical path to consider entities that do not fit with the standardization process of the tests, and that eventually are cast out (Star 1991). Organizing Virtual Singapore as a laboratory supposes that elements that cannot be measured by the network of sensors on which it relies are left out. Turning San Francisco into a 'real-time city' makes the whole city a laboratory in a way that imagines the role of public bodies (including above all the municipal transportation authorities) as coordinators able to ensure that supplies and demands of urban services are permanently optimized. To most of these public bodies, such a perspective is often framed as an alternative to costly and controversial long-term public investments in transportation infrastructures (Laurent and Talvard 2017). It indeed frames the role of public authorities in a way that excludes long-term action.

Audiences

There is no city experiment without associated demonstrations. City experiments, like other experiments (Shapin and Schaffer 1985; Barry 1999; Rosental 2013), need to assemble an audience expected to attest that their outcomes have value. Simulations in Singapore offer a virtual platform for the production of public proofs addressed to a community of experimenters made of government bodies eager to ground their intervention in the urban environment on tested (if virtual) facts. The audience of the tests is not limited to government bodies though.

Another audience is envisioned by the simulations' designers, namely potential stakeholders of the initiative being tested. Eventually, and in line with longstanding practices of collaboration between foreign companies and Singapore's government (Akrich et al. 2017), Virtual Singapore also serves as a demonstration addressed to customers and investors whereby Dassault System may publicly prove the value of its expertise. In San Francisco, the MuniMobile experiment is meant to produce proofs for transportation managers to act on pricing mechanisms and transportation administration. In a similar fashion as Dassault Systems, the City Innovate Foundation is also a global actor involved in different places and using interventions in one site as a demonstration of what it can do in another. As such, the tests are also meant for all the experimenters involved to provide demonstrations of their ability to act on the city.

Examining the audience component of city experiments offers a way out of two of the difficulties we might encounter when studying smart cities. First, when analyzing audiences, there is little room for asking questions such as whether or not the initiatives at stake are 'mere hype'. As they necessarily comprise the assemblage of public proofs, and an external gaze to witness them, city experiments are necessarily construed as 'hype'. What matters then, for both the actors involved and the analysts studying them, is less whether or not this 'hype' has 'real' grounds than who it manages to convince, convey and eventually transform, and by what means. Second, the study of city experiments' audiences offers an opportunity to avoid questions related to whether the analysis is (or should be) 'micro' or 'macro', 'local' or 'global'. As one cannot understand city experiments without accounting for the audiences that they assemble, they are part of particular spaces within which they are expected to have value. This latter point leads us to our final reflection. We can now get back to our initial questions, and discuss the ways in which the analysis of city experiments offers us a path to answer them.

How do city experiments matter, and to whom?

After having characterized Virtual Singapore and MuniMobile as city experiments, and broken down their components, we can now explore how the analysis of city experiments helps us answer our initial questions: How to analyze city experiments, not as standalone innovative projects, but as components of wider evolutions of urban policies? How are these initiatives connected to the political and economic ordering of the city? What do they tell us about potential alternatives being left out in that process?

A way of approaching these questions is to explore how city experiments matter, and to whom. Of course, this is a question raised by the actors themselves, but it is also relevant as an analytical interrogation, in order to identify relevant sites where contemporary cities are transformed. Studying how city experiments matter and to whom is also a way of examining a crucial issue: are these experiments only first steps before larger deployments? Or can one identify a mode of governing cities that would be characterized by a permanent experimental state? San Francisco and Singapore provide elements that lead us to the second half of this alternative, yet in ways that significantly differ.

San Francisco and real-time democracy

The variety of experimenters intervening in the MuniMobile initiative consider it important in that it takes part in a renewed understanding of the urban organization. Indeed, they naturally connect it to a diversity of city experiments in San Francisco. When we interviewed the head of SFMTA's innovation office, he immediately invited us to talk with some of his colleagues at the Office of Civic Innovation at San Francisco city hall. There, he told us, we could complete our understanding of why initiatives such as those he had just presented to us were important in San Francisco. At the Office of Civic Innovation, which was created in 2012 in the wake of the election of the late Edwin Lee as mayor of San Francisco, we were presented with a series of initiatives aimed to test potential solutions to urban problems, through various partnerships with start-ups, thanks to a new Open Data program. In San Francisco, we encountered other initiatives undertaken by the SFMTA, often in partnership with other public bodies, and meant to act in adaptive ways. Programs such as 'pavement to parks', 'a collaborative effort between the San Francisco Planning Department, the Department of Public Works, and the Municipal Transportation Agency',[8] seek to involve local inhabitants in the test of small-scale urban infrastructures in dedicated areas of public space.

As we studied the experimenters of the MuniMobile experiment, the entities that were being tested, the laboratory that it relied on, and the audiences it assembled, we were drawn to other city experiments. MuniMobile mattered in that it was connected to these other initiatives, which together aim to turn San Francisco into a self-proclaimed 'capital of innovation', where urban problems and solutions are permanently re-defined and re-adjusted. In this context, city experiments are not just primary trials before a definitive extension of a given technical solution, but technologies of government (Rose and Miller 1992). They are the tools whereby public bodies act on people, and which turn them into particular political subjects, namely individual ones expected to contribute to the identifications of urban problems and solutions. Understanding this was not only a way to re-situate city experiments, but also to better account for the nature of the political, economic and material ordering at stake in the 'capital of innovation'. If MuniMobile is indeed a component of a 'real-time city', what the set of initiatives in which it is situated draws is a type of ordering that makes the real-time adjustment of urban problems and solutions the core task for governing the city. One can see here a problematization of the sources of democratic legitimacy, as well as a proposition for the identification of the active participants of urban life – namely those who mobilize to make urban problems explicit, and/or propose solutions to them. The 'real-time democracy' that emerges here (Laurent and Talvard 2017) is also the outcome of economic ordering processes, as private actors make urban issues a new source of market demand, and, perhaps more fundamentally, as inhabitants are expected to adopt economic modes of reasoning, following incentives, or acting as entrepreneurs to propose new solutions for urban problems.

Singapore and the making of a global laboratory

In Singapore, projects based on simulating the city, or part thereof, in which government bodies are engaged not only comprise Virtual Singapore, but also a modelling tool developed by the French company EDF in collaboration with the House and Development Board (HDB), and various modelling initiatives conducted at the Singapore MIT Alliance for Research and Technology (SMART) in partnership with government bodies such as the Land Transport Authority. The number of these projects, the networks of sensors on which they rely, the sheer amount of data they gather, and their integration into a 'Smart Nation' program might well be components of what a recent book characterizes as a 'smart state' (Calder 2016), thereby reaffirming what others had claimed in the early days of the smart city trend, that Singapore had the potential to become the model smart city (Mahizhnan 1999).

Whether or not this is indeed the case is less important here than what the city experiment lens allows us to account for. A first straightforward remark is that alongside Virtual Singapore aimed at simulating the entire city, other projects offer more detailed information on some features, such as the EDF simulation, which aims to serve as a platform for HDB to test building innovation, and for local stakeholders to confront various choices related to building layout. These other simulation projects could be described using the same categories as those discussed in the previous section. We would then be led to examine connections between these various city experiments, as, for instance, public bodies are involved in several of them, or companies compete to attract would be customers or investors. What emerges then is a desirable horizon of intervention for the Singapore public bodies, whereby simulation would offer a technological tool on which to base the government of the city, for the sake of political subjects expected not only to be passive simulated entities, but also contributors to the collection of data and as would-be users of the platform.

As real-time democracy in San Francisco is an outcome of both political and economic ordering processes, this type of political ordering is also economic. Indeed, the value of Virtual Singapore for the actors involved is tied to another laboratory that emerges from the collection of city experiments, namely the island of Singapore itself. While global companies use the city of Singapore as a test-bed for experimenting with their technologies (here simulation methods), public bodies deliberately use the characterization of Singapore as a laboratory to attract these companies. The analysis of Virtual Singapore is thus not only that of a single city experiment, but leads us to reflect on the aggregation of them, and eventually on the making of Singapore as the outcome of deliberate experimental strategies. These experimental strategies have been tied to the definition of Singapore as an independent city-state, able to become a global laboratory for multinational corporations to test their technologies. They are now part of a redefinition of

Singapore's instruments of government to include virtual tools. Singapore offers yet another case where city experiments are not a first step before mainstreaming, but a central component of how the city is expected to be governed. But whereas San Francisco provided an illustration of techniques of government based on real-time interventions, Singapore makes experiments a condition for the city-state to ensure its long-term stability.

Alternative cities

The political and economic ordering processes that we identified out of the Virtual Singapore and MuniMobile cases are also choices for the desirable city, which have little reason to be consensual and/or uniformly stable. In San Francisco, the affirmation of innovation as an engine for urban life is often met by scepticism, if not violent protest. The city experiments we mention can be contrasted with others, performed by concerned groups and activists (De Kosnik 2014; Maharawal 2014), and perhaps best understood as counter-experiments. Activists protesting the gentrification of the city have been active in the 'anti-eviction mapping project', which gathers data and maps them to illustrate the transformation of the city. This project displays connections between evictions and other evolutions, such as the growing role of private actors in transportation. This anti-eviction mapping project is a way for activists to oppose the optimization of flows circulating in the city characteristic of real-time democracy by supporting another type of democratic organization, namely community building. Activists use data to demonstrate the need for political action against the transformations of the city. This demonstration aims to persuade a local audience to join an active community. Activists' interventions here can be seen as a powerful counter-experiment, and as such offer an alternative vision of the city.

Virtual Singapore offers no example of counter-experiments. Yet it is a telling illustration of the problematic transformation of the global island laboratory. The official discourse calls people in Singapore to act as innovators 'and to co-create with business corporate bodies',[9] actively taking part in technological innovation and participating in the identification of urban problems and solutions. Tools such as Virtual Singapore are meant to serve as platforms for various stakeholders to intervene in the urban life. One can identify here a tension between opening up simulation tools to external contributions (for would-be entrepreneurs, or political discussions about city choices, or foreign actors) and maintaining control. This tension is at the heart of the stabilization of city experiments in Singapore. While it might offer entry points to re-thinking the nature of political intervention in the city state at both descriptive and normative levels, it also shows that analyzing city experiments is also investigating stabilization processes, and potential sites of friction.

Conclusion

In this chapter, we have proposed to contribute and dialogue with the large amount of works contemplating, urging for, or critically examining the move towards smart cities by focusing on city experiments. Drawing on the STS literature on laboratory and tests practices (Latour 1983; Shapin and Schaffer 1985; Pinch 1993), we suggested that a focus on city experiments offers relevant entry points for the study of contemporary urban transformations. Such an STS-inspired approach builds on the recent invitation to explore 'urban experimentations' as an emerging mode of governance (Karvonen and van Heur 2014; Evans et al. 2016), and develops it in several ways. As it takes seriously the key role of experiments in smart city projects, it proposes to study the production of knowledge about the city, as it is articulated with processes of economic, material and political reorderings. The 'smart' label might cover a wide range of domains, and leads one to examine what is 'smart' and what is not, what is 'real' and what is 'mere hype'. By contrast, city experiments can be empirically accounted for by carefully examining a series of concrete components (e.g. experimenters, experimental subjects and objects, laboratories, audiences). Such an approach thus provides some insights into the investigation of city experiments in practical and theoretical terms. In addition, the analysis of city experiments connects many elements that comprise, but are not limited to, what are commonly seen as components of smart cities. Not only does the investigation point to a range of actors that is far beyond the key players usually made visible (funders, ICT firms, and local start-ups), but it also stresses the ecology of political and economic reorderings – and their articulation to international networks in situated, local urban initiatives – in which city experiments take a significant place.

Notes

1 https://www.nrf.gov.sg/programmes/virtual-singapore
2 This project is entitled 'City experiments: new mobility practices and urban infrastructures'. The empirical material used in this chapter comes from a collective fieldwork conducted successively in San Francisco (February and June 2016) and Singapore (February 2017 and February 2018). We conducted interviews in public bodies, private companies, and civil society groups. These interviews were complemented by the relevant public documentation and press materials. We thank the participants to the collective fieldwork: Madeleine Akrich, Stève Bernardin, Jérôme Denis, Liliana Doganova, Félix Talvard, and the graduate students of the Public Affairs and Innovation program at Mines ParisTech.
3 https://www.nrf.gov.sg/programmes/virtual-singapore
4 https://www.sfmta.com/sites/default/files/agendaitems/2015/11-3-15%20Item%2010. 4%20MuniMobile%20app.pdf
5 W.S.N., Deputy Department Head, Urban Systems at the Institute for Infocomm Research, A*Star, 14 February 2017.
6 W.S.N., Deputy Department Head, Urban Systems at the Institute for Infocomm Research, A*Star, 14 February 2017.
7 Thus, the SFMTA regularly sets up agreement with private companies (e.g. transportation app providers) and public universities, whereby the latter use the data of the former for the benefit of the SFMTA but without disclosing the data.
8 http://pavementtoparks.org/about/
9 V.N., Deputy Head, Smart Nation Programme Office, 8 February 2017.

References

Akrich, M., J. Denis, L. Doganova, B. Laurent, and D. Pontille, 2017. "Can an Island Nation Be a Global Test-Bed? The Politics of Experimentation in Singapore." Society for the Social Studies of Science conference, STS (In)Sensibilities, Boston, 31 August–2 September.

Barry, A. 1999. "Demonstrations: Sites and Sights of Direct Action." *Economy and Society* 28 (1), 75–94.

Calder, K.E. 2016. *Singapore: Smart City, Smart State*. Washington DC: Brookings Institution Press.

Callon, M. ed. 1989. *La science et ses réseaux. Genèse et circulation des faits scientifiques*. Paris: La Découverte.

Callon, M. 1998. "An Essay on Framing and Overflowing: Economic Externalities Revisited by Sociology." *The Sociological Review* 46: 244–269.

Callon, M. 2009. "Civilizing Markets: Carbon Trading Between in Vitro and in Vivo Experiments." *Accounting, Organizations and Society* 34(3): 535–548.

Callon, M. and B. Latour. 1981. "Unscrewing the Big Leviathan; or How Actors Macro-structure Reality, and How Sociologists Help Them to Do So?" In *Advances in Social Theory and Methodology*, edited by K. Knorr and A. Cicourel, 277–303. London: Routledge and Kegan Paul.

Callon, M., and F. Muniesa. 2007. "Economic Experiments and the Construction of Markets." In *Do Economists Make Markets? On the Performativity of Economics*, edited by D. MacKenzie, F. Muniesa and L. Siu, 163–189. Princeton: Princeton University Press.

Callon, M., C. Méadel, and V. Rabeharisoa. 2002. "The Economy of Qualities." *Economy and Society* 31(2): 194–217.

Callon, M., P. Lascoumes, and Y. Barthe. 2009. *Acting in an Uncertain World: An Essay on Technical Democracy*. Cambridge, MA: MIT Press.

Coletta, C. 2017. "Open-Ended and Continuous Urban Experimentation Through Networked Big Data Infrastructures: the Case of LPWANs." Working paper, Ulysses Workshop, Paris.

De Kosnik, A. 2014. "Disrupting Technological Privilege: The 2013–2014 San Francisco Google Bus Protests." *Performance Research* 19(6): 99–107.

Doubleday, R., and B. Wynne. 2011. "Despotism and Democracy in the UK: Experiments in Reframing Relations Between the State, Science and Citizens." In *Reframing Rights: The Constitutional Implications of Technological Change*, edited by S. Jasanoff, 239–261. Cambridge, MA: MIT Press.

Evans, J., A. Karvonen, and R. Raven, eds. 2016. *The Experimental City*. London: Routledge.

Gieryn, T. 2006. "City as Truth-Spot: Laboratories and Field-Sites in Urban Studies." *Social Studies of Science* 36(1): 5–38.

Halpern, O., J. LeCavalier, N. Calvillo, and W. Pietsch. 2013. "Test-bed Urbanism." *Public Culture* 25(270): 272–306.

Ho, E. 2016. "Smart Subjects for a Smart Nation? Governing (Smart) Mentalities in Singapore." *Urban Studies* 54(13): 3101–3118.

Karvonen, A., and B. van Heur. 2014. "Urban Laboratories: Experiments in Reworking Cities." *International Journal of Urban and Regional Research* 38(2): 379–392.

Kitchin, R. 2014. "The Real-Time City? Big Data and Smart Urbanism." *Geojournal* 79(1): 1–14.

Kitchin, R. 2016. "The Ethics of Smart Cities and Urban Science." *Philosophical Transactions of the Royal Society A: Mathematical, Physical and Engineering Sciences* 374(2083): 1–15.

Latour, B. 1983. "Give Me a Laboratory and I Will Raise the World." In *Science Observed: Perspectives on the Social Study of Science*, edited by K. Knorr-Cetina and M. Mulkay, 141–170. London: Sage.

Latour, B. 1987. *Science in Action. How to Follow Scientists and Engineers through Society*. Cambridge: Harvard University Press.

Laurent, B. 2011. "Technologies of Democracy: Experiments and Demonstrations." *Science and Engineering Ethics* 17(4): 649–666.

Laurent, B. 2016. "Political Experiments that Matter: Ordering Democracy from Experimental Sites." *Social Studies of Science* 46(5): 773–794.

Laurent, B. and M. Tironi. 2015. "A Field Test and its Displacements. Accounting for an Experimental Mode of Industrial Innovation." *CoDesign* 11(3–4): 208–221.

Laurent, B. and F. Talvard. 2017. "Real-Time Democracy. Imagining the City of Permanent Innovation." i3 Working Papers Series, 17-CSI-01.

Lezaun, J. 2006. "Creating a New Object of Government: Making Genetically Modified Organisms Traceable." *Social Studies of Science* 36(4): 499–531.

Lezaun, J. and L. Soneryd. 2007. "Consulting Citizens: Technologies of Elicitation and the Mobility of Publics." *Public Understanding of Science* 16(3): 279–297.

Maharawal, M. 2014. "Protest of Gentrification and Eviction Technologies in San Francisco." *Progressive Planning* 199: 20–24.

Mahizhnan, A. 1999. "Smart Cities: the Singapore Case." *Cities* 16(1): 13–18.

Marres, N. 2012. *Material Participation: Technology, the Environment and Everyday Publics*. New York: Palgrave Macmillan.

Mitchell, T. 2005. "The Work of Economics: How a Discipline Makes its World." *Archives Européennes de Sociologie* 46(2): 297–320.

Park, R.E. 1929. "The City as a Social Laboratory." In *Chicago: an Experiment in Social Science Research*, edited by T.V. Smith and L.D. White. Chicago, IL: University of Chicago Press.

Pinch, T. 1993. "'Testing – One, Two, Three … Testing': Toward a Sociology of Testing." *Science, Technology, & Human Values* 18(1): 25–41.

Rose, M. and P. Miller. 1992. "Political Power Beyond the State: Problematics of Government." *British Journal of Sociology* 43(2): 173–205.

Rosental, C. 2013. "Toward a Sociology of Public Demonstrations." *Sociological Theory* 31(4): 343–365.

Shapin, S., and S. Schaffer. 1985. *Leviathan and the Air-Pump: Hobbes, Boyle, and the Experimental Life*. Princeton, NJ: Princeton University Press.

Star, S.L. 1991. "Power, Technology and the Phenomenology of Conventions: on Being Allergic to Onions." In *A Sociology of Monsters? Essays on Power, Technology and Domination*, edited by J. Law, 26–56. London and New York: Routledge.

Tironi, M., and T. Sánchez Criado. 2015. "Of Sensors and Sensitivities. Towards a Cosmopolitics of 'Smart Cities'?" *Tecnoscienza: Italian Journal of Science & Technology Studies* 6(1): 89–108.

8

UNIVERSITY CAMPUSES AS TESTBEDS OF SMART URBAN INNOVATION

Andrew Karvonen, Chris Martin and James Evans

Introduction

Universities are emerging as influential actors in the co-production of smart cities. Academic researchers provide expertise on the technical, economic, and social aspects of smart technologies and networks. They also have the ability to evaluate and assess the performance of smart interventions (Cocchia and Dameri, 2016). In addition, they liaise with the general public to communicate the broader benefits of smart urban development and to engage the public through smart city co-creation (Evans et al., 2015; Voytenko et al., 2016; Martin, Evans and Karvonen, 2018). As such, universities play multiple roles in the "quadruple helix" of knowledge-based, data-intensive urban development, alongside the public and private sectors, as well as civil society.

Beyond their position as researchers and public liaisons, universities play a significant but underappreciated role in *situating* smart cities. Higher education campuses serve as an ideal real-world platform to trial urban innovations because they: (1) comprise a large, single-owner estate; (2) include a collection of buildings and infrastructure networks that are managed in-house; (3) feed into applied research and teaching activities; and (4) enhance the institutional reputation of the university. In this chapter, we focus on the role of university campuses in situating smart urban development. By drawing on literatures on urban laboratories and experimentation as well as universities and knowledge production, we explore how campus-based projects are reframing universities as testbeds of smart urban innovation.

We begin the chapter by interpreting smart urban development as a mode of urban experimentation where ICT is being implemented to fundamentally alter the operation of cities. University campuses serve as bounded spaces or real-world laboratories where smart experiments are designed, built, and operated. We then provide a case study of a European smart cities project that uses two university campuses in Manchester (UK) to trial an integrated suite of energy, transport, and ICT systems. The project leverages the campuses as testbeds of innovation and reveals advantages and disadvantages of this particular urban environment to roll out smart technologies and networks. Campuses provide a "protected space" where innovations can be designed and installed relatively quickly with a limited number of stakeholders (Smith and Raven, 2012; Raven et al., 2016). However, they often have tenuous and sometimes problematic connections to the surrounding urban fabric. This situating of innovation activities has important implications for the governance, spatial development, and realisation of smart urbanisation and broader processes of urban development.

University campuses as smart urban testbeds

Smart urban development projects can be interpreted as part of a broader contemporary agenda on urban experimentation and sustainable transitions (see Kullman, 2013; Karvonen and van Heur, 2014; Bulkeley et al., 2015; Evans et al., 2015; Bulkeley, Berardi, and Dangelico, 2016; Evans, Karvonen, and Raven, 2016; Voytenko et al., 2016). There is a shared understanding that cities are a key arena to address persistent and complex issues relating to climate change, social inequality, economic stagnation, public health, and so on. Urban stakeholders promote experimentation as a catalyst for change where visible and tangible interventions can be undertaken to develop and improve cities (Karvonen, Evans, and van Heur, 2014). As Bulkeley and colleagues (2015, 50) note, "making experiments is an attempt to negotiate the perceived scale divide between the unfolding of the problem and the possibilities of intervention". It is through experiments that pathways to more desirable urban futures can be realised.

The rise of smart urban development, particularly over the last five years, involves a range of activities that feed into this experimental drive in cities. "Smart" promises to upgrade existing infrastructure networks through integration, interaction, and efficiency to make them fit for purpose in the twenty-first century (Albino et al., 2014; Martin, Evans, and Karvonen, 2018). The digitalisation of the city involves the generation of large datasets that can be used to measure and assess a wide range of processes, informing evidence-based local policymaking and governance (Kitchin, 2014; Hodson, Evans and Schliwa, forthcoming). Moreover, the democratic impulse of the smart agenda calls for deeper engagement with the general public through co-production activities. There are many parallels here with the notion of "living labs" and the realisation of situated, co-produced innovation activities (Nevens et al., 2013; Evans et al., 2015; Bulkeley et al., 2016; Voytenko et al., 2016; Perry et al., 2018).

It is important to remember that smart urban development does not occur in a vacuum; it is *situated* in particular places (Karvonen, Cugurullo, and Caprotti, 2019). Early notions of smart cities involved comprehensive visions of entire urban areas benefiting from an all-encompassing digital layer to coordinate urban metabolic processes. Exemplars such as Masdar City, Songdo, and the IBM Smarter Cities project in Rio de Janeiro frame smart urban development on a broad scale. More recently, the "actually existing smart city" (Shelton, Wiig, and Zook, 2015) has emerged in multiple locales. These projects tend to be more modest in scale, comprising a neighbourhood, a district, or a designated special purpose zone. The disadvantage of downscaling is that it makes "smart" less ambitious and all-encompassing. However, the restricted spatial and temporal reach of smaller projects accelerates innovation processes by avoiding financial and legal barriers. This makes it possible to design, execute, and assess smart city strategies in a timely and cost-effective manner.

University campuses are increasingly identified as ideal sites for smart interventions. As Evans and colleagues (2015, 1) note, "campuses offer amenable real-world locations in which to conduct applied research". A 2016 ranking of UK smart cities by Huawei identified ten leading municipalities and all except for Peterborough have an internationally leading university (Huawei, 2016). Exemplars of high-profile smart city/university collaborations in the UK include the University of Newcastle's Newcastle Science Central, the University of Glasgow's Future City Glasgow, and Bristol University's Bristol is Open. There is significant diversity in the aims and strategies pursued by these projects, but they share a collaborative approach that includes public, private and higher education stakeholders to realise urban innovation. In this sense, the pursuit of urban knowledge promised in smart urbanisation serves to bridge the "local-global divide" of universities (Perry, 2008) and make them central actors in local urban development processes.

While the smart agenda feeds into higher education's mission to conduct world-leading research, there are also compelling *economic* reasons for universities to use their campuses for smart projects. As cities move from industrial economies to knowledge economies, universities are being perceived as anchor institutions that can contribute more substantially to urban development (City Growth Commission, 2014). Melhuish (2015, 6) notes that "cities and towns are becoming increasingly expectant of, and reliant upon universities to represent and promote their own urban interests at regional, national and international levels". Simultaneously, public funding for universities is declining and universities are looking to other sources of income to support their teaching and research activities. "Smart" also contributes to the increasingly prominent role that universities play in urban regeneration (Benneworth, Charles, and Madanipour, 2010; Madanipour, 2011; Goddard and Vallance, 2013; Melhuish, 2015). The campus, the physical embodiment of higher education, becomes a symbol and a site for a city's future reputation and standing when compared to its international peers.

The notion of universities as urban stakeholders reflects the fact that these institutions are not simply platforms on which teaching and research activities are undertaken. Universities have significant influence on broader economic development, employment opportunities, infrastructure upgrades, and the long-term national and global reputation of the cities in which they are located. Increasingly, universities are targeted to bolster a city's "knowledge economy" (Perry, 2008;

May and Perry, 2011). Van Heur (2010, 1714) notes that there is a shared understanding that "local interactions between researchers, firm members and/or citizens need to be supported in order for the economic and social valorisation of knowledge on the urban and regional scale to take place". Universities are not simply another component of the urban landscape but are key partners in realising the emerging knowledge economy (Perry, 2008; May and Perry, 2011).

In some of these cases, there is a drive to realise a "civic urban model" of university development, where the boundaries between the campus and the city are less defined (Goddard, 2009; van Heur, 2010). Here, the university is positioned in collaboration with other urban stakeholders "to develop, test and then diffuse in a specific locality, city or region the various technological, social and policy solutions required to drive a physical transformation of the urban environment" (Trencher, Yarime, and Kharrazi, 2013, 40). This points to a direct connection between the spatial configuration of universities and the immediate impact on their surroundings (Benneworth, Charles, and Madanipour, 2010). Campuses are protected spaces, often outside of the jurisdiction of local authorities and thus have the flexibility to trial new ideas. They are autonomous and function in many ways as small towns, with infrastructure provision and collective services provided by a dedicated estates department. Campus experiments have the potential to reduce operating costs while enhancing research and teaching activities. Meanwhile, the emphasis on the pursuit of new knowledge provides license to try new things under the guise of learning.

The integration of universities into urban development agendas is further complicated by the higher education sector's third mission of social responsibility (Jongbloed, Enders and Salerno, 2008; Trencher et al., 2014). Working as an urban stakeholder involves a commitment to priorities ranging from economic development and technology transfer to community engagement and social equality. This raises challenging questions about which groups actually benefit from a university's participation in urban regeneration activities. The public and private sectors as well as civil society can all be potential beneficiaries but it is rarely the case that all of these groups benefit equally (or at all). Smart city advocates promise economic development opportunities and lower operating costs for cities, and more recently, opportunities for the general public to engage in co-production activities (Caragliu, Del Bo, and Nijkamp, 2011; Townsend, 2013; Carvalho, 2015; Cowley, Joss, and Dayot, 2018). Thus, universities can leverage smart urban development to demonstrate their worth to society while also bolstering their reputation nationally and internationally. The future of the city and the university become tightly intertwined through the pursuit of smart urban development.

Overall, the emphasis on the university campus as part of urban development is infiltrating the core missions of research, teaching, and social responsibility in higher education. This feeds into ideas of applied learning with the education agenda of higher education spilling out beyond its boundaries and engaging in "place-based, real world problem solving and engaged research" (Trencher, Yarime, and Kharrazi, 2013, 41). Universities are not just "in" the city but are "of" the city (Goddard and

Vallance, 2013) and "smart" serves as an alluring opportunity to solidify the relationship between the university and its non-academic surroundings.

To provide a concrete illustration of how "smart" is influencing the role of universities in cities, the following section summarises on-going activities in Manchester where two university campuses are serving as platforms for smart city development. The authors are deeply involved in various smart city projects and the findings reflect their experiences as researchers and stakeholders. The experiences from Manchester provide a clear example of how universities are engaged in smart urban development, not only because of their specialised knowledge about technologies, cities, and society, but also because of the geographical and physical opportunities afforded by the campuses to situate "smart" in an accessible and visible real-world setting.

Universities and smart urban development in Manchester

In Manchester, the campuses of the University of Manchester (UoM) and Manchester Metropolitan University (MMU) are a dominant part of the urban core. Located adjacent to the central business district on Oxford Road, the campuses comprise almost 300 buildings and over 90,000 students and staff, contributing a shared annual income of over £1.25 billion. Both institutions have aggressive long-range master planning ambitions to modernise their campuses, with completed or planned investments exceeding £1.5b over the next decade (Table 8.1). In 2007, the universities formalised their role in the city's urban development activities by joining Corridor Manchester, a public-private partnership that includes the Manchester City Council, the Royal Northern College of Music, the NHS Hospital Trust, Bruntwood (a commercial property owner) and Arup (Corridor Manchester 2018).

Corridor Manchester is a partnership of organisations that are physically located within a 243-hectare area that is centred on Oxford Road and spills out to the south of Manchester's central business district (Figure 8.1). The area is designated as

TABLE 8.1 Representative statistics of the University of Manchester and Manchester Metropolitan University

	UoM	MMU
Number of buildings	229	40
Number of students	39,700	37,000
Number of staff	12,315	4,500
Annual income (£m)*	987	298
Campus investment (£m)**	1000	550

Source: UoM (2012, 2017); MMU (2016, 2017)

*The time period for UoM is 2016-17 and for MMU is 2015–16
**The UoM investment is for 2012–2022 and the MMU investment is for 2008–2014 (£350m) and 2017–2027 (£200m)

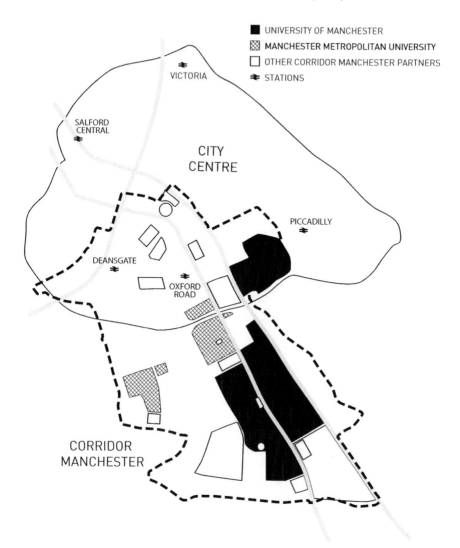

FIGURE 8.1 Map of Corridor Manchester
Source: based on Corridor Manchester (2018)

the site of the future knowledge economy in the city through development of existing economic and cultural assets. It is the latest manifestation of Manchester's citywide economic strategy that builds on the "knowledge capital" agenda of the early 2000s (May and Perry, 2006; Perry, 2008). There is a collective drive to recast the storied industrial history of Manchester into a twenty-first century globally competitive city (Deas, 2014; Robson, 2016). All of the partners (except for Arup) have significant real estate holdings and are collaborating to realise Manchester's long-term economic strategy by their leveraging existing institutional assets in new ways. In effect, they recognise that coordinating their spatial development activities will reap great rewards while producing a compelling innovation storyline to underpin Manchester's future.

Smart urban development neatly aligns with Corridor Manchester's focus on the knowledge economy. It also builds on several smart projects completed by academic researchers in the past few years that used the campuses and surrounding area to test new digital applications related to green infrastructure, high speed wireless communication, and real-time environmental sensing (Evans and Karvonen, 2014; Paskaleva et al., 2017; Cowley, Joss, and Dayot, 2018; Burton, Karvonen, and Caprotti, 2019). These independent activities fed into a formal smart city agenda in 2014 when Manchester, Eindhoven, and Stavanger were awarded a €25m Horizon 2020 project from the European Commission. The central aim of the Triangulum project is to develop and evaluate low-carbon smart districts in each city over a five-year period (2015–2020) by integrating energy, transport and ICT through an integrated/shared datahub (Triangulum 2018). The three "Lighthouse cities" (Manchester, Eindhoven, and Stavanger) are developing and applying a common data collection and evaluation platform and are sharing their experiences and expertise with three "Follower cities" (Sabadell, Prague, and Leipzig). The lessons from the project will also be developed into a framework for other cities to follow (Haarstad, 2017).[1]

In Manchester's part of the Triangulum project, the UoM and MMU campuses are the site of the low-carbon smart interventions. This was a logical choice as the campuses were located within the Corridor Manchester boundaries and were already a physical presence within an existing special purpose district. Moreover, the campuses provided a platform to install and test a range of smart technologies and strategies including renewable energy technologies, energy efficient refurbishment of historic buildings, electric vehicle charging stations, electric cargo bicycles for logistics, a "virtual" power plant, and so on (Triangulum, 2018) (Figure 8.2). All of the interventions will be monitored and the data will be collected in a central datahub for analysis. The work contributes to ongoing low-carbon and sustainability initiatives on each campus to realise more resource-efficient estates.[2] Moreover, the project bolsters the research reputation of each university, creates formal research and operations links between the two universities, and serves as a physical demonstration of the innovation ambitions of the city as a whole. While it is too early to evaluate the project, the activities to date reveal a number of intriguing implications for collaboration and co-production as it relates to smart urban development.

Using the campuses as laboratories or testbeds of innovation requires close collaboration between researchers and the estates department on each campus. Both sets of actors are employed by the same organisation but "estates teams often only see universities as spatial and operational entities which pose particular issues around maintenance and running costs" (Melhuish, 2015, 15). There is a clear separation of objectives between the *knowledge production* of university academics and the *property management* of the estates departments. Triangulum blurs the boundaries between research and operations by calling for a new, co-managed estate that is at

FIGURE 8.2 Electric cargo bikes (top) will operate on renewable energy generated on campus buildings (bottom)

Source: authors

once a platform for teaching and research but also a research object in itself. The researchers see the campus as a platform to test technologies *in situ*. It serves as a real-world laboratory that can produce novel datasets and evidence related to the efficacy of smart strategies. The estates team is understandably more risk-averse as their goal is to provide a functioning campus for students, staff, and visitors. While they appreciate the infrastructure upgrades provided by Triangulum, they also see the smart interventions as a disruption to their existing approach to campus management.

The choices of technologies themselves are largely unproblematic because they are off-the-shelf and "tried and tested" (photovoltaics, electric vehicles, etc.). However, understanding how to integrate them into the existing infrastructure services and how to monitor their performance has proven to be a major task for the project team. For example, one of the Triangulum interventions involved a fuel cell as a renewable energy strategy. Siemens proposed to purchase and install the fuel cell on campus and then hand over operations to the UoM estates team. However, this deviated from UoM's conventional process of issuing a tender for contract, awarding a contract, and overseeing installation by a private contractor. Eventually the impasse was resolved by reclassifying the fuel cell as "research equipment", thereby transferring liability to an academic researcher. This example reveals the practicalities of integrating "smart" in existing institutional structures. Reflecting on the challenges of working on university estates, one academic researcher argues that "university estates need to be repositioned as actual research infrastructures rather than simply as supporting research infrastructures".

In addition to requiring internal collaboration between the estates team and academics on each campus, the Triangulum project requires collaboration *between* UoM and MMU to design, build and operate interventions that span both campuses (e.g., virtual power plant, electric cargo bikes for logistics, shared datahub). This involves the development of new strategies to co-manage the adjacent estates to develop and maintain shared infrastructure services. The estates teams from each university are charged with understanding how their respective campuses are operated and managed differently and, more importantly, where commonalities can be leveraged. Meanwhile, the researchers are asked to work against the grain of the existing university cultures that frequently pit one against the other in national and international academic league tables. At the same time, all parties recognise the advantages of working together and the opportunities provided by their adjacent estates.

Beyond the collaboration within and between the Manchester universities, a central aim of the Triangulum project is to foster the *co-production* of urban innovation between academic and non-academic stakeholders. "Co-production involves stakeholders understanding each other's contexts, in order to work together to frame research that delivers more effective solutions" (Evans et al., 2015, 1). Manchester City Council (MCC) serves as the overall coordinator of Manchester's Triangulum activities and frames the project as one of urban development. Smart interventions provide tangible evidence of MCC's long-term ambitions for the city's future, both economically and environmentally (Manchester Smarter City Programme, 2018; Burton, Karvonen, and Caprotti, 2019). The inclusion of the universities as well as private industry (Siemens for energy, Clicks and Links for data architecture) comprises a public-private partnership that promises a new mode of governance that is founded on collaboration. MCC serves as the enabler rather than the director of urban development, encouraging the partners to work together to realise the central aim of Triangulum: to develop and evaluate a low-carbon smart district. MCC chairs monthly meetings to discuss the progress of the various interventions and serves as an intermediary between project partners. The meetings reveal very different organisational cultures and expectations for the project and many discussions involve the development of a shared understanding of what the project actually entails and how to install and monitor the interventions within a limited timeframe.

Interestingly, the public and private sectors seem more attuned to co-production as they are accustomed to collaborating with partners. Meanwhile, co-production is a novel activity for the university estates personnel who have struggled to align their internal objectives of campus management with broader urban development objectives. The location of Manchester's Triangulum interventions on the university campuses largely precludes the need for wider public involvement. The smart technologies can simply be dropped in without extended consultation because the campuses are single-owner estates. This is both an advantage and a disadvantage. The campus as a bounded site of innovation facilitates the rapid installation and monitoring of smart technologies but provides few opportunities for broader buy-in and participation of the general public. Campus users (students, staff, and visitors) are represented by the estates departments and the academic researchers. Future plans to engage the public in Triangulum involve the creation of a publicly accessible data portal where anyone can access the data generated by the project to develop apps and an energy consumption app aimed at students who reside in one of the university's halls of residence. This represents only a minimal degree of co-production and suggests that the general public is not a key stakeholder in the project or the smart city agenda as a whole.

In the future, there will undoubtedly be opportunities to extend the smart agenda beyond the campus boundaries to include neighbouring areas. However, the universities have a chequered history with their surrounding neighbours. The neighbouring wards are characterised as low-income with a significant amount of social deprivation. The neighbouring residents see the universities as elitist and out of touch or blame them for the problems caused by large student populations living in their neighbourhoods. Meanwhile, they have not benefited from the education and research activities that are central to the universities' missions. Thus, the universities have had mixed experiences in engaging with residents in these wards. This divide is also evident in the look and feel of the built environment, with stark differences between the aging housing stock and the new, modern campus buildings. These cleavages will continue to be a formidable challenge as the smart agenda extends beyond the campus boundaries and into adjacent neighbourhoods.

Conclusions

In July 2016, a consortium of Manchester stakeholders launched a new Internet of Things project called CityVerve (2018) with £10m of UK Government funding. Twenty-one partners, including MCC, UoM, Siemens, and multiple local and international technology partners will build upon the smart agenda of the Triangulum project with additional interventions in transport and travel, culture and the public realm, health and social care, and energy and environment. The project provides further support for Manchester's global ambitions to be an exemplar smart city of the twenty-first century while requiring additional integration of the higher education sector with other urban stakeholders.

As cities turn to experimentation and smart urban development for a range of reasons, there is an increasing role for higher education to serve as "change agents" in urban sustainable development (Stephens et al., 2008). This involves research expertise but also the positioning of the physical campuses as testbeds of innovation. The experiences of Triangulum in Manchester highlight the opportunities and challenges of using university campuses to design, build, and assess smart interventions that combine energy, transportation, and ICT. The project continues to be a work in progress but a number of issues have emerged on the role of university campuses as sites of smart urban development. These involve internal collaboration between academic and estates staff, external collaborations between the two universities, broader collaboration between the public and private sectors, and the still nascent co-production of smart city activities with civil society.

Situating smart urban development on campuses presents opportunities as well as challenges. It provides a protected space of innovation where smart technologies can be installed and put into operation relatively quickly. It creates stronger links between the universities and other urban stakeholders and bolsters the reputations of all involved, creating a more integrated and compelling urban narrative of innovation and change. However, these bounded spaces preclude the need for collaboration with civil society. It is not clear how the smart interventions can be rolled out beyond the campuses and how they will be received by neighbouring residents. The campuses are a great place for "getting things done" because consultation and collaboration can be achieved efficiently with a limited number of stakeholders. Meanwhile, demonstrating the relevance of the smart city agenda to civil society remains a task for future projects.

Moreover, the logic of funding bodies such as the European Commission assumes that smart solutions that are being trialled on the university campuses in Manchester will be upscaled to the city as a whole. However, it is unclear how the Triangulum project will influence the long-term development of Manchester. How will the learning from the smart interventions on the university campuses be scaled up and transferred to other parts of the city? Does this project reinforce a particular narrative of urban development that focuses on the connection between technological innovation and decarbonisation? Does the Triangulum project point towards a new form of governance that is realised through public-private partnerships and collaboration? And is there room for the public in the smart urbanisation agenda? It remains to be seen how the campus as testbed for smart urban development will influence cities of the future.

Notes

1 The notions of "Lighthouse cities" and "Follower cities" as well as the combination of energy, transportation, and ICT as embodying smart urban development were prescribed by the European Commission in its call for proposals. In subsequent funding calls, the European Commission added a fourth element of green infrastructure. See the Horizon 2020 website on Smart and Sustainable Cities for further information.
2 For information on campus sustainability and greening activities, see http://www.sustaina bility.manchester.ac.uk and http://www.mmu.ac.uk/environment/

References

Albino, Vito, Umberto Berardi and Rosa Maria Dangelico. 2014. "Smart Cities: Definitions, Dimensions, Performance, and Initiatives." *Journal of Urban Technology* 22(1): 3–21.

Benneworth, Paul, David Charles and Ali Madanipour. 2010. "Building Localized Interactions between Universities and Cities through University Spatial Development." *European Planning Studies* 18(10): 1611–1629.

Bulkeley, Harriet, Vanesa Castán Broto and Gareth A.S. Edwards. 2015. *An Urban Politics of Climate Change: Experimentation and the Governing of Socio-Technical Transitions*. London: Routledge.

Bulkeley, Harriet, Lars Coenen, Niki Frantzeskaki, Christian Hartmann, Annica Kronsell, Lindsay Mai, Simon Marvin, Kes McCormick, Frank van Steenbergen and Yuliya Voytenko Palgan. 2016. "Urban Living Labs: Governing Urban Sustainability Transitions." *Current Opinion in Environmental Sustainability* 22: 13–17.

Burton, Kerry, Andrew Karvonen and Federico Caprotti. 2019. "Smart Goes Green: Digitalising Environmental Agendas in Bristol and Manchester." In *Inside Smart Cities: Place, Politics and Urban Innovation*, edited by Andrew Karvonen, Federico Cugurullo and Federico Caprotti. 117–132. London: Routledge.

Caragliu, Andrea, Chiara Del Bo and Peter Nijkamp. 2011. "Smart Cities in Europe." *Journal of Urban Technology* 18(2): 65–82.

Carvalho, Luis. 2015. "Smart Cities from Scratch? A Socio-technical Perspective." *Cambridge Journal of Regions, Economy and Society* 8: 43–60.

City Growth Commission. 2014. *Universities: The Knowledge to Power Metros*. October 2014, London: City Growth Commission.

CityVerve. 2018. CityVerve website. Accessed 12 April 2018. http://www.cityverve.org.uk

Cocchia, Annalisa and Renata Paola Dameri. 2016. "Exploring Smart City Vision by University, Industry and Government." In *Blurring the Boundaries through Digital Innovation*, edited by Fabrizio D'Ascenzo, Massimo Magni, Alessandra Lazazzara, and Stefano Za, 259–270. Switzerland: Springer.

Corridor Manchester. 2018. "Corridor Manchester Strategic Vision to 2025." Accessed 12 April 2018. Available http://www.corridormanchester.com

Cowley, Robert, Simon Joss and Youri Dayot. 2018. "The Smart City and Its Publics: Insights from across Six UK Cities." *Urban Research & Practice* 11(1): 53–77.

Deas, Iain. 2014. "The Search for Territorial Fixes in Subnational Governance: City-regions and the Disputed Emergence of Post-political Consensus in Manchester, England." *Urban Studies* 51(11): 2285–2314.

Evans, James, and Andrew Karvonen. 2014. "'Give Me a Laboratory and I Will Lower Your Carbon Footprint!' – Urban Laboratories and the Governance of Low Carbon Futures." *International Journal of Urban and Regional Research* 38(2): 413–430.

Evans, James, Ross Jones, Andrew Karvonen, Lucy Millard and Jana Wendler. 2015. "Living Labs and Co-production: University Campuses as Platforms for Sustainability Science." *Current Opinion in Environmental Sustainability* 16: 1–6.

Evans, James, Andrew Karvonen and Rob Raven, eds. 2016. *The Experimental City*. London: Routledge.

Goddard, John. 2009. *Re-inventing the Civic University*. London: National Endowment for Science, Technology and the Arts.

Goddard, John and Paul Vallance. 2013. *The University and the City*. London: Routledge.

Haarstad, Håvard. 2017. "Constructing the Sustainable City: Examining the Role of Sustainability in the 'Smart City' Discourse." *Journal of Environmental Policy & Planning* 19(4): 423–437.

Hodson, Mike, James Evans and Gabriele Schliwa. Forthcoming. "Conditioning Experimentation: The Struggle for Place-Based Discretion in Shaping Urban Transport Infrastructures." *Environment and Planning C: Politics and Space*. doi:10.1177/2399654418765480.

Huawei. 2016. "London and Bristol Crowned UK's Leading Smart Cities." Huawei. Accessed 26 July 2016. http://www.huawei.com/en/news/2016/5/UKs-leading-smart-cities

Jongbloed, Ben, Jürgen Enders and Carlo Salerno. 2008. "Higher Education and its Communities: Interconnections, Interdependencies and a Research Agenda." *Higher Education* 56(3): 303–324.

Karvonen, Andrew, and Bas van Heur. 2014. "Urban Laboratories: Experiments in Reworking Cities." *International Journal of Urban and Regional Research* 38(2): 379–392.

Karvonen, Andrew, Federico Cugurullo and Federico Caprotti, eds. 2019. *Inside Smart Cities: Place, Politics and Urban Innovation*. London: Routledge.

Karvonen, Andrew, James Evans and Bas van Heur. 2014. "The Politics of Urban Experiments: Radical Change or Business as Usual?" In *After Sustainable Cities?*, edited by Mike Hodson and Simon Marvin, 104–115. London: Routledge.

Kitchin, Rob. 2014. "The Real-time City? Big Data and Smart Urbanism." *GeoJournal* 79(1): 1–14.

Kullman, Kim. 2013. "Geographies of Experiment/Experimental Geographies: A Rough Guide." *Geography Compass* 7(12): 879–894.

Madanipour, Ali. 2011. *Knowledge Economy and the City: Spaces of Knowledge*. London: Routledge.

Manchester Smarter City Programme. 2018. Manchester Smarter Manchester Programme website. Accessed 12 April 2018. http://www.manchester.gov.uk/smartercity

Martin, Chris, James Evans and Andrew Karvonen. 2018. "Smart and Sustainable? Five Tensions in the Visions and Practices of the Smart-Sustainable City in Europe and North America." *Technological Forecasting & Social Change* 133: 269–278.

May, Tim and Beth Perry. 2006. "Cities, Knowledge and Universities: Transformations in the Image of the Intangible." *Social Epistemology* 20(3–4): 259–282.

May, Tim and Beth Perry. 2011. "Urban Research in the Knowledge Economy: Content, Context and Outlook." *Built Environment* 37(3): 352–367.

Melhuish, Claire. 2015. *Case Studies in University-led Urban Regeneration*. London: UCL Urban Laboratory.

MMU (Manchester Metropolitan University). 2016. *Manchester Metropolitan University Annual Report and Financial Statements Year Ended 31 July 2016*. Manchester: Manchester Metropolitan University.

MMU (Manchester Metropolitan University). 2017. *Manchester Metropolitan University Estate Strategy 2017–2017*. Manchester: Manchester Metropolitan University.

Nevens, Frank, Niki Frantzeskaki, Leen Gorissen and Derk Loorbach. 2013. "Urban Transition Labs: Co-creating Transformative Action for Sustainable Cities." *Journal of Cleaner Production* 50: 111–122.

Paskaleva, Krassimira, James Evans, Christopher Martin, Trond Linjordet, Dujuan Yang and Andrew Karvonen. 2017. "Data Governance in the Sustainable Smart City." *Informatics* 4(4): 41.

Perry, Beth. 2008. "Academic Knowledge and Urban Development: Theory, Policy and Practice." In *Knowledge-Based Urban Development: Planning and Applications in the Information Era*, edited by Tan Yigitcanlar, Koray Velibeyoglu and Scott Baum, 21–41. London: Information Science Reference.

Perry, Beth, Zarina Patel, Ylva Norén Bretzer and Merritt Polk. 2018. "Organising for Co-Production: Local Interaction Platforms for Urban Sustainability." *Politics and Governance* 6(1): 189–198.

Raven, Rob, Florian Kern, Bram Verhees and Adrian Smith. 2016. "Niche Construction and Empowerment through Socio-political Work: A Meta-analysis of Six Low-carbon Technology Cases." *Environmental Innovation and Societal Transitions* 18: 164–180.

Robson, Brian. 2016. "The Resurgent Entrepreneurial City." In *Manchester: Making the Modern City*, edited by Alan Kidd and Terry Wyke, 347–396. Liverpool: Liverpool University Press.

Shelton, Taylor, Alan Wiig and Matthew Zook. 2015. "The 'Actually Existing Smart City'." *Cambridge Journal of Region, Economy, and Society* 8: 13–25.

Smith, Adrian and Rob Raven. 2012. "What is Protective Space? Reconsidering Niches in Transitions to Sustainability." *Research Policy* 41(6): 1025–1036.

Stephens, Jennie C., Maria E. Hernandez, Mikael Román, Amanda C. Graham and Roland W. Scholz. 2008. "Higher Education as a Change Agent for Sustainability in Different Cultures and Contexts." *International Journal of Sustainability in Higher Education* 9(3): 317–338.

Townsend, Anthony M. 2013. *Smart Cities: Big Data, Civic Hackers, and the Quest for a New Utopia*. New York: W.W. Norton and Company.

Trencher, Gregory P., Masaru Yarime and Ali Kharrazi. 2013. "Co-creating Sustainability: Cross-sector University Collaborations for Driving Sustainable Urban Transformations." *Journal of Cleaner Production* 50: 40–55.

Trencher, Gregory, Masaru Yarime, Kes B. McCormick, Christopher N.H. Doll and Steven B. Kraines. 2014. "Beyond the Third Mission: Exploring the Emerging University Function of Co-creation for Sustainability." *Science and Public Policy* 41(2): 151–179.

Triangulum. 2018. Triangulum website. Accessed 12 April 2018. http://www.triangulum-project.eu

UoM (University of Manchester). 2012. *University of Manchester Master Plan 2012–2022*. Manchester: University of Manchester.

UoM (University of Manchester). 2017. *University of Manchester Facts and Figures 2017*. Manchester: University of Manchester.

van Heur, Bas. 2010. "The Built Environment of Higher Education and Research: Architecture and the Expectation of Innovation." *Geography Compass* 4(12): 1713–1724.

Voytenko, Yuliya, Kes McCormick, James Evans and Gabriele Schliwa. 2016. "Urban Living Labs for Sustainability and Low Carbon Cities in Europe: Towards a Research Agenda." *Journal of Cleaner Production* 123: 45–54.

PART II

Smart cities, citizenship and ethics

9

WHO ARE THE END-USE(R)S OF SMART CITIES?

A synthesis of conversations in Amsterdam

Christine Richter, Linnet Taylor, Shazade Jameson and Carmen Pérez del Pulgar

Introduction

Today, withdrawing from digital space would mean giving up on countless pleasures and conveniences afforded by communication and navigation devices. Even if one wanted to withdraw, living offline has become rather difficult. Around the world urban life has become digitized and datafied to a degree that any attempt at living even for a few days without engagement with digital space would likely require a withdrawal from urban life altogether: from travel, work, and personal relations as we nowadays experience and live them. Many urbanites produce digital data through almost everything they do. We get up in the morning and use a mobile phone that is constantly emitting information to check our email, the news, and social media. We travel to work using an electronic travel card or in a car with various GPS and digital systems. We walk down streets where signals from our phones and other devices are captured and read by wifi beacons and MAC address sensors, and our images by CCTV. We use apps that emit details of our location, we tweet, we tag, we check in. We make phone calls through particular antennas set up by our mobile phone providers. We interact with the city digitally by paying our taxes, living in our houses, using city services, and offering feedback to the authorities. All day, digital signatures are embedded in the technologies we use, emitted as we communicate and move around, and signaled by most of our activities. The picture that builds up about us in the course of every day is both behavioral and spatial in ways that are often opaque to us. Actual and possible effects of digitalization and datafication of urban life are critically debated in scholarly and policy circles; and Liesbet Van Zoonen (2015) has observed that city governments today are faced with a super-wicked problem of data governance (Levin et al. 2012). In this context citizens are both contributors to the digitalization and datafication, as well as being affected by these processes.

Yet, we still know relatively little – given the global spread of smart cities and their interconnectedness – about residents' perceptions of the smart city and their experiences in their daily crossings between physical and digital spaces. How voluntary or forced, conscious or unconscious, desired or undesired is people's engagement with the smart city? What are people's experiences and thoughts, concerns and emotions? In order to address a future where people make different choices about engaging with digital technologies, in a world where the city is becoming more programmable and digitally integrated as technology continues to advance (Kitchin and Dodge 2011), we therefore set out to ask, how residents of Amsterdam, the Netherlands, perceive the emerging digital data infrastructure that weaves its way through the urban fabric and how they feel about and respond to the uses of their digital data. This chapter follows up from a report published in June 2016 (Taylor et al. 2016), and a subsequent public debate in Amsterdam in the same month. Throughout the study, and across groups of respondents, as well as during the public debate a general sense of "ambivalence" and "insecurity" permeated the conversations. During the debate, one researcher, when asked to summarize her views, began as follows: "What I keep hearing is concerns, concerns, concerns." Several participants agreed with our perception that focus group discussions and public debate not only provided a platform for people to "finally discuss these matters," but were also "highly emotional," in the words of participants. It is this sense of ambivalence and feeling of insecurity, which we seek to further unpack in this chapter.[1] An understanding of emotional responses is important, Sabine Roeser (2016, in *De Correspondent*, 23 February) argues, because emotions derive from what people value and find important; and as such offer sources for reflection also for politicians and policy makers.

Before summarizing the main themes of our conversations with Amsterdam residents in section three of the chapter, we briefly describe the study's background and conceptual underpinnings. We conclude with a brief argument on how to reimagine the smart city with reference to urban studies literature.

Research context and methodological notes

The research was conducted through expert interviews and focus groups in Amsterdam during 2015. Over the course of 2014–15 we also participated in a range of events and discussions to do with smart city technologies, charting the actors engaging in the field and the debates emerging from different sectors.

Amsterdam has historically been and continues to be a thriving "global city," acting as a commercial and financial hub (Sassen 2008), and has made significant advances in digitizing, automatizing, and datafying urban life. As such the city often serves as a reference for the development of smart cities elsewhere in the world. The past years have witnessed a lively debate in Amsterdam especially over the question of how to balance between protecting citizens' privacy in digital data flows, on the one hand, and leveraging commercial, science and technology, and innovation sectors for urban services delivery on the other. Across the city and the

Randstad region more broadly (Rotterdam, The Hague, Utrecht), designers, artists, political activists, data scientists, hacker communities, academics and others have begun to engage in various ways in making sense of digital urban life (see for example Gr1p.org). Amsterdam is a city of high real estate prices and housing competition, and a place of social inequality, with inclusionary as well as exclusionary dynamics in social, economic and spatial terms. These dynamics are gaining a new dimension with the emergence of digital socio-spaces adding to the complexities of urban governance.

As an analytical pathway into these complexities we can conceptualize the smart city as an urban information infrastructure, because information systems and infrastructures have come to transcend the boundaries of formally circumscribed organizations, such as one company, one government department, or one country. Rather than being *a priori* designed and built from scratch, the development of such infrastructure evolves continuously through the interplay between technical and human agents, a process which follows unanticipated paths and results in political choices and human values becoming hidden in the system's nature and logic, so that the impacts on society are difficult to trace (Bowker and Star 2000; Avgerou and McGrath 2007). The development of information infrastructure always excludes some groups of people (Aanestad, Monteiro, and Nielsen 2007; Star 1999). The initial questions informing this study therefore included, what kind of governance of digital data creates an equal playing field for the elderly, the young, the vulnerable? For non-users of smart technologies, non-citizens, speakers of other languages?

We began the research with a series of 20 interviews with experts in data and urban governance, followed by a scenario-building exercise in which we used that information to think about what data use scenarios might look like in the future.[2] We then conducted a series of eight focus groups, with six to ten people in each. In convening the focus groups, we aimed to determine which groups were missing from, or marginalized by, current discussions and practices of smart city development, and also those whose lives might be most affected by an increase in urban datafication. Our discussions highlighted several groups: non-natives (EU and non-EU immigrants); people at higher risk of being profiled (ethnic and religious minorities); those who opted out of using the technologies currently seen as necessary for citizen involvement in the smart city (people who do not own/use smartphones); those who operate in highly regulated professions (sex workers, also at a higher risk of being profiled), freelancers who are responsible for their own working environment and data management, people working in technology development (tech developers of a large Dutch energy provider), and high school children. The project was conducted partly in Dutch, but mostly in English: the expert interviews were conducted in English, but the events we attended and the focus group discussions were often in a mixture of Dutch and English, and about 20 per cent of our respondents spoke only Dutch during the research.[3]

Our analysis for this chapter is inspired by a framework originally developed by Ribes and Finholt (2009) to analyze and understand tensions experienced by participants in the development of cyber infrastructure in natural scientist communities. We write "inspired," because there is an important difference between the development of a digital skin of cities (Rabari and Storper 2014) and intra- or inter-organizational information system design. In the digital landscape of cities, we are confronted with a scenario, where citizens are producers, co-designers, as well as end-users of digital technology and data,[4] and their participation spans between being voluntary and forced, and between conscious and unconscious. This is a different positionality compared to the conscious participation in the development of information systems and infrastructure through collaborative efforts among participants, who are aware of the general goals and strategies to develop the system, who discuss and influence data usability and data uses, and whom system designers may explicitly invite to partake in what Ribes and Finholt call "infrastructuring."

We identified four tensions across the interviews and focus groups through repeated readings of the transcripts and discussions among researchers:

- between conveniences afforded by digital engagement and the risks of being tracked;
- between becoming visible and the invisibility of those watching;
- between individualized data sharing practices and the structural forces of digitalization;
- between a homogeneity of digital citizenry and a dispersal of human citizen concerns.

The following section discusses these tensions through a summary along the lines of two main themes.

Conversations with residents of a smart city

The first two tensions reflect insecurity in terms of not knowing who is collecting and using one's data and for what purposes. In the following, we discuss these tensions under the theme "perspectives on use(r)s from the other end." The other two tensions refer to the collective experience of lives lived increasingly in digital space while the paths, which one can, should or wants to take into the digital world are highly individualistic and at the same time hidden beneath "representations" made up of digital data. We discuss these tensions under the theme of "citizen-ries in the shadow of data."

Perspectives on use(r)s from the other end

The residents of a smart city are often referred to as the "users," "end-users," consumers or beneficiaries. This is reflected in discussions with residents from the point of view of digital data-based service provisions of various kinds. Many respondents discussed, sometimes enthusiastically, the conveniences and opportunities afforded by digital infrastructure, but recognized at the same time that this comes at the cost of giving up not only one's data, but also one's privacy, in return:

> I think we accept to give up our data when it really aids us in daily living, like stuff like Google Now for instance. It says like "leave now for this and that meeting", I find that aggregating these data sources [your agenda, if there are traffic jams on your route, weather, etc.], I find that this is really smart, it's really helpful to have that stuff ... and I am willing to give on privacy for these use-cases.
>
> *(Technology developers focus group, 3 December 2015)*

Insecurity pertains especially to trade-offs that need to be made between safety and convenience afforded by the use of digital data technology and related services, on one hand, and privacy, on the other. The concern for privacy here reflects a discomfort and discontent with not knowing who is or will be using one's data. To know whether one's safety is protected in return for personal information otherwise considered too private to share or whether one is being profiled requires knowing the interests of the users of the data. The opaqueness in terms of data uses and users is compounded by increasingly little contact on a human level during the exchange of data and information for various purposes as expressed by a resident of Dutch origin:

> I have very little touch points with the city of Amsterdam. Nearly everything I need to do with the city is either completely automated without any touch points or the rare following up about your driving licence or passport. That's all.
>
> *(Technology developers, 3 December 2015)*

Decisions on the possible trade-offs between being seen and not being seen, being on or off the map, are made – if possible at all – in blindness. In the digital city the users of data are more or less unknown and therefore unaccountable to the residents being mapped and watched. Respondents made a distinction here between data collected and used by private versus public sectors, often being more concerned about data collection and use by the former:

> [the city collects our data] to assess what services are needed – transport capacity, disease reporting – I don't feel spied on by the state. If I go to a public service place and they have my data, that's alright. I mind if companies have my data.
>
> *(Non-users of smart phones, 10 September 2015)*

This differentiation between private/public records, however, is unrealistic given current data streams across the public/private boundaries. It is the socio-technical assemblages, into which visible recording devices such as CCTV or smart lamp poles are embedded, that remain invisible to people. And yet it is this very knowledge of what happens inside and especially behind a camera, or who is using the data for what purpose, which people require in order to express, whether they are comfortable and choose if they are willing to "provide" data or not. One participant of the public debate of our report captured this tension in a nutshell with the remark: "I am tired of being told, sorry, cannot do anything about that. It's the [computer] system doing that."

In their role as data providers to the smart city residents are mainly concerned about the users and uses of their data; and these "end-users/uses" of personal data remain to a large extent both opaque and in constant flux. There is no master designer at work here – at least not in any visible form: not one system of traffic signs, lanes and lights to regulate data flows, or one concerted and pre-designed population census that takes place at specified intervals in time, nor do we encounter the data collectors at the door with survey forms in hand anymore. The insecurities expressed in discussions are a reflection of the lack of accountability structures in the emerging digital network, into which one's life is becoming embedded and plugged.

Citizenries in the shadow of data

Another type of insecurity, which we identified across respondent groups, relates to the contextual forces at a larger urban societal level, which require the individual to "participate" in the digital sphere, on one hand, and the individualistic nature of data sharing practices and decisions on whether, when, and how to share one's digital data on the other.

Most obviously people discussed the near impossibility of disengaging from digital space. This was discussed especially in relation to the necessity to enter digital space to build and maintain social networks: both private and professional, as well as for voluntary work and membership in various associations. Also once the digital space has been entered, the choices to navigate are perceived as limited by respondents in the sense that the use of an app or access to a website often require prod-user/customer to "click agree" whether one agrees with the conditions put forth by a digital service provider or not.

Where people see possibilities and need for choices, they experience at the same time an increasing pressure and individualization due to the need to self-manage digital data flows and sharing under circumstances and conditions that are difficult to understand. People's varying backgrounds obviously further add to individualized choice making and data sharing practices as well as related concerns. For example, privacy may come at a price affordable only to some. A paper ticket purchased via cash payment would provide more anonymity to the traveler and his travel routes, but it costs more than using the electronic card. Similarly, an anonymized electronic card does not allow the traveler to subscribe to fare discounts. The nature and dynamics of how a person's professional and private life relate play a role in the individual practices of data sharing and choices that can be made and/

or are desirable. This was an important point of discussion, especially among the sex worker group, but found expression also in other respondent groups, for example in the case of a freelance software developer, who recognizes the need to make some personal details available digitally in order to support his profession:

> I come from an open-source background, and in an open source background, it's very common to put everything online … you create and people get to know you from what you are doing … so not telling about what you're doing, but doing it. But as a company you need to promote yourself a little bit more than just put online the code you're making …, because people that take the decision whether to hire you or not don't always understand the code. So you need to tell more about yourself than just putting your code online.
>
> *(Freelance software developer, interviewed 26 June 2015)*

In sum, while engagement with the city increasingly means engaging with the digital sphere, people's capacities, preferences, and backgrounds require them to do so in very diverse ways and largely through self-management of various data flows as far as this "management" is possible.

It is at this point, where a core challenge in smart city creation emerges. While citizens – in the form of data providers and as "digital data points" – become part of a digital mass, their concerns as human citizens – "behind the data," so to speak – increasingly atomize and become less visible. One technology developer stated: "I think we are virtually invisible, at least on a digital level" (3 December 2015).

This point of view is interesting because it contrasts an increasing sense of personal invisibility in digitized systems with the increasing digital visibility that comes with our emission of more types of data. In such systems, the city can identify us, but it cannot see who we are. Historian Jan Holvast, interviewed for this project, explained how the Dutch census boycott of 1970 occurred (Anderetijden 2011). At the time, the Dutch census was boycotted for three reasons, which are interesting to note as triggers, because they are being replicated by current datafication practices. First, the 1970 census was computerized and made it possible to examine the population in new ways by correlating variables, while also asking more in-depth questions to add new variables to the analysis. Second, the census deployed a questionnaire and punch cards similar to those used by IBM during the Nazi occupation of the Netherlands during World War II. And third, the 1970 census was compulsory. The history of the boycott demonstrates the deeply embedded insecurity about being counted, categorized and recorded that is being reawakened by datafication.

This insecurity was voiced by all our interviewees without exception, including technology developers, data scientists, academic researchers involved in smart city projects and city officials themselves. At the same time, however, it is possible to question how socially interdependent people are willing and able to be today, in comparison to the Amsterdam community of 1970. Holvast notes that "the most important difference between now and then is that then we were talking about our privacy, and now we are talking about my privacy".

So, what we see in the smart city then is a digitally highly networked society, which is, at the same time a highly individualized citizenship. The overemphasis on the possibilities of fast, easy, and "neat" categorizations of people and their individual or collective concerns on the basis of digital data "representations" leaves the human citizen's concerns at one and the same time atomized and in the shadows of the kind of public spaces that could give voice to human concerns and pluralistic political debate.[5]

Remembering the urban to reimagine the smart city

The majority of focus group participants acknowledged the conveniences afforded by the smart city: be it the fast and easy finding of the next train connection through online apps or the convenience afforded by using digital calendars. But what the discussions equally evoked was the question of how far we have reached a "tipping point of convenience" in smart city creation, where the price paid in terms of privacy, personal choice making, and the quality of citizen-government interactions is becoming too high. The notion of "I have nothing to hide" surfaced across focus groups in different discussion contexts. But here too, the momentary comfort gave way to discussing different circumstances, in which the question of what is to be hidden or not is no longer one's own choice, and where the visibilities created through automatic inferences drawn from data have little to do with what I might think I have to hide or not.[6]

Creating a democratic city livable for its citizens, questions beyond the labels of "convenience, efficiency, and security" need to be addressed through continued public debate. Both focus groups as well as public debates in Amsterdam, that have been taking place in past years, showed us the need among residents to reflect on the themes summarized in this chapter (among others) in a democratic quest for navigational paths through the digital-physical labyrinth of smart cities. Rather than seeing the city as data emitted and produced by urban residents, we need to remember the city as residence of people and as urban/political space (Brenner 2009) – both public and private, physical and social – where political debate rooted in human ambivalence and ambiguity takes place – online and offline.

A number of concrete recommendations at municipal level for the case of Amsterdam, but potentially applicable elsewhere, are published in our 2016 report. However, we also recognize that the questions at hand go beyond the jurisdictional capacities of one municipality or even one nation-state. Within existing jurisdictional boundaries, the digitalization of the public sector is sparking new constellations of professionals and "hybridizing private and public actors" (Bauman et al. 2014). While writing about "the case of Amsterdam" most of our discussions left the boundaries of the municipality. Smart cities are spaces, where the global infiltrates the local and vice versa through intersecting flows of capital, finance, and information still rooted in the human and material of each city (Sassen 2008). The smart city comes to represent developments and systems that care little for administrative boundaries relating people to larger and partially de-nationalized "network[s] of networked metropolitan regions" (Townsend 2001). Therefore creating the smart city involves also a potential re-thinking of jurisdictional boundaries.

Along these lines we argue that the processes and practices of creating smart cities in future ask us to think of "smart" not only as digital data network, but also as a "people infrastructure" (Simone 2004) and of the city not only as efficient and convenient, but also as a democratic and pluralistic arena for people to think and institutionalize new templates of accountability and jurisdictional maps for navigating our lives lived in cyberphysical space.

Acknowledgements

Principal investigators of this project are Prof. Isa Baud and Dr. Linnet Taylor. We also gratefully acknowledge contributions and input during the course of the research from Dr. Karin Pfeffer, Alexandra Ruina, Christopher Livett, Nathalia Vredeveld, Dionne Poulussen, expert interviewees and focus group participants. The project was funded through Maps4Society (Kleine Innovatieve Projecten).

Notes

1 For related investigations in the Dutch context regarding emotional responses to technological change and innovation, see for instance a recent research project at the Rijksuniversiteit Groningen, "Developing socially responsible innovations: The role of values and moral emotions" (http://www.rug.nl/gmw/psychology/value-emotion-innovation/).
2 A summary of these scenarios can be read in the report: Taylor et al. (2016, pp. 9–11).
3 Further details can be read in the report: Taylor et al. (2016).
4 In this sense it would be fair to use the term "produser" (see for example Coleman et al. 2009). However, our discussions and interview focused on people's perceptions regarding the data they produce, more or less voluntarily or not, and more or less consciously or not.
5 Mireille Hildebrandt (2017, p. 26) writes that "the large-scale introduction of so-called cyberphysical systems that generate the novel onlife world, further confuses and confounds the individual human subjects that use these systems while they (cyberphysical systems) use them (the humans whose machine-readable behaviors are mined to drive the functionality of these systems)."
6 For a more elaborate argument see Solove (2007).

References

Aanestad, M., E. Monteiro, and P. Nielsen. 2007. "Information Infrastructures and Public Goods: Analytical and Practical Implications for SDI." *Information Technology for Development* 13(1): 7–25.
Anderetijden. 2011. "De burger in kaart – De Volkstelling in 1971." 30 September. http://www.npogeschiedenis.nl/andere-tijden/afleveringen/2011-2012/Volkstelling.html.
Avgerou, C., and K. McGrath. 2007. "Power, rationality, and the art of living through sociotechnical change." *MIS Quarterly* 31(2): 295–315.

Bauman, Z., D. Bigo, P. Esteves, E. Guild, V. Jabri, D. Lyon and R.B.J. Walker. 2014. "After Snowden: rethinking the impact of surveillance." *International Political Sociology* 8(2): 121–144.

Bowker, G. C., and S.L. Star. 2000. *Sorting Things Out – Classification and its Consequences.* Cambridge, MA: MIT Press.

Brenner, N. 2009. "What is critical urban theory?" *City* 13(2–3): 198–207.

Coleman, D., Y. Georgiadou and J. Labonte. 2009. "Volunteered Geographic Information: The Nature and Motivation of Produsers." *International Journal of Spatial Data Infrastructures Research* 4: 332–358.

Hildebrandt, M. 2017. "The Virtuality of Territorial Borders." *Utrecht Law Review* 13(2): 13–27.

Kitchin, R., and M. Dodge. 2011. *Code/space: Software and Everyday Life.* Cambridge, MA: MIT Press.

Levin, K., B. Cashore, S. Bernstein and G. Auld. 2012. "Overcoming the tragedy of super wicked problems: constraining our future selves to ameliorate global climate change." *Policy Sciences* 45(2): 123–152.

Rabari, C. and M. Storper. 2014. "The digital skin of cities: urban theory and research in the age of the sensored and metered city, ubiquitous computing and big data." *Cambridge Journal of Regions, Economy and Society* 8: 27–42.

Ribes, D. and T. A. Finholt. 2009. "The long now of technology infrastructure: Articulating tensions in development." *Journal of the Association for Information Systems* 10(5): 375–398.

Roeser, S. 2016. "Bang voor robots? Gebruik die angst." *De Correspondent*, 23 February. https://decorrespondent.nl/4069/Bang-voor-robots-Gebruik-die-angst/873551511261-11f042b5.

Sassen, S. 2008. "The global city: the de-nationalizing of time and space." http://90.146.8.18/en/archiv_files/20021/e2002_018.pdf. Accessed: 5 September 2017.

Simone, A. 2004. "People as infrastructure: Intersecting fragments in Johannesburg." *Public Culture* 16(3): 407–428.

Solove, D. J. 2007. "'I've got nothing to hide' and other misunderstandings of privacy." *San Diego Law Review* 44: 745. Available at: https://papers.ssrn.com/sol3/Papers.cfm?abstract_id=998565.

Star, S. L. 1999. "The ethnography of infrastructure." *American Behavioral Scientist* 43(3): 377–391.

Taylor, L., C. Richter, S. Jameson and C. Perez de Pulgar. 2016. *Customers, Users or Citizens? Inclusion, Spatial Data and Governance in the Smart City.* http://ssrn.com/abstract=2792565.

Townsend, A.M. 2001. "The Internet and the rise of the new network cities, 1969–1999." *Environment and Planning B: Planning and Design* 28(1): 39–58.

Van Zoonen, L. 2015. "Big, Open and Linked Data (BOLD) challenges for urban governance." Paper presented at the Data Power Conference, University of Sheffield, June 22–23.

10

'CITYZENS BECOME NETIZENS'

Hashtag citizenships in the making of India's 100 smart cities

Ayona Datta

Introduction

In May 2014, a new ruling party came to power in India on the basis of their promises of good governance and economic growth. The creation of 100 smart cities formed the backbone of these promises, which sought to 'leapfrog' India into a future of innovation, entrepreneurialism and endless prosperity. Seeking to produce the 'smart city' and the 'smart citizen' as conjoined aspects of an urban age, this programme seeks to apply a range of digital technologies from e-governance to smart utility networks to produce ubiquitously networked cities. The Indian definition of the 'smart city' however, significantly plays down the global imaginary of a ubiquitously connected Internet of Things (IoT) and big data to emphasise the importance of local situatedness. Indeed, the Guidelines note,

> there is no universally accepted definition of a Smart City. It means different things to different people. The conceptualisation of Smart City, therefore, varies from city to city and country to country, depending on the level of development, willingness to change and reform, resources and aspirations of the city residents.
>
> *(GoI, 2015: 5)*

Delivering this rhetoric in practice requires a number of manoeuvres. First since over 80 per cent of Indian citizens are currently on the negative side of the digital divide, they need to be drawn into digital space in order to produce a 'user base' for smart city services. Indeed in India, only 0.2 billion of the 1.2 billion strong population are connected to information and communication systems. This digital divide is geographically, socially and economically uneven – across rural/urban divides, across generations, caste and religious communities, and across middle and working classes.

Crucially the digital divide is also a gender divide (Antonio and Tuffley 2014), which sees the take up of ICT at a higher pace among urban middle class young men.

However as Calzada and Cobo (2015) argue, 'being digitally connected should not be perceived as gaining social capital.' In other words, digital access requires a fundamental transformation in the nature and parameters of citizenship, transforming the horizontal citizen-citizen interactions while restructuring vertical relationships between state, urban governments and civil society. Thus Cardullo and Kitchin (2018: 1) point out that 'most "citizen-centric" smart city initiatives are rooted in stewardship, civic paternalism, and a neoliberal conception of citizenship that prior-itizes consumption choice and individual autonomy'. While the lack of digital access is disempowering, access to digital space is not automatically empowering. On the contrary, citizenship in digital space can be reduced to a passive consumerism of likes, tweets, retweets and shares at best, and surveillance, trolling, threats of violence at worst. Lerman (2013: 59) notes that 'these technologies may create a new kind of voicelessness, where certain groups' preferences and behaviors receive little or no consideration when powerful actors decide how to distribute goods and services and how to reform public and private institutions.'

This chapter examines the making of India's 100 smart cities through what I call 'hashtag citizenships' – the production of idealised urban citizens through a range of interactive apps, infographics, competitions and online consultations that sustain a 'corporate storytelling' (Söderström et al., 2014) around the smart city. This is as much a visual statecraft as it is an opportunistic redefinition of the very terms and parameters of citizenship in India. I argue that the citizens of the smart city are framed and sustained through a technique of discursively and visually coded representations that seek to mime actually existing citizenships in digital space. I suggest therefore that the production of smart citizens in the future Indian city has become synonymous with the production of a postcolonial technocratic sub-jectivity, which needs to be critically investigated.

Smart citizen as postcolonial subject

The figure of the smart citizen in India reinforces historical and contemporary paradoxes of identity and belonging. This is because the notion of citizenship is a relatively new concept in India. Under colonial rule, bodies and identities of Indians existed as 'lesser' subjects, and were 'scientifically' categorised by caste, religious and ethnic markers (Chatterjee, 2004). Civil society and citizenship within an equal public sphere were lar-gely absent, and any claims to citizenship by colonial subjects were primarily conceived through civil disobedience. Upon independence in 1947, the Indian Constitution explicitly provided universal rights to all citizens while simultaneously evoking rights to positive discrimination in social and political spheres (such as education, employment, housing, representation in democratic politics and so on) for those historically margin-alised by caste, religious or gender ideologies. Indian Citizenship is now caught between the search for a uniform civil society under the rubric of universalised rights and the demand for differentiated rights for those who have historically faced social and economic marginalisation in society (Jayal, 2013). Smart cities provide the 'map of citizenship' (Holston and Appadurai, 1999) in a digital urban age, articulating its features and its moral and performative dimensions across physical and virtual spaces.

The imaginary of the smart citizen revolves around a particular demographic – a group that has been outspokenly supportive of the use of ICT and smart cities. As Calzada and Cobo (2015, p. 26) argue, they have been variously referred to as 'the net generation (Tapscott, 2009), digital natives (Prensky, 2001), millennials (Oblinger and Oblinger, 2005), Google generation (Rowlands et al., 2008), and many others (Jones et al., 2010).' The imaginary of the smart citizen in India revolves around this particular demographic of 'digital natives', a loose group of young upwardly mobile middle-classes who are mostly male, but now also increasingly female. They constitute a generation in post-liberalised India who belong to a 'techno-world' of newfound online and offline consumer identities (Fernandes, 2006). As I have argued elsewhere (Datta, 2015), this demographic shift is significant in India, which for the first time in its history is set to become the youngest country in the world by 2020 with 64 per cent of its population in the working age group (IRIS-UN 2013). India's digitally savvy youth are empowered by their 'pride' in driving the corporate IT sector leading to a techo-political belonging to the nation-state. In this scenario, the IT industry is constructed as one, with a more ethical position than a corrupt state (Dasgupta, 2015), legitimising technology (rather than state) as the benefactor of social welfare. Thus, citizenship has become a 'gift of the state' (Jayal, 2013); that is, it is no longer claimed as a right, but given to those deemed worthy of self-governance. As I suggest in this chapter, digital citizenship then is constructed as a rite of passage to be included in the smart city.

This chapter is based on a horizon scanning of publicly available smart city applications (on the Ministry of Urban Development website in India) made by different urban municipalities that were submitted towards the 100 smart cities challenge. Beyond the various proposals for the smart city, these applications showed the range of citizen consultation workshops that had been conducted by urban governments. The data on the number and nature of these consultations drives a large part of the analysis. This is supplemented by a range of textual and visual material publicly available from government and private sector websites to trace the production of smart citizens as an essential component of India's smart urban future. Often seen as independent consultancy/media representations, I nonetheless bring this into dialogue with the state sponsored smart city applications because the state and the corporate are often indistinguishable in these smart city applications, as I will elaborate later. The findings then are driven by discursive analysis of the documents, applications and citizen consultations in terms of their references to and descriptions of the smart citizen.

'Cityzens become netizens'

In February 2016 as the first set of 20 winning cities were announced, MoUD announced that the 100 smart cities challenge had kick-started the process of 'cityzens becoming netizens' (Naidu, 2016). The Ministry reported that a total of

15.2 million citizens participated in the preparation of smart city plans at various stages. The national smart cities mission had tapped into the digital sphere to produce millions of digital citizens projected to become smart citizens in the future. Although these statistics were at a scale not achieved or attempted earlier, it still constituted a small share of the total urban populations (about 12 per cent of the total population of the participating cities). But who were these smart citizens of the future? How were they discursively and performatively produced? What was their role in the future smart city?

Very early on, the draft concept note on smart cities stated that the intention was 'to promote cities that … give a decent quality of life to its citizens' (GoI 2015: 5). Indeed, it emphasised that quality of life in smart cities would be at par with European standards, indicating that despite its situated rhetoric, the Indian smart cities mission had set for itself the parameters of western modernity and urbanism. The federal Ministry of Urban Development (MoUD) website monitored citizen engagement statistics across all cities. The MoUD in consultation with US based Bloomberg Philanthropies prepared a 43-part questionnaire which was used to garner information from citizens in each city in terms of their preferences. Compared to other evaluation categories in the smart cities challenge, 'citizen participation' had the third highest weightage of 16 per cent after 'feasibility and cost-effectiveness of proposals' (30 per cent) and 'result orientation' (20 per cent). Other criteria such as 'smartness of proposal' (10 per cent), 'strategic plan' (10 per cent), 'vision and goals' (5 per cent), 'evidence-based city profiling and key performance indicators' (5 per cent), and 'processes followed' (4 per cent) came much lower in the priority list. Not only that, digital presence was a key criterion of citizen participation as evident in the assessment questions: 'How much of social media, community, mobile governance have been used during citizen consultation?' and 'How well does the Vision articulate the use of information and communication technologies to improve public service delivery and improve the quality of life of local citizens?' (GoI 2015: 33).

This then was not just digital access, rather a collaboration with urban governance for and by digital technology. As Hansen and Stepputat (2001, 63) argue:

> Rather than giving liberty and citizenship to all and basing government on the autonomous individual, liberal projects in postcolonial states have tended to establish a distinction between 1) populations that were suitable for liberal (self)government, 2) populations that could improve or improve themselves to a point in which they could manage autonomy, and 3) populations judged to be beyond the scope of improvement.

This nomenclature of citizenship when applied to smart citizenship identifies digital natives as category 1 – those who are already able to fulfil their duties in digital space and able to self-govern their actions. However, it is category 2 that now forms the terrain of coercion and conversion into digital citizens. As I will argue, this group are the young socially mobile middle-class men who have the potential to acquire digital skills, be convinced of the smart city imperative, and collaborate with urban governance in digital space. This is the population that is valuable to the future smart city. This population needs to be: (1) counted; and (2) further guided into 'acceptable' patterns of behaviour across online and offline spaces.

'Counting' smart citizens

The first indications of the production of 'netizens' became apparent in the draft preceding the final smart city guidelines in 2014. The 'Smart City Mission document' as it was called went through a number of iterations from concept notes to draft guidelines to a final public document. Crucially, the 'netizen' also underwent a set of transformations. The draft concept note identified the smart city as 'not only described by the level of qualification or education of the citizens but also by the quality of social interactions regarding integration and public life and the openness towards the "outer" world' (MoUD, 2014, p. 9). It further noted that it was important to have urban citizens in the digital sphere since online participation will lead to '[s]ocial pressure on other citizens [that] can often remove resistance and facilitate a greater degree of civic discipline' (MoUD, 2014). These explicit links between digital participation and digital surveillance were dropped in the final Smart City mission guidelines, to describe a smart citizen:

> The Proposal development will lead to creation of a smart citizenry. The proposal will be citizen-driven from the beginning, achieved through citizen consultations, including active participation of groups of people, such as Residents Welfare Associations, Tax Payers Associations, Senior Citizens and Slum Dwellers Associations. During consultations, issues, needs and priorities of citizens and groups of people will be identified and citizen-driven solutions generated.
>
> *(GoI, 2015: 22)*

This focus on 'smart citizenry' reflects the general transformation in processes of deliberative democracy which Kitchin (2015) observes have a 'discursive emphasis' on 'inclusivity and citizen empowerment' without necessarily any real impacts on democratic participation. The process of enumerating this 'smart citizenry' relied on what Dan Hill (2012) has called a 'push button democracy' where online endorsement is seen to stand for democratic deliberation in the public sphere. With the announcement of the nominated 100 smart cities, overnight each city began their own 'enumeration' process through which an urban population was incorporated into the logics of digital governance. This enumeration occurred across digital and material publics, with municipalities summoning its urban residents to participate in online 'citizen consultations' to produce what I will call here 'hashtag citizens'. These consultations were both online and face-to-face, virtual and analogue. Each city carried out extensive public mobilisation events (smart city walks and marathons, essay, poster and logo competitions). They conducted surveys in middle-class neighbourhoods as well as informal settlements, in government run schools and colleges and in marginal city wards. The public were invited to meetings and workshops with local councillors and civil servants through newspaper announcements, through neighbourhood residential associations, through slum dwellers' organisations, trader's associations and so on.

One of the key platforms where these processes came together was the MoUD website, which hosted the smart city proposals and citizen consultations with over 2 million online comments received across 98 cities. The language of consultations on the digital platforms was English, although responses were sometimes in Hindi or other regional languages. Despite being a small share of the total urban population of these cities, this nevertheless revealed the huge shift towards digital citizenship. For example, by the end of 2015, Chandigarh Municipal Corporation reported that there had been about 20,000 MyGov submissions with over 56,000 Facebook likes, 260 tweets and 400 views of You-Tube videos of their smart cities proposal. In Navi Mumbai, the municipal corporation outlined a set of 10 questions,[1] which its residents had to prioritise on a scale of 1–5. The municipality held over 110 'Consultation Events', including face-to-face open forums, discussion groups, questionnaire surveys with citizens at ward level, schools, colleges, institutes, professional bodies, and so on. The municipality claimed that about 408,000 citizens joined in their online and face-to-face consultations. Online consultations were carried out through the MoUD website where over 1425 suggestions for how to make Navi Mumbai a smart city were received. The municipal corporation also used social media (Facebook, Twitter, Instagram, Pinterest) to garner support for their proposals.

Capturing online citizens and enumerating the data on consultations, documented the transformation of a territorial 'population' into digital citizens. Enumeration promoted participation as a 'category of governance' (Chatterjee, 2004) which stood for 'democratic' urban transformation. Online systems were seen to replace earlier analogue systems of documentation, form filling, bureaucracy and 'red tape' (Gupta 2012). This online population was the material of a digital society – hashtagged digital subjects with a digital signature, the foundation of a 'smart citizenry'.

The 100 smart cities challenge animates forms of citizenship that claim to establish flexible and democratic systems of governance using otherwise inflexible systems of connection and communication between state and citizen. While data on cities and citizens is politically, socially, culturally and historically produced, they are nevertheless used to stand for a rationality of a networked vision of the city. This exercise of enumeration produced what Kitchin et al. (2015: 6) call 'the city as visualised facts – that is reshaping how managers and citizens come to know and govern cities.' In this, the objective was not as Granier and Kudo (2016) point out 'to involve citizens in city governance, but rather to make them participate in the co-production of public services, mainly energy production and distribution.'

Prescribing smart citizenship

The citizen consultations highlighted three key processes in the making of smart citizenship. First, that counting a digital population set the pedagogic terrain of smart citizenship which believed that citizens 'need to be educated by city leaders as to the benefits IT can bring' (Hollands, 2015). This was evident in the smart city guidelines which underlined key duties of 'smart people':

The Smart Cities Mission requires smart people who actively participate in governance and reforms. Citizen involvement is much more than a ceremonial participation in governance. Smart people involve themselves in the definition of the Smart City, decisions on deploying Smart Solutions, implementing reforms, doing more with less and oversight during implementing and designing post-project structures in order to make the Smart City developments sustainable.

(GoI, 2015: 18)

The introduction of 'smart people' in the policy, reflects a shift from the ordinary citizen to the tech-savvy, entrepreneurial and judicious citizen working for and on behalf of state enterprise, innovation and growth. 'Smart people' are seen to be central to the state's alignment with digital governance. It reflects what Vanolo (2016) notes as the desire of the state to 'speak about the citizens of smart cities, and speak in the name of them, but very little is known about citizens' real desires and aspirations.' In this role, smart people were collaborators and endorsers of the smart city, rather than critical and active citizens. Thus, instead of testing smart cities as the site of democratic participation, smart citizens were constructed as allies of state-private sector experiments in urban governance.

Next, the digitally networked citizen became the instrument for the realisation of smart cities. While citizen consultations were instrumental in making visible the presence of ordinary citizens in India's digital space, their self-transformation into 'smart citizens' was enacted through specific codes of performance. This included remaining vigilant and active about the city's health, sanitation and infrastructure. Several cities such as Ahmedabad, Pune and others had been running online complaints and grievance addressing systems through their e-governance websites since the 2000s, which were then integrated into the smart city governance model. Ordinary citizens had used their urban e-governance services to pay for bills, access services, and file complaints since the 2000s. Digital citizens were defined as those who took advantage of these systems and actively alerted the municipality (often just by uploading pictures on the e-governance sites) to the breakdown of sewage systems or malfunctioning of its transport or even crime. New smart citizenship performances were defined through their deep participation in online and offline spaces. The former included participation via social media, online quizzes, blog posts, logo designs and so on. The latter included running smart city marathons, encouraging children to take part in poster or essay competitions, filling in survey questionnaires and providing feedback to city authorities on what their smart city should include.

In Pune for example, Sakal Times, a media group ran a 'Simply Smart' programme that included a series of competitions (variously called – smart city, smart citizen, smart family) in collaboration with Delivering Change Foundation (owned by the CEO of Sakal Times) with the prize-winning ceremony presided over by Tel Aviv's Chief Knowledge Officer, Zohar Sharon during the Israeli government visit to India in 2015 (Pawar, 2015b). Sharon, in his presentation on the Israeli smart city stressed the need for a 'change in mentality' among ordinary citizens for the smart city to be successfully implemented in India. Albeit a private sector endeavour, the smart city event was endorsed and supported by a heavy state presence, becoming a space of international business exchange and deal-making between political, entrepreneurial and social elites. Such events which took place across several cities highlighted that there was no longer a distinct separation between the state and private sector in prescribing the parameters of citizenship.

The Sakal Times infographic of the smart citizen encourages Indian citizens to perform a newly found digital identity (see Figure 10.1). Framed through the representation of a young male professional, the smart citizen is defined by their actions as 'green, honest, polite, social, bright, healthy and virtuous'. Their thoughts are to 'be the change, stay on course, feel the need, meet the world, yearn to learn, follow the sun, and pass it on'. In this visual and discursive framing, smart citizens are simultaneously careerist and heroic – they are start-up and tech entrepreneurs, wired in, connected and defined by their online presence and canny. This framing offers parameters that the millions of young urban voters can identify with and make meaningful for themselves. It offers the possibility of an Indian smart city dream that can repeatedly produce successful entrepreneurs who have risen above the inequalities of caste, class and religion. It represented a civic-cyber personality who engages in crowdsourcing for knowledge and participates actively in the sharing economy. This smart citizen is a figure without history in India, but ironically also an embodiment of the history of its social and political inequalities. In doing so it becomes a caricature of itself.

Figure 10.2, from the MoUD-run MyGov.in website, merges the performance of the smart citizen with the 'role model' or an idealised Indian smart citizen – the Prime Minister himself. The incorporation of the quiz into the performative measurement of smart citizenship rewards the winners with an encounter with the original smart citizen himself, one who was able to overcome social and economic barriers through personal resolve. The wording on the advertisement – 'yes it's a tough quiz, but wouldn't you make this effort to meet the Prime Minister?' implies that this performance might not be easy, it might be ridden with obstacles, but the rewards of the effort far outweigh the costs. This is the final requirement of smart citizenship which requires drive, ambition, learning by doing and entrepreneurial skills to achieve high rewards in the future. Here digital citizenship is a reward earned through hard work – literally a 'gift of the state' (Jayal, 2013).

The final example (see Figure 10.3) is the billboard in Chandigarh Railway station which explicitly represents the young middle-class population running the marathon for the smart city. The marathon is branded and endorsed by several corporate companies and calls for the embodied participation of a digitally savvy population to come onto the physical spaces of the city in support of the smart city vision. Ironically, the homeless or working class have no visual or rhetorical space within this framing, only outside it. These are category 3 of Hansen and Stepputat's (2001: 63) framing – 'populations judged to be beyond the scope of improvement'.

'SIMPLY SMART' CITIZENS, WHAT ARE THEIR ACTIONS?

GREEN

Segregate their home waste, avoid market plastic and store personal trash until they find a dustbin

HONEST

Never deceive, cheat or steal from their own city and build their city a nationally acclaimed reputation

POLITE

Refrain from verbal abuse, serious threats or grievous hurt (physical or emotional) to fellow citizens

SOCIAL

Obey rules (e.g., hygiene), respect laws (e.g., traffic) and actively participate in community services

BRIGHT

Eliminate paper (e.g., digitizes bank and bills) and conserves energy (e.g., utilizes solar and wind) in life.

HEALTHY

Prioritise nutrition, vivacity, hygiene, fitness and health, thus promoting well being among their peers

VIRTUOUS

Oppose immoral conduct in public and religious places in society and they mobilise others against it.

'SIMPLY SMART' CITIZENS, WHAT ARE THEIR THOUGHTS?

#3 BE THE CHANGE

If your city is deficient, you are its **EFFICIENCY**. You start the fire and good times are up to what you do.

#4 YEARN TO LEARN

Keep collecting and experimenting with new ideas, concepts and experiences. Keep **LEARNING** lifelong.

#5 FOLLOW THE SUN

Find the right mentor that motivates you, the right idea that captivates you. We all need a **CATALYST**.

#2 STAY ON COURSE

Live life with a sense of **BALANCE** and conscience. May it be work-life, career interests, self interests, play

#6 MEET THE WORLD

Make the **ECOSPHERE** your oyster, your canvas, your concourse

#7 PASS IT ON

Turn the wheels of life through the course of time. All the good you gather is a gift for **DELIVERY** ahead.

#1 FEEL THE NEED

Be human enough to hold on to true **EMOTION**. A great city needs good humans who feel for it.

FIGURE 10.1 Smart citizen by Sakal Times
Source: Pawar (2015a)

FIGURE 10.2 Smart city competition run by MoUD

Hashtag citizenships

The making of 100 smart cities in India has initiated a radical transformation in the understanding of what constitutes citizenship in an urban age. So far, this has largely been a process of capturing those outside of data structures within systematic processes of performative citizenship and 'push-button democracy' (Hill, 2012). The performative demands of smart citizenship suggest that it entails more than just digital access to a territorial population; rather it involves a coordinated strategy in transforming how citizens react and respond to states' smart city initiatives. This raises a key question – can there be a smart citizen outside of the structures of power embodied by digital technologies?

I have argued here that the instant production of the huge number of digital citizens through the smart city consultations underlines digital signature as the endgame of democratic participation. This promotes a reductionist version of democratic governance where a range of top-down citizen consultations, citizen forums, and citizen engagement platforms begin to stand for citizenship per se. It assumes that the removal of the digital divide is the key to resolving challenges of

FIGURE 10.3 Chandigarh railway station, 2016
Source: Photo by Author

participation of those often left behind by urban development. It merges participation and deliberation as one and the same or uses them interchangeably to refer
to a set of complex politics around urban citizenship, planning and governance. In
the citizen consultations, smart citizenship becomes a benign space of hashtagging
responsibilities that can be achieved only through data connectivity.

New forms of digital citizenship in the smart city are framed through the ratio-
nalisation and normative categorisation of what cities should look like in the future
and what it means to be a 'smart citizen' in this projected future. It is sustained
through a technique of visually coded representations that seek to mime actually
existing citizenships through ICT. In doing so, it mobilises smart cities and citizenships through various degrees of distanciation from the veracities of actually existing
citizenships. The 100 smart cities challenge seeks to produce the 'smart city' and the
'smart citizen' as two sides of the postcolonial urban condition, and in doing so
establishes new modes of governmentality over its territories and citizens. While the
'quest for citizenship in India has been conducted in tandem with a quest for
democratic modernity' (Jayal 2013: 274), the smart city consultations in India shift
the traditional location of citizenship practices from civil and political society to
digital society. In doing so, it upholds contemporary neoliberal shifts in redrawing
the political limits of citizenship, in particular its boundaries of participation and
democratisation, and therefore the actors who embody and perform this. The smart
citizen is born from a burgeoning global market in smart cities – simultaneously

individual and entrepreneurial, supported by the aspirations of local political and social elites, and complicated by local translations of its meanings and consequences within society. The smart citizen is not simply a relation between the city and citizen, it emerges from larger shifts in relationship between state and citizen, between state and corporates and between citizen and citizen.

Note

1 What Priority would you assign to developing a unique identity of Smart Navi Mumbai; What Priority would you assign towards development of Infra, employment, business, trading, corporate & commercial growth; What Priority would you assign towards water supply management; What Priority would you assign towards sanitation & waste management; What Priority would you assign towards smart & safe transport; What Priority would you assign towards smart energy management; What Priority would you assign towards preservation of environment; What Priority would you assign towards Social infrastructure; What Priority would you assign towards development of housing facility; What Priority would you assign towards government services, e-governance, safety & security, IT connectivity.

Acknowledgements

This paper has been facilitated by funding from the Arts and Humanities Research Council (PI ref: AH/N007395/1). A different version of this was published in *Transactions of the Institute of British Geographers* and published with the title 'The "digital turn" in postcolonial urbanism: Smart citizenship in the making of India's 100 smart cities'. DOI: 10.1111/tran.12225. I am grateful to city stakeholders in India for the insights and debates that contributed to this paper and to the 'Creating Smart Cities' Workshop in Maynooth for the opportunity to write this chapter.

References

Antonio, A. and Tuffley, D. 2014. The gender digital divide in developing countries. *Future Internet* 6: 673–687.

Calzada, I. and Cobo, C. 2015. Unplugging: Deconstructing the Smart City. *Journal of Urban Technology* 22. 1: 22–43.

Cardullo, P. and Kitchin, R. 2018, online first. Being a 'citizen' in the smart city: Up and down the scaffold of smart citizen participation in Dublin, Ireland. *GeoJournal*. doi:10.1007/s10708–10018–9845–9848.

Chatterjee, P. 2004. *The Politics of the Governed: Reflections on Popular Politics in Most of the World*. New York: Columbia University Press.

Dasgupta, S. 2015. *BITS of Belonging: Information Technology, Water, and Neoliberal Governance in India*. Philadelphia: Temple University Press.

Datta, A. 2015. A 100 smart cities, a 100 utopias. *Dialogues in Human Geography* 5. 1: 49–53.

Fernandes, L. 2006. *India's New Middle Class*. Minneapolis: University of Minnesota Press.

GoI. 2015. *Smart City Mission Statement and Guidelines*. New Delhi, India: Ministry of Urban Development, Government of India.

Granier, B. and Kudo, H. 2016. How are citizens involved in smart cities? Analysing citizen participation in Japanese 'Smart Communities'. *Information Polity* 21(1): 61–76.

Gupta, A. 2012. *Red Tape: Bureaucracy, Structural Violence, and Poverty in India*. Durham, NC: Duke University Press.

Hansen, T.B. and Stepputat, F. eds. 2001. *States of Imagination: Ethnographic Explorations of the Postcolonial State*. Durham, NC: Duke University Press.

Hill, D. 2012. *Dark Matter and Trojan Horses: A Strategic Design Vocabulary*. Moscow: Strelka Press.

Hollands, R. 2015. Critical interventions into the corporate smart city. *Cambridge Journal of Regions, Economy and Society* 8: 61–77.

Holston, J. and Appadurai, A. 1999. Introduction: Cities and Citizenship. In Holston, J. (ed.), *Cities and Citizenship*. Durham, NC: Duke University Press.

IRIS-UN. 2013. *State of the Urban Youth, India 2012*. Mumbai: Iris Knowledge Foundation.

Jayal, N.G. 2013. *Citizenship and Its Discontents: An Indian History*. Cambridge, MA: Harvard University Press.

Jones, C., Ramanau, R., Cross, S. and Healing, G. 2010. Net generation or digital natives: Is there a distinct new generation entering university? *Computers & Education* 54(3): 722–732.

Kitchin, R. 2015. Making sense of smart cities: addressing present shortcomings. *Cambridge Journal of Regions, Economy and Society* 8: 131–136.

Kitchin, R., Lauriault, T.P. and McArdle, G. 2015. Knowing and governing cities through urban indicators, city benchmarking and real-time dashboards. *Regional Studies, Regional Science* 2. 1: 6–28.

Lerman, J. 2013. Big data and its exclusions. *Stanford Law Review* 66: 55–63.

MoUD. 2014. Draft Concept Note on Smart City Scheme. Updated September 2014. Delhi: Ministry of Urban Development.

Naidu, V. 2016. Smart City Challenge has kick-started a revolution in urban landscape. *Economic Times*, 2 February. http://blogs.economictimes.indiatimes.com/et-commentary/smart-ci ty-challenge-has-kick-started-a-revolution-in-urban-landscape/ (accessed 28 February 2018).

Oblinger, D.G. and Oblinger, J.L. 2005. *Educating the Net Generation*. Boulder, CO: Educause.

Pawar, A. 2015a. Citizens resolve to make Pune a Smart City. Sakal Media Group. 9 March. http://www.sakalmediagroup.com/citizens-resolve-to-make-pune-a-smart-city/ (accessed 28 February 2018).

Pawar, A. 2015b. Smart Governance, Smart City. Sakal Media Group. 9 April. http://www. sakalmediagroup.com/smart-governance-smart-city/ (accessed 28 February 2018).

Prensky, M. 2001. Digital natives, digital immigrants Part 1. *On the Horizon* 9(5): 1–6.

Rowlands, I., Nicholas, D., Williams, P., Huntington, P., Fieldhouse, M., Gunter, B., Withey, R., Jamali, H., Dobrowolski, T. and Tenopir, C. 2008. The Google generation: the information behaviour of the researcher of the future. *Aslib Proceedings* 60(4): 290–310.

Söderström, O., Paasche, T. and Klauser, F. 2014. Smart cities as corporate storytelling. *City* 18. 3: 307–320.

Tapscott, D. 2009. *Grown Up Digital: How the Net Generation is Changing Your World*. New York: McGraw-Hill.

Vanolo, A. 2016. 'Is there anybody out there?' The place and role of citizens in tomorrow's smart cities. *Futures* 82: 26–36.

11

FROM SMART CITIES TO SMART CITIZENS?

Searching for the 'actually existing smart citizen' in Atlanta, Georgia

Taylor Shelton and Thomas Lodato

The emergence of the smart citizen

At this juncture, pointing out the disconnect between the promise of the 'smart city' and its actual implementation is rather uncontroversial. Although they masquerade as a public good, smart city efforts are largely indistinguishable from earlier iterations of neoliberal urbanism (Hollands 2008, 2015; Greenfield 2013; Söderström et al. 2014; Viitanen and Kingston 2014). So rather than providing a cure-all to struggling cities, the smart city instead reinscribes already substantial urban social and spatial inequalities by privileging free market, technology-centric, and expert-driven forms of urban planning and governance, forcing cities to compete for resources in new ways (Halpern et al. 2013; Kitchin 2014; Datta 2015; McNeill 2015; Wiig 2015, 2016; Shelton and Clark 2016).

In response to the mounting criticism along these lines, a number of individuals and entities have attempted to pivot this ongoing discussion of 'smartness' from one of 'smart cities' to that of 'smart citizens', a shift crystallized in Dan Hill's (2013) blogpost-qua-manifesto entitled "On the smart city; Or, a 'manifesto' for smart citizens instead". Though certainly not alone in pushing for this discursive shift, Hill's commentary is particularly important in its stark dichotomy between the vision of the smart city on the one hand, and that of the smart citizen on the other; a recognition that the former is, in effect, too far gone to save, and that only by shifting both our discourse and interventions to be more citizen-centric can we actually achieve any meaningful change. But increasingly, the 'smart citizen' discourse isn't mobilized solely in opposition to more conventional smart city imaginaries. Indeed, as Kitchin (2015, 133) has noted, even "smart city vendors such as IBM and Cisco have started to alter the discursive emphasis of some of their initiatives from being top-down managerially focused to stressing inclusivity and empowerment".

But, as with much of the broader literature on smart cities, discussions around 'smart citizens' have thus far been fairly generic and speculative, often more normative than analytical, failing to deal with the more concrete ways that citizens are (or are not) actually integrated into the making of the smart city (cf. Gabrys 2014, Taylor et al. 2016 and Vanolo 2016, for exceptions to this rule). So, extending Shelton, Zook, and Wiig (2015)'s call for more attention to the variety of ways that the smart city ideal is realized in particular historically and geographically specific ways, this chapter sets out to understand the 'actually existing smart citizen'. Through an examination of ongoing smart cities efforts in Atlanta, Georgia, we argue that while the 'smart citizen' is most often seen as a kind of foil for those more stereotypically top-down, neoliberal, and repressive visions of the smart city, the 'actually existing smart citizen' plays a much messier and more ambivalent role in practice. In particular, we identify two key moments for, or instantiations of, the 'actually existing smart citizen': (1) the way the more general figure of 'the citizen' is deployed by key actors and institutions in the context of smart city policy-making, and (2) the ways that actual citizens are, or are not, participating in such decision- and policy-making processes around smart city strategies.

Searching for the 'actually existing smart citizen'

In order to trace the two primary means by which we are able to identify the 'actually existing smart citizen', we turn to the case of Atlanta, Georgia and our experiences observing and, at times, participating in the development and discussion of smart city initiatives there. Atlanta represents, in many ways, precisely the kind of 'actually existing smart city' that Shelton, Zook, and Wiig (2015) attempt to call attention to. Long known as the capital of the New South and "the city too busy to hate" – an ostensible bastion of relative progressivism in a conservative region – Atlanta remains one of the country's most segregated and unequal cities, shaped by the persistent legacies of racism and 'white flight' that characterized the city's political struggles in the mid-20th century (Kruse 2005; Berman 2015; Pooley 2015). Even as the city was innovative in its methods of encouraging citizen participation – especially from its majority black populace – through the development of a system of 'neighborhood planning units' (or NPUs) in the mid-1970s, the NPU system has slowly been diluted such that the average citizen remains largely on the outside of being able to meaningfully influence planning or political decisions within the city (Isaf 2015). This pattern of development points towards the fact that Atlanta and its broader metropolitan area have a long way to go to become 'smart', though the city isn't necessarily unique in this respect.

At the same time, however, under Mayor Kasim Reed, the city has joined the growing trend of cities attempting to *position* themselves as 'smart', most often as a means of promoting economic development through inter-urban competition (cf. Wiig 2016). In recent years, Atlanta has participated in a variety of smart city networks and technical assistance programs, from being host to one of the initial Innovation Delivery Teams from Bloomberg Philanthropies in 2011, to the IBM

Smarter Cities Challenge in 2012, the Code for America fellowship program and City Energy Project beginning in 2014, as well as the White House's MetroLab Network in 2015 and, most recently, the Rockefeller Foundation's 100 Resilient Cities program in 2016. Though the city was unsuccessful in its bid for $50 million as part of the US Department of Transportation's Smart Cities Challenge competition in 2016, Atlanta *is* one of just three cities (along with Chicago and Dallas) to be tapped as partners in AT&T's nascent Smart Cities Framework partnership (AT&T 2016). This wide-ranging participation in these various kinds of smart cities initiatives puts Atlanta among the nation's leaders in this kind of activity, further underscoring its centrality within these discussions nationwide.

Together, these initiatives provide the setting in which our observations have taken place. In particular, our empirical work draws on attendance and participation at workshops and roundtables about smart cities, some with a deliberate emphasis on developing policy ideas that can be implemented by the city government, others with a more abstract goal of increasing awareness about these initiatives among different groups spread throughout the city.[1] This section uses these observations as a way of addressing the continued gap in empirical evidence with regards to how citizens are integrated into smart city planning and implementation exercises, both discursively and materially.

The general citizen

In February 2016, the City of Atlanta convened a two-day workshop on the campus of the Georgia Institute of Technology meant to envision the future of Atlanta's smart city efforts. The workshop was organized by the City of Atlanta's Innovation Delivery Team (or i-team), "a special projects team that drives progress on the Mayor's top-priority challenges" that "was initially formed through a grant from Bloomberg Philanthropies" (City of Atlanta n.d.). Though organized by the Atlanta i-team, the workshop was largely run by a team of three consultants from Barcelona – widely recognized as one of the world's 'smartest cities' – who were there to impart their place-based expertise to Atlanta.

The workshop opened with three instances that demonstrate the variety of different ways that citizens and ideas of citizenship were deployed discursively at the workshop. During his welcome message, the first speaker from the Atlanta i-team explained that "we should all come to this as Atlantans". For municipal employees in different departments, the sentiment stressed how "our silos" – the variety of official, disciplinary, and even geographic affiliations of the participants – might impede the discussion. For those visiting from outside the city, the comment invoked a type of temporary citizenship that made the ostensibly place-based concerns of the City of Atlanta their concerns as well. The first speaker concluded by thanking the participants "for being here to shape our future".

During an overview of the schedule and goals of the workshop, the second speaker explained that "everything we're doing is for our citizens". Here the citizen was invoked under the auspices of stewardship: those in the room were endowed with the responsibility of overseeing the well-being of Atlanta's citizens above all else. Motivated by such a responsibility to the citizens of Atlanta, the second speaker continued that the various challenges facing the city should be understood as "opportunities" rather than problems. In the third and final instance, one of the consultants from Barcelona remarked that "ultimately this is about what's best for the citizens of Atlanta". Here, the figure of the citizen comes to the fore through a type of civic paternalism, where "what's best" for Atlantans is decided on their behalf by those in the room, even if these individuals were not from the city or were unfamiliar with the various problems and struggles taking place within the city. All of that is to say that the figure of the citizen, if not the 'smart citizen' in particular, loomed large in the way workshop organizers, facilitators and participants framed their ideas and motivations.

And yet, despite all the attention to the citizen, at times during the workshop, it was not clear who the citizens being discussed actually were. On the second day of the workshop, participants were divided into small groups to create proposals for new smart city policies and services. To give structure to the proposals, participants used one-page worksheets with various boxes such as "Idea Name" (title of the proposal), "Associated Challenge" (what challenge this proposal responded to), and "Partners and Roles Involved" (what institutional partnerships would be necessary for the idea's implementation). One box was titled "Benefits for city/citizens". As an example, one of the consultants from Barcelona showed a finished worksheet for a mobile application for tourists. This box contained two benefits: (1) "Inform about fancy places to visit and how to get there" and (2) "Increase economic activity around the city by attracting more tourists". It is worth noting that given the equivalence of city and citizens, this example focuses on tourists – that is, non-citizens or non-residents – and their economic impact on the city, without explicating how citizens might benefit directly from the application or indirectly from the presence of well-informed tourists.

Once the activity was in full-swing, one of us worked on a small team discussing a proposal for citywide data portal. When asking the group a seemingly simple question – "what do we mean by data here?" – the immediate response from one group member was "all of the data", while another responded simply with "big data". The subsequent exchange revealed that it was not that people in the group were *unable* to be specific – eventually deciding that the data portal could focus on public data otherwise accessible through FOIA requests or third-party data providers – but instead that group members were *unwilling* to preclude any particular type of data in the event that *someone* might find it useful and meaningful. As a result, the box on the worksheet titled "Target to whom it is addressed" was filled out with just the word "citizens". But the group discussion surrounding this project was more illustrative. One city employee was adamant about monetizing the data portal, an imperative he attributed to the mayor. Giving the example of businesses requesting monthly building permit reports, as well as citizens requesting information on a one-off basis, the use of "citizens" as the target served as a placeholder by demonstrating the city's accountability to the public. While ostensibly laudable, this left the true purpose of the proposal – generating monthly revenue from real estate developers, contractors or other business people – hidden under a veneer of citizen participation.

These two proposed interventions highlight an important lacuna within the workshop, and the city's smart city policymaking more generally. That is, the question of *which citizens in particular* went both unasked and unanswered. The titling of one box as "Benefits for city/citizens" conflates the geographic context of the city with the fractured interests of the municipal government and the variety of differently-positioned citizens within its borders. When applied to the sample proposal of a tourist-oriented smartphone application, this conflation insinuates a kind of trickle-down effect, where what is good for the city (as a center of economic activity) is automatically good for the city's citizens. Even were this causal relationship assumed to be true, the reality is that all citizens don't benefit equally from the tourist economy, and even those directly engaged in this economic sector are subject to considerable power differentials. A similar logic is at play in the example of the proposed data portal. In the group's unwillingness to be specific due to a fear of excluding someone, they failed to consider the impact that already-existing forms of social exclusion might have on different citizens' abilities to access and use such an application. They failed to consider that not all citizens might be equally predisposed to, or even technically capable of, using a web portal to access public records, or how traditional, analog FOIA requests might be handled relative to the maintenance of the portal. Indeed, the relationship between potential users of such a data portal and the broadest conception of 'citizens' in the city of Atlanta went unexplored. Even more, although the team implicitly saw businesses as the prototypical users of the data portal, they never addressed the potential that a data portal focused on generating revenue from local businesses might exclude many citizens from making use of it. So even in trying not to exclude anyone a priori, the proposal ultimately embedded problematic assumptions about equity, access, and resource allocation that are characteristic of most conversations about smart cities and smart citizens.

Together, these examples illustrate the prominence of what we call *the general citizen* within discussions of smart cities. At best, the general citizen is vague and poorly defined, lacking the kind of specificity that would demonstrate a *meaningful* attention to issues of inequality and difference that are, or at least ought to be, at the core of discussions around urban governance. At worst, we observed the general citizen being used as a vessel for stereotypes and groundless assumptions that reinscribe existing power relations and hierarchies under the auspices of paying attention to the people who make up a city. Rather than being a foil to more conventional, top-down smart city ideas, the figure of the general citizen actually serves as a means by which the status quo can largely be perpetuated, allowing decision-makers to feel as though they have adequately attended to the concerns of citizens simply because they've not deliberately or explicitly excluded anyone. That is, the discursive centrality of 'the citizen' to some otherwise-conventional smart city efforts provides a kind of justification or insulation from criticism while making little substantive difference in the design or implementation of the policy itself. Indeed, the rhetorical deployment of the general citizen is powerful precisely insofar as it is accompanied by the *absence* of actual citizens who might call into question the kinds of unproblematized assumptions and generally paternalistic approach discussed above.

The absent citizen

While the ways that on-the-ground actors are deploying the discourse of the smart citizen, even in a generic way, when justifying their work are undoubtedly an important aspect of the story, it is important to pair the figure of the general citizen with that of *the absent citizen*. For all of the discussion of citizens within some circles, the citizen continues to remain marginal to the actually existing smart city. Even though this absence is clearly evident at the discursive level, it takes on an even greater significance when paired with the reality of how actual citizens are largely absent from important discussions and decision-making efforts, which are left to be shaped by experts of one kind or another.

At a roundtable lunch discussion hosted by a local entrepreneurial organization in the summer of 2016, representatives from the municipal government, private sector and civil society organizations were present to discuss how they're engaging with the idea of smart cities and the future of government. Two moments from this event highlight the continued absence of citizens from some smart city discourses, even as they are being prominently invoked elsewhere. First, a representative from the Code for Atlanta group, ostensibly representing the most citizen-centric perspective of any of the panelists, was tasked with opening the roundtable by providing an overview of the civic hacking movement. In listing the potential beneficiaries of or constituencies for Code for Atlanta's work, government employees, researchers, journalists, entrepreneurs and innovators were included. Of course, notably absent from this list are *citizens*.

Later on at this same meeting, the entrepreneur on the panel, himself the head of a smart transportation company, posed a question to himself: "what's the core of a smart city?" He proceeded to mention the examples of an ambulance trying to get where it's going, or bureaucrats in city hall trying to figure out how to time the traffic lights. While one could reasonably interpret these examples as important – if somewhat mundane – things that could help to make everyday routines easier for people in the city, they are also indicative of the extent to which citizens are not actually mentioned as being a substantive element of the smart city. That is, the things mentioned as being at the core of the smart city highlight the extent to which the smart city is and remains, precisely as Dan Hill mentions in his original invocation of the smart citizen, primarily about the efficiency of urban infrastructural systems, not the people living in these cities. By focusing on the optimization of the surface transportation network, a largely technical exercise aided by new kinds of data-collection and automated analysis, this vision pushes to the side questions of who actually uses this infrastructure (e.g., primarily car owners) and how the current state of this system has been shaped by intensely political decisions made in the past (e.g., to privilege automobile transportation over other ways of moving around the city), naturalizing these historical and contemporary exclusions.

The exclusion of citizens from the proverbial table is perpetuated not only through discourse, but also through material practices involved in the construction of the actually existing smart city. While this chapter has thus far documented instances where citizens were both discursively centered and absent, arguably the most notable part of our experience in observing smart city events has been the distinct absence of people participating in these workshops, meetings, and discussions in their capacity *as citizens*, rather than through some other institutional or organizational capacity. This dynamic was particularly notable at the smart cities visioning workshop discussed previously. While nearly all of the attendees were indeed citizens (or, at the very least, residents) of Atlanta, all came to the workshop by special invitation, due to the expertise and organizational affiliation they brought to the table. They were representatives from some, though not all, municipal departments, such as the Atlanta Police Department and the city's Office of Sustainability, the city's two public universities and various business and non-governmental organizations. That is, though citizens were indeed involved, they were invited *as experts*. Unsurprisingly, drawing from such a group of citizens-qua-experts does not yield a representative sample of the city's population, either demographically or spatially, and thus works to further engrain particular kinds of bias into the planning and policymaking process from the start.

Even more, none of the participants in this workshop, nor in the other workshops and meetings we observed, were even elected representatives, but were instead municipal bureaucrats or informal representatives of certain organizations (e.g. the Code for Atlanta representative discussed above). One workshop participant told us at the end of the first day that they had hoped for more participation among different kinds of people, as "the cutting edge" of smart cities is all about "social inclusion". But this individual also said that as much as they hoped students or people of color, among others, would be present for such a meeting, they also hoped for more participation from the private sector. So while it is perhaps a positive sign that some participants were able to recognize some of the constituencies missing from the room, such a response also highlights the challenges to making everyday citizens the center of any smart city effort.

A similar absence was noted in the Startup Atlanta event. In its most basic set-up, the panel was composed of four men, all of whom had a particular expertise and organizational affiliation that led to their inclusion. During the Q&A session at the end of the panel, a woman of color in the audience remarked that "these types of events always seem to draw the same group of people". While it is somewhat ambiguous what exactly she meant by 'same', the implication is that conversations about these topics tend to be dominated by white men, whether they be invited panelists or simply members of the audience, who are already well-connected in the city and its technology sector. Her comment alludes to a categorical and systemic homogeneity, the recognition and vocalization of which is particularly stark in contrast to the comments made by panelists at this event, which demonstrated a lack of facility in discussing issues of citizenship, inequality and difference within the context of the smart city.

Indeed, just as important as the line of questioning about how this lack of representativeness might be rectified were the responses from the panelists. The representative from the City of Atlanta's i-team noted that in order to include these more marginalized groups, the city was partnering with organizations in Atlanta's historic Westside, a conglomeration of largely poor and African-American neighborhoods just to the west of downtown. Specifically, he mentioned the Westside Future Fund, a local business elite-led organization that's attempting to ameliorate some of the negative impacts associated with the construction of the new Mercedes Benz Stadium and associated redevelopment activities at the Westside's periphery, though certainly not the group that one would call the most representative of long-term residents who have historically been marginalized within the city's planning process. On the other hand, the aforementioned smart transportation executive turned the question about a lack of citizen participation into a question of a lack of venture capital funding. His assumption was, in effect, that the city's technology community could only be inclusive when there was more money to go around.

But citizens are not *entirely* absent from this 'actually existing smart city'. Initiatives like the Westside Communities Alliance's Data Dashboard[2] show that citizens and community organizations *are* actively enmeshing themselves in some of the overarching discourses and practices of smart cities and data-driven governance. With the goal of "allow[ing the] community to use data vibrantly, well and in its own interest", the Data Dashboard is explicitly positioned as tool for the Westside community to use in its fight against gentrification and encroachment by the Mercedes Benz Stadium project (O'Connell 2017). By integrating not just quantitative data, but also qualitative and archival data, and also centering this data at the geographic scale of Atlanta's neighborhood planning units in order to be more legible to residents and relevant to policy discussions, the Data Dashboard represents a means by which citizens can tell their own stories, demonstrating the interconnectedness of different issues that they confront on an everyday basis, such as the relationship between housing affordability, jobs and transit accessibility.

But even as Westside residents, precisely the kind of citizens that tend to be absent from official city visioning workshops or tech community roundtables, are constructing their alternative vision of what the (smart) city might look like, they also remain largely separate from the broader discourse of the smart city, and the institutions that are responsible for creating it. As one WCA staffer noted at the public launch of the Data Dashboard at Georgia Tech in the winter of 2016, the Data Dashboard project has largely been ignored by the city and by major funders who might be able to provide resources that would help to extend its technical capabilities and allow for more outreach activity around its use. Implicit in this comment was its direction at some of the very same business-led and elite institutions mentioned above by city officials as the lone examples of how the city is attempting to engage with marginalized populations. So while there is on the one hand a clear presence of something approximating 'actually existing smart citizens' – people using and engaging with data in order to make alternative representations of, and claims on, their neighborhoods and the city as a whole – these citizens and their efforts remain largely ignored and outside of the formal institutions responsible for creating the smart city. This is perhaps due in part to their oppositional nature, or the fact that at the same time as they adopt some of the rhetoric and practices of 'smartness', they also politicize these discourses, disrupting one of the fundamental tenets of the smart city as it is commonly operationalized.

Conclusion

Ultimately, all of this points towards the idea that, in practice, the 'actually existing smart citizen' might not *really* exist at all. At the very least, the emerging alternative discourse around smart citizenship is clearly not matched by the realities of how citizens are discussed and enrolled in the process of making the smart city in Atlanta. Instead, we can see a much more ambivalent relationship between the smart city and its citizens than is often recognized. Even where 'smart citizens' actually *do* exist, they don't seem to be recognized as such, and remain largely on the periphery of these structures of power and decision-making processes, revealing the limits to the smart city and its ability to reckon with disparate voices and political claims. As such, a necessary, but likely insufficient, first step to building a smart city that is truly of, by, and for citizens would be to pay more than lip-service to their participation. Municipal governments and any other institutions involved in such processes should actively center diverse, underrepresented and otherwise marginalized voices in the visioning and planning of the smart city, ensuring that plans are not simply imposed top-down onto citizens.

That being said, we would argue that focusing only on the presence or absence of citizens in these settings belies the more general problem of the 'smart citizen' discourse. While failing to include the voices of 'average' citizens in decision-making processes, or ignoring those who attempt to participate, is an important failing for these initiatives, it is important to note that inclusion in such processes will not necessary yield a better, or even different, result. The more general problems lies in the fact that like the smart city discourse in general, the smart citizen discourse assumes that all problems are simply problems of execution or implementation: we simply need 'the right technology' and 'the right people' to make things work. If something is not working, we simply need to change the technology and/or the people.

The problem is instead more structural, as the smart citizen discourse fails to consider, and ultimately obscures, that increasing inclusion for some does not preclude continued exclusion for others. This should come as no surprise, for the various iterations of the 'actually existing smart city' emerge out of, or exist within, cities where these kinds of exclusions have been the rule, rather than the exception, for years and years. As Mark Shepherd and Antonina Simeti have argued, "[i]n the end, both the Smart City and the Smart Citizen result in the same rhetorical paralysis" (Shepherd and Simeti 2014, 17), as their seeming opposition to one another belies both their common grounding in market- and technology-centric ways of approaching contemporary urban problems, as well as their divorce from the actual practices of citizenship and city-making. To achieve truly just, equitable and democratic cities, these underlying dynamics must be challenged and overturned, whether through 'smart' technologies or other means.

Notes

1 The authors' participation in these events was, at least in the case of the city's visioning workshop, a direct result of our affiliation with Georgia Tech's Center for Urban Innovation, which played a consultative or supporting role in these visioning processes. As an institution, Georgia Tech occupies a contradictory place in the 'actually existing smart city' of Atlanta; sometimes as a direct actor, as in the development of Tech Square, sometimes as a supporter of larger governmental initiatives as with the redevelopment of the Techwood Homes site immediately south of campus or the smart cities visioning workshop discussed in this chapter, and sometimes as something of an oppositional force, as with the work of the Westside Communities Alliance or various faculty and staff who lend their efforts to community organizations who oppose these more top-down initiatives. While our presence at the events described herein was primarily for the purposes of research, our expertise allowed us access to these spaces, and at times allowed us to raise our own questions about the city's priorities or approaches to certain issues.
2 http://wcadatadashboard.iac.gatech.edu/Home/

Acknowledgements

Portions of this chapter are adapted from Shelton, Taylor and Thomas Lodato, "Actually existing smart citizens: expertise and (non)participation in the making of the smart city", Forthcoming in *City*.

References

AT&T. 2016. "AT&T Launches Smart Cities Framework with New Strategic Alliances, Spotlight Cities, and Integrated Vertical Solutions". Press Release, January 5. http://about.att.com/story/launches_smart_cities_framework.html

Berman, Mark. 2015. "Atlanta is the Country's Most Unequal City Again." *The Washington Post*, March 17. https://www.washingtonpost.com/news/post-nation/wp/2015/03/17/altanta-is-the-countrys-most-unequal-city-again/

City of Atlanta. "Office of Innovation Delivery and Performance." Accessed 24 April 2018. http://www.atlantaga.gov/index.aspx?page=133

Datta, Ayona. 2015. "New Urban Utopias of Postcolonial India: 'Entrepreneurial Urbanization' in Dholera Smart City, Gujarat." *Dialogues in Human Geography* 5(1): 3–22.

Gabrys, Jennifer. 2014. "Programming Environments: Environmentality and Citizen Sensing in the Smart City." *Environment and Planning D: Society and Space* 32(1): 30–48.

Greenfield, Adam. 2013. *Against the Smart City*. New York: Do Projects.

Halpern, Orit, Jesse LeCavalier, Nerea Calvillo and Wolfgang Pietsch. 2013. "Test-Bed Urbanism." *Public Culture* 25(2): 272–306.

Hill, Dan. 2013. "On the Smart City; Or, a 'Manifesto' for Smart Citizens Instead." *Cityofsound*, February 1. http://www.cityofsound.com/blog/2013/02/on-the-smart-city-a-call-for-smart-citizens-instead.html

Hollands, Robert G. 2008. "Will the Real Smart City Please Stand up? Intelligent, Progressive or Entrepreneurial?" *City* 12(3): 303–320.

Hollands, Robert G. 2015. "Critical Interventions into the Corporate Smart City." *Cambridge Journal of Regions, Economy and Society* 8(1): 61–77.

Isaf, Robert. 2015. "Wither the NPU?". *Creative Loafing Atlanta*, March 26. https://creativeloafing.com/content-232252-Neighborhoods—Wither-the-NPU?

Kitchin, Rob. 2014. "The Real-Time City? Big Data and Smart Urbanism." *GeoJournal* 79(1): 1–14.

Kitchin, Rob. 2015. "Making Sense of Smart Cities: Addressing Present Shortcomings." *Cambridge Journal of Regions, Economy and Society* 8(1): 131–136.

Kruse, Kevin M. 2005. *White Flight: Atlanta and the Making of Modern Conservatism.* Princeton, NJ: Princeton University Press.

McNeill, Donald. 2015. "Global Firms and Smart Technologies: IBM and the Reduction of Cities." *Transactions of the Institute of British Geographers* 40(4): 562–574.

O'Connell, Katie. 2017. "The Difference Data Makes: Combatting Inequality with the Westside Communities Alliance Data Dashboard". *Atlanta Studies*, March 30. https://scholarblogs.emory.edu/atlantastudies/2017/03/30/the-difference-data-makes-combatting-inequality-with-the-westside-communities-alliance-data-dashboard/

Pooley, Karen. 2015. "Segregation's New Geography: The Atlanta Metro Region, Race, and the Declining Prospects for Upward Mobility." *Southern Spaces*, April 15. https://southernspaces.org/2015/segregations-new-geography-atlanta-metro-region-race-and-declining-prospects-upward-mobility

Shelton, Taylor, and Jennifer Clark. 2016. "Technocratic Values and Uneven Development in the 'Smart City.'" *Metropolitics*, May 10. http://www.metropolitiques.eu/Technocratic-Values-and-Uneven.html

Shelton, Taylor, Matthew Zook and Alan Wiig. 2015. "The 'Actually Existing Smart City.'" *Cambridge Journal of Regions, Economy and Society* 8(1): 13–25.

Shepherd, Mark and Antonina Simeti. 2014. "What's so Smart about the Smart Citizen?". In *Smart Citizens*, edited by Drew Hemment and Anthony Townsend, 13–18. Manchester: FutureEverything.

Söderström, Ola, Till Paasche and Francisco Klauser. 2014. "Smart Cities as Corporate Storytelling." *City* 18(3): 307–320.

Taylor, Linnet, Christine Richter, Shazade Jameson and Carmen Perez de Pulgar. 2016. "Customers, Users or Citizens? Inclusion, Spatial Data and Governance in the Smart City." Maps4Society Final Project Report. University of Amsterdam. http://papers.ssrn.com/sol3/papers.cfm?abstract_id=2792565

Vanolo, Alberto. 2016. "Is There Anybody out There? The Place and Role of Citizens in Tomorrow's Smart Cities." *Futures* 82: 26–36.

Viitanen, Jenni, and Richard Kingston. 2014. "Smart Cities and Green Growth: Outsourcing Democratic and Environmental Resilience to the Global Technology Sector." *Environment and Planning A* 46(4): 803–819.

Wiig, Alan. 2015. "IBM's Smart City as Techno-Utopian Policy Mobility." *City* 19(2–3): 258–273.

Wiig, Alan. 2016. "The Empty Rhetoric of the Smart City: From Digital Inclusion to Economic Promotion in Philadelphia." *Urban Geography* 37(4): 535–553.

12

PROMISES, PRACTICES AND PROBLEMS OF COLLABORATIVE INFRASTRUCTURING

The case of Dublin City Council (DCC) Beta and Code for Ireland

Sung-Yueh Perng

Introduction

Smart cities so far have largely been imagined and implemented by public-private partnerships between municipalities and multinational corporations. Technological innovations featured in smart city initiatives often promote improved urban life and new prospects of community engagement. However, being citizens in smart cities can be tokenistic, merely providing data and ideas through citizen engagement technologies or acting as an object of urban experimentation (Evans, 2016; Cardullo and Kitchin, 2018).

This chapter raises questions concerning if we can imagine and experiment a different making of smart cities – one that is more collaborative, involving diverse actors, viewpoints and practices. If so, what are the benefits, drawbacks and unintended consequences of such city making practices? Answering these questions, the chapter explores the practices and problems emerging from experimenting an alternative form of city making: collaborative infrastructuring. It discusses several key issues in attempting a new city making mechanism, including experiments, collaboration and infrastructuring. The chapter then examines a case study of a collaboration between an experimental government initiative, Dublin City Council (DCC) Beta, and a civic hacking organisation based in Dublin, Code for Ireland, to demonstrate how collaborative infrastructuring might be implemented, how diverse viewpoints and practices can be aligned, and what issues might emerge from such experiments. In doing so, the chapter aims to demonstrate the promising futures and future problems of collaborative infrastructuring as an alternative way of making smart cities.

Experimentation, civic hacking and collaborative infrastructuring

The chapter draws on, but differentiates, two approaches to experiments in cities. Urban experimentation is concerned with the political economy of knowledge production as selective parts of a city are transformed into 'living labs' (Bulkeley and Castán Broto, 2013; Evans and Karvonen, 2014). Public experimentation focuses on public participation in civic or bottom-up initiatives as practices for speculating and enacting futures (Büscher et al., 2011; Gabrys, 2016).

Studies on urban experiments observe that living laboratories are designed with expert knowledge in the research and private sectors and aim to manage contingency and uncertainty through adaptive learning (learning-by-doing) for rendering cities governable (Evans and Karvonen, 2014). The design of urban experiments thus causes concerns regarding how they can preferentially reward people, places and (public and private) partnerships in support of growth-first urban development (Bulkeley and Castán Broto, 2013; Evans, 2016). While sharing similar concerns, research on public experiments focuses on the experiments' exploratory, indeterminate and speculative aspects of creating opportunities to imagine and experience socially desirable futures. Büscher et al. (2011: 134) conceive 'public experimentality' as opportunities where the public can take active part in articulating and materialising desirable socio-technical futures in ways that are 'not just through academic sociological critique or top-down design, but through stimulating awareness, ongoing public reflection and social innovation'. For Gabrys, experimentality is considered as an ontogenetic process that is not merely concerned with 'detecting information "out there" but about "tuning" the subjects and conditions of experience to new registers of becoming' (Gabrys, 2016: 32). Environmental sensing practices, the focus of her research, are thus about indeterminacy, in the sense of exploring and considering if speculative encounters are generated to 'offer up opportunities for creative and practical as much as analytical engagements' for future environmental and political actions (Gabrys, 2016: 272).

Civic hacking, among other bottom-up initiatives in smart city contexts (Gabrys, 2016: Ch. 7), can be considered a public experiment that challenges established ways of governing a city. Civic hacking incorporates the sensitivity and culture towards transparency and openness from early free and open source software (F/OSS) (Coleman, 2013; Kelty, 2008), and also further develops a 'utopian realist' approach to politics by 'bringing the hidden workings of abstract systems to light and improve their functioning' (Schrock, 2016). Civic hacking seeks to go beyond 'proto-publics' that are contingently and temporarily formed by, and highly dependent on, individual civic hackathons (Lodato and DiSalvo, 2016) by undertaking a longer-term approach and establishing partnerships with sympathetic staff or units within the government to form 'recursive publics' (Kelty, 2008).

Local governments might value civic hacking or civic hackathons as an opportunity for public engagement (Robinson and Johnson, 2016). However, its long-term approach to collaboration with the government does not necessarily translate into change in organisational structure or culture within the government for taking collective responsibility with the public (Perng and Kitchin, 2018). Further concerns are raised regarding the social, governmental and political economic consequences of these initiatives. The 'value' of releasing government data is often considered in terms of commercial re-use and thus the governmental generation, archival and release of data become mechanisms of deregulation and neoliberalisation of urban governance (Bates, 2012). The long-term effects, extents of change and the decline of government responsibility are also concerns for the incorporation of civic hacking as an added model for local governments to address community problems (Johnson and Robinson, 2014).

These issues lead to questions concerning the possibility of a more collaborative relationship between citizens and governments in shaping future cities and if 'public experimentality' can be invoked to explore such a possibility. Drawing on recent work in participatory design (Karasti, 2014; Le Dantec and DiSalvo, 2013), I propose to analyse the opening up of city making processes through the lens of 'collaborative infrastructuring'.

There are several key aspects to collaborative infrastructuring. It comprises continual and situated, as well as dynamic and contested, processes. Conducting experiments of infrastructure making requires time to establish collaborative relationships, develop trust, and deploy prototypes. Collaborative infrastructuring therefore comprises continual attempts and situated socio-technical arrangements for enabling trials and prototypes.

Furthermore, collaborative practices inevitably bring in incompatible voices, visions and actions, leading to contested socio-technical relationships and unexpected consequences. The agonistic relationships do not necessarily rest upon the opposition between 'the government' and 'the people'. Rather, tension can arise from competing alliances mobilising individuals, initiatives and governmental agencies to set up social, technological and institutional arrangements in support of their own views and practices (Barry, 2013). Accordingly, examinations on collaborative infrastructuring have to remain sensitive to 'socio-material assembly that deals with "matters of concern" … and the alignment of controversies, ready for unexpected use, opening up new ways of thinking and behaving' (Björgvinsson et al., 2010: 41–3).

The spatial and temporal scaling of trials can be another source of concern for collaborative infrastructuring. In developing prototypes, decisions about the technologies to use, places of testing them and the length of trials, all have consequential effects on the experimenting of desirable futures. The spatio-temporal scaling of prototypes entails the reconfiguration of the places, times, people, organisations and knowledge around prototypes, thereby producing 'grounded imagination' for involved actors to experience futures that are otherwise unimaginable or unknowable (Büscher et al., 2004). Spatio-temporal scaling can also lead to consequences contradictory to the ethical or societal values of collaborative infrastructuring. As exemplified by the various open movements, initiatives promoting social and ethical values of a more transparent government can become instruments of neoliberal urban governance that establish technological and commercial means for capitalising on the generation and release of public data. 'Grounding imagination' is thus instrumental in not only reflecting upon the trial experiences, but also disclosing unanticipated practices, consequences and challenges in relation to realising wider societal and ethical values.

Accordingly, the values of collaborative infrastructuring are 'the product of engagement with the technology, by directly or indirectly implicated publics' and 'subject to processes of change and negotiations' (Liegl et al., 2016: 87–92). Values perceived at the outset can become contested and uncertain later on, which has knock-on effects on whether the futures and visions as initially promised are still attainable in social, ethical and pragmatic terms. Further exploring these issues, the remainder of the chapter discusses the complex enactments of values, futures and urban governance with the case study of DCC Beta and its 'Traffic Light Box Artworks' project.

DCC Beta as collaborative infrastructuring

DCC Beta is an initiative led by City Architects, a division of the city council responsible for architectural and urban design. Against the doubts of the capability of 'municipal governments to achieve transformational change' (Fainstein, 2014: 14), DCC Beta carried out the Box project, seeking to transform city street-scape by giving mundane traffic light boxes a paint-over and reflecting the neighbourhood in the artworks (for an example of a repainted box, see Figures 12.1A and 12.1B). DCC Beta started in 2012 and has been organised outside of 'Smart Dublin', the city-region's administrative unit formalised in 2015 for coordinating smart city initiatives (Coletta et al., 2018). The collaboration unfolding in the Box project demonstrates the possibility of experiencing collaborative ways of shaping future cities through experimentation and also discloses how politics might emerge from the process.

Considering traffic light boxes as part of urban infrastructure, the rationale behind the project strikes a chord with the narratives in support of 'intelligent'

FIGURE 12.1A Traffic light boxes before with DCC Beta logo
Source: https://dubcitybeta.wordpress.com/2012/01/19/traffic-light-box-artworks/

FIGURE 12.1B Traffic light boxes after artworks
Source: https://dubcitybeta.wordpress.com/2012/01/19/traffic-light-box-artworks/

urban infrastructure. In Hewlett-Packard's white paper on smart cities, for example, smart infrastructure 'takes a city's cultural, socioeconomic, environmental, and
geographical realities into account and requires collaboration between stakeholders – from policy makers to citizens', as well as enjoying an extended 'life span'
and reducing 'maintenance costs' (HP, 2016: 3–10). In a similar tone, traffic light
boxes were an issue for DCC because they 'tend to attract graffiti and stickers,
etc – and end up looking very ugly. The Council repaints them regularly (frequency depending on the abuse they're receiving obviously), which creates a cost
for the Council'.[1] Addressing these issues, the project outlines a diverse range of
values from the perspectives of the city government, communities and local artists:

• Save the Council money;
• Enhance the area around … making it more attractive;
• Strengthen the identity of the area in the minds of the people that live, work,
  visit and pass through;
• Provide an outlet for artists to exhibit their work.

Like other urban laboratories, DCC Beta seeks to improve physical, cultural and
digital spaces in the city by carrying out various trials, e.g. 'rain boxes' for rainwater
management, 'parklets' for repurposing parking space for public use, and the Box
project. However, contrary to many urban laboratories, these areas receive little
'laboratorisation' before trials commence (Karvonen and van Heur, 2014): they do
not receive investment for new, 'intelligent' infrastructure, nor do they have spatial
and epistemic boundaries created for cross-site comparison. Critically, DCC Beta is

experimental in that it questions how local governance should work by conducting trials to explore alternative city-making processes, rather than treating urban experiments as an instrument to consolidate the Council's authoritative and expert position. As the coordinator commented in an interview, such exploration is key for staff and the (local) state to become responsive to the ideas they receive:

> So if that person in that city government doesn't know or isn't familiar with how to trial something, ... how do you assess whether a temporary intervention is a policy that you can adopt or not? ... So I think it is important for the emphasis to be on the local government, on the city staff.

For exploring rather than reducing uncertainty and indeterminacy, DCC Beta does not have projects or goals predetermined by senior management. Instead, it receives trial ideas and design suggestions directly from people living or working in the city and also from staff who identify problems as they carry out their duties. This facilitates the broadening of actors, viewpoints and skills in shaping how (a part of) local government might operate differently to improve urban spaces. DCC Beta also prepares 'report cards' for each trial to reflect upon the aims, processes, costs, benefits and concerns that it has observed and received from the public during or after the trials, including a report card to evaluate DCC Beta itself. These report cards are published online after each trial and are also displayed at the locations of the trials to avoid bias towards feedback from digital platforms.

Furthermore, while many other 'utility box art' projects in other cities are led either by local governments or artists, the Box project seeks to grow both DCC Beta and Code for Ireland through their collaboration, as well as showcasing the paintings created by a wide range of contributors, including residents, students, amateurs or professionals.[2] To this end, the DCC Beta coordinator attended the monthly meetup of Code for Ireland in November 2014, where he introduced the project and recruited volunteers. At this point, the project had already had a previous round of online and in-person consultation and a trial.[3] At the meetup, the discussion focused on the technical specs for the prototype required for showing about 20 traffic light boxes and allowing an interactive platform with more details about the contributors to be added later. By 2016, more than 40 traffic light boxes were painted and the responsibility of maintaining the prototype and the project is taken up by a community group as a street art project (http://dublincanvas.com/map/).

Co-creating values and uncertainties in collaborative infrastructuring

Conducting DCC Beta and the Box project as a public experiment provides an opportunity to articulate issues that can emerge from the aligning of different spatio-temporal scales and the scaling of experiments. This section details several ways in which collaborative infrastructuring is a product of the negotiation of trust, value, responsibility and urban futures.

Trust and temporalities of change

From very early on, temporalities of change, which are constitutive of, but often mutually contradictory in urban everyday life, have been the central concerns that motivate collaborative infrastructuring. The interview with DCC Beta coordinator demonstrates that, while physical changes in a city do occur, people have been frustrated by the slow pace of any small change towards a better urban environment. These frustrations are shared by DCC staff too, which motivates them to experiment possible ways to 'speed up' change:

> [A]t a conference, [a speaker] showed a picture of Grafton Street 40 years ago and said, look how far we have come? Yes absolutely it has changed, but that was 40 years ago as well. ... So instead of thinking in terms of decades, how can we think in terms of months? I don't have an exact time, but ... each time you may be a bit faster than the time before and you learn something new.

DCC Beta's experiment of speeding up change requires an 'infrastructure of trust' (Felt and Fochler, 2008). DCC Beta has to earn and maintain it so as to ensure that the public understands that the planning and procedure put in place for the experiments. The branding of 'beta' is a crucial instrument in this regard. The term 'beta' is chosen to denote that the experiments are imperfect and also an instrument to learn from the deployment, as the coordinator explained:

> I wanted to create a brand in its own right, so that when people see it they can implicitly trust it, they know it is going to follow a certain set procedure. It will have a certain ethos and all of that. So, that is why I wanted a specific name as opposed to trial or prototype or pilot.

The branding as an infrastructure of trust is maintained in several ways. During the time a Beta project is tested, a printed DCC Beta logo will be displayed at the site of experiments (see Figure 12.1A) so that people know the project is not a one-off event, but is part of an ongoing, experimental governmental initiative. Also, DCC Beta's website explains its motivation, its ethos, the procedures before a Beta project is rolled out, and the steps already taken in relation to specific projects, in addition to the 'report cards' that review the processes. The logo, documentation, reports and website thus are assembled as an infrastructure of trust while the physical streetscape is undergoing experimentation and change.

Entangling 'values': For whom and how?

In a situation where value can be re-enacted in alternative legal, social, technical and ethical terms, the processes of achieving it can produce concerns regarding who benefits and how. In civic hacking and open data initiatives, 'value' can certainly be recognised in monetary terms (Bates, 2012; Gregg, 2015). In the case of

DCC Beta, value in monetary terms can be readily associated with purchasing new digital content or technology from outside of a government organisation, which has established procurement processes to follow.

However, DCC Beta opted for partnering with a civic hacking organisation as an experiment to build a symbiotic relationship. This creates uncertainty because it enters uncharted territory and the decision can lead to wider societal concerns in relation to government policies and practices in austerity, such as exploiting wilful and free labour and neoliberalising the government.

However, like issues, values are entangled and '*jointly and antagonistically* implicated' in the pragmatic associations that might not be fully reducible to one another (Marres, 2007: 733; original emphasis). If exploitation and the neoliberalisation of the government are already concerns that collaborative infrastructuring has to negotiate, there are further complications emerging from the involvement of disparate sensibilities and practices of value as DCC Beta develops. For example, there is a worry that procurement procedures are too 'formal' for DCC Beta's 'trial-and-error' approach. As the coordinator commented: 'But when it came to a digital prototype, … do I go out and try to procure it, be it a tender or … I am sure I could but often it is slightly too formal.'

Also, by undertaking formal procurement where contracts will more than likely be obtained by private companies, the opportunity of growing communities and government agencies together for experimenting a more open and inclusive government will be lost. As the coordinator continued to comment:

> Equally, I think there might be a symbiotic relationship there whereby actually something like Code for Ireland gets real projects via the city council but actually help Code for Ireland as a concept itself. They know they are working on a real problem somewhere and they actually see it develop, get implemented or not or whatever.

Accordingly, the refusal to bring DCC Beta to closer alignment with government procurement protocols, or potentially market-let urban development, provides an opportunity to trial practical arrangements to grow a symbiotic relationship that is fair and reciprocal. For example, there are costs incurred by painting the boxes and participation in building the platform prototype. In practice, this means making explicit the contributions of residents or artists who took part in the project, as well as creating tangible values from their participation. As the coordinator expressed in the excerpt below, DCC Beta recognises the efforts of the contributors, including residents, artists and civic hackers, and explores possible 'returns' for them:

> … if people are taking time out of their year to paint a box, they ideally would at least have their box mentioned and you could think of things like treasure hunts with people going around all those boxes. If someone could click on a box they could find out who the person who painted it was, maybe they could follow them on social media or whatever. Or maybe when you see

a box you could buy a print of that box straight away, maybe that is a side door income stream.

Indeed, DCC benefits from such a project by saving the human and financial costs of painting the boxes. But, for the coordinator, DCC's responsibility then shifts towards trialling possible social, monetary, technological and ethical arrangements to support collaborative infrastructuring. By recognising and creating values associated with the artworks and the prototype, what is also envisioned and trialled is the possibility of establishing a sustainable scaling up of an experimental project to maintain its momentum. The goal for DCC Beta then is for the interested parties to 'grow it themselves' so that the government does not interfere with how they understand and organise the project, how they interpret their place identity, or how the artworks relate to the identity.

Civic hacking and government responsibility

How value is entangled in collaborative infrastructuring can be further articulated by examining the tension of taking or withdrawing from government responsibility. 'Grow it themselves' seems to confirm the criticism that local government can avoid its responsibility through adopting civic hacking for engaging the public (Johnson and Robinson, 2014). But growing a symbiotic relationship also requires work in that the (local) state has to consider how its roles and responsibilities should be reconfigured and whether they are appropriate for a collaboration in infrastructure making. This transition of responsibility is observable in the interview excerpt below:

> … I mean what are we interested in as a city council? We are interested in maybe picking which boxes get painted and which don't. Maybe the refresh rate, that they are always of a certain quality, that the paint isn't getting really old or that the artwork isn't offensive to people or something.

To be sure, there will be other issues emerging as individual trials go on. They might concern, for example, the ownership over the decisions about rates, qualities or offensiveness of the painted artworks, which has important consequences regarding whose views and life are legitimised during public experimentation. The 'value' of growing a symbiotic relationship then becomes less concerned with determining and attributing values by adopting existing social or ethical frames. Instead, it rests on the articulation and enactment of values and the reassembling of institutional, technological, spatio-temporal, monetary or ethical arrangements to scale collaborative infrastructuring spatially and temporally.

Co-creating promising futures and future problems

Collaborative infrastructuring generates promising futures and future problems in the scaling of the ethical, material, spatio-temporal and socio-technical arrangements of the trials. The 'situational contingencies' and 'performative effects' that occur during the experiments are a 'practice of *doing politics*' (Voß and Amelung, 2016: 763; original emphasis). It can disrupt established orders of organisational norms, skills, expertise and knowledge and lead to an uncertain future, however desirable a vision is initially.

The issue regarding appropriate ways of procurement surfaces again. In earlier experiments, some other DCC staff found it difficult to follow formal procurement procedures for rolling out calls for tenders in a way similar to commissioning art pieces by the city council. Although the staff had obtained permission from other relevant departments, other problems emerged as the coordinator reflected:

> So, we trialled it two slightly different ways, one was internally, our own staff in the area offices trying to roll it out themselves. And I think they actually found that quite difficult because how did they put the call out? Are they supposed to create their own sub-section on their own website? Are they supposed to ...? It was quite a specific set of skills required for it, it was difficult to ... They already had their everyday jobs and suddenly they had this extra piece of work to do.

The difficulty of implementing the calls is due to any government's multiplicity (Law and Singleton, 2014), rather than staff inability. Government agencies are tasked differently and thus develop and possess disparate sets of skills and expertise. This strengthens staff proficiency at routine tasks, but not ad hoc ones that arise as public experimentation unfolds. The question regarding whether to create more sub-units or incorporate new tasks to existing workload is also one that oscillates between scaling organisations (by creating more sub-sections in the city council) or staff (by demanding upskilling). This difficulty in organisational change to incorporate public experimentation is an added layer of challenge to existing ones, such as organisational silos or 'multiple overlapping visions and forces that continually jostle with one another, sometimes aligning, other times competing' (Kitchin et al., 2016: 99).

Furthermore, from early on in the project, traffic light boxes are perceived as one among many other physical objects in the city that can be repurposed. For example, walls have always been on the list and only a small number of them in the inner city had been re-painted. This trial was not on the same scale as the traffic light boxes and did not have a dedicated platform to showcase the repainted walls. However, whether experimenting with the walls or other things, the trials would lead to different considerations and implementation when scaling. As the DCC Beta coordinator commented, when scaling has the intention to include a different set of things in the infrastructural network, it would incur changes to other parts in the infrastructure, leading to further social, governmental, legal and administrative issues:

> ... but there is a whole set of other things that you need to look ... what assets are involved, liability or ownership, who do you sue if something goes

wrong and so on. So a whole set of things there that need to be discussed. That is partly still only being figured out a little bit.

In addition to these issues, there are subsequent excitement and further uncertainties when DCC Beta was adopted as a formal procedure within the council in 2015. The positive includes a small but steady budget, support from senior management of the council, and a steering group that enrols more units of the council into DCC Beta. However, as the experimentation grows larger, it remains uncertain as to the legitimate time that participating DCC staff could spend on the initiative. Also, when DCC Beta was only a concept in trial, the inclusion and prioritisation of requests could be conducted informally since the involved individuals and communities were small. But when DCC Beta is formally adopted by the council, providing transparency concerning how requests are processed and how decisions should be made become a demanding and difficult task.

Conflicting spatio-temporal scaling again adds further challenges to articulating the future for the city and DCC Beta. Whether individual trials are to stay in a local community or have the potential for city-wide roll-out, they are designed and tested locally. This has several unexpected effects. People who experience the trials might think the trials are small and limited in scope, whereas DCC Beta as a trial itself aims at providing the whole city with an alternative city making mechanism. Also, trials are conducted on the scale of months to allow review and modification, and therefore the public might lose sight of DCC Beta's intention to grow it as a long-term project, occurring on the scale of years to a decade. Adding onto the growing of the trials is the scaling up of participants for more inclusive, diverse and reflexive feedback for future adjustment. However, citizen panels are 'political and not neutral instruments' because the design of the panel 'is a decision of political process', which is firmly situated in, as demonstrated throughout the chapter, '[d]ifferences in worldviews and philosophical orientations' regarding what constitutes legitimate opinions and concerns (Mann et al., 2014: 40). Also, it is hoped that DCC Beta will align more closely with Smart Dublin to provide solutions to the challenges proposed by the council that can straddle civic paternalism that plagues many smart city initiatives (Cardullo and Kitchin, 2018).

Conclusion

DCC Beta and the Box project are analysed in this chapter to address questions concerning the possibility of a collaborative shaping of infrastructures and urban futures. DCC Beta and its projects are conducted as experiments that bring diverse actors, practices and viewpoints into the exploration of an alternative city making process where the infrastructuring of prototypes, trust, skills and value generates promising futures and future problems. The chapter demonstrates how value, trust and responsibility in collaborative infrastructuring materialise and are also contested in practical arrangements. Also, the spatio-temporal scaling of prototypes has been complicated by the difficulty in the scaling of staff skills, human and budgetary resources, and organisational remits, structures and protocols. Furthermore, after DCC Beta grows in momentum, scope and resources and subsequently becomes tasked with citizen engagement by DCC, it remains to be seen whether the procedure established through the trials can persist as an instrument for a collaborative making of urban futures.

The examination of DCC Beta and the collaborative infrastructuring it trials makes reference to other smart city experiments that celebrate citizenship as their focus. The point of unpacking DCC Beta then is also to emphasise urban everyday life as a productive site of innovation and promising future, which includes disclosing future problems and the problem of scaling – issues that are often glossed over in other state-led and corporate-endorsed experimentation and yet deserve wider attention.

Notes

1 For this and quotes below, see https://dubcitybeta.wordpress.com/2012/01/19/traffi c-light-box-artworks/ (accessed 8 July 2016).
2 See, for example, that in Toronto and Calgary in https://www1.toronto.ca/wps/portal/ contentonly?vgnextoid=b33498b613412410VgnVCM10000071d60f89RCRD,http:// www.calgary.ca/CSPS/Recreation/Pages/Public-Art/Utility-Box-Public-Art-Program. aspx, and a short list of such projects in other cities https://en.wikipedia.org/wiki/Uti lity_box_art (accessed 7 September 2017).
3 For more details about the initial stage of the project, see the project's report card https:// dubcitybeta.files.wordpress.com/2014/09/traffic-light-boxes-report-card-public.pdf (accessed 8 July 2016).

Acknowledgements

The chapter is supported by The Programmable City project, funded by a European Research Council Advanced investigator award (ERC-2012-AdG-323636-SOFTCITY) and Reshaping Cities through Data and Experiments project, funded by an Irish Research Council Ulysses award. I would also like to thank Thad Miller and Rider Foley for shaping the ideas in the chapter.

References

Barry, A. 2013. *Material Politics: Disputes along the Pipeline*. Oxford: Wiley Blackwell.
Bates, J. 2012. "'This is What Modern Deregulation Looks Like': Co-optation and Contestation in the Shaping of the UK's Open Government Data Initiative." *The Journal of Community Informatics*, 8(2).
Björgvinsson, E., Ehn, P. and HillgrenP.-A. 2010. "Participatory Design and 'Democratizing Innovation." *Proceedings of the 11th Participatory Design Conference*, 41–50. Sydney.
Bulkeley, H., and Castán Broto, V. 2013. "Government by Experiment? Global Cities and the Governing of Climate Change." *Transactions of the Institute of British Geographers* 38(3): 361–375.
Büscher, M., Eriksen, M. A., Kristensen, J. F., et al. 2004. "Ways of Grounding Imagination." *Proceedings of the Eighth Conference on Participatory Design*, 193–203. Toronto.

Büscher, M., Coulton, P., Hemment, D., et al. 2011. "Mobile, Experimental, Public." In Büscher, M., Urry, J. and Witchger, K. (eds), *Mobile Methods*. London: Routledge.

Cardullo, P., and Kitchin, R. 2018. "Being a 'Citizen' in the Smart City: Up and Down the Scaffold of Smart Citizen Participation in Dublin, Ireland." *GeoJournal*. doi:10.1007/s10708–10018–9845–9848.

Coleman, E. G. 2013. *Coding Freedom: The Ethics and Aesthetics of Hacking*. Princeton, NJ: Princeton University Press.

Coletta, C., Heaphy, L. and Kitchin, R. 2018. "From the Accidental to Articulated Smart City: The Creation and Work of 'Smart Dublin'." *European Urban and Regional Studies*. Online first. doi:10.1177/0969776418785214.

Evans, J. 2016. "Trials and Tribulations: Problematizing the City through/as Urban Experimentation." *Geography Compass* 10(10): 429–443.

Evans, J., and Karvonen, A. 2014. "'Give Me a Laboratory and I Will Lower Your Carbon Footprint!' — Urban Laboratories and the Governance of Low-Carbon Futures." *International Journal of Urban and Regional Research* 38(2): 413–430.

Fainstein, S.S. 2014. "The Just City." *International Journal of Urban Sciences* 18(1): 1–18.

Felt, U., and Fochler, M. 2008. "The Bottom-up Meanings of the Concept of Public Participation in Science and Technology." *Science and Public Policy* 35(7): 489–499.

Gabrys, J. 2016. *Program Earth: Environmental Sensing Technology and the Making of a Computational Planet*. Minneapolis, MN: University of Minnesota Press.

Gregg, M. 2015. "Hack for Good: Speculative Labour, App Development and the Burden of Austerity." *The Fibreculture Journal* 25: 185–202.

HP. 2016. *Smart Cities and the Internet of Things*. Palo Alto, CA: HP.

Johnson, P., and Robinson, P. 2014. "Civic Hackathons: Innovation, Procurement, or Civic Engagement?" *Review of Policy Research* 31(4): 349–357.

Karasti, H. 2014. "Infrastructuring in Participatory Design." *Proceedings of the 13th Participatory Design Conference*, 141–150. Windhoek, Namibia.

Karvonen, A., and van Heur, B. 2014. "Urban Laboratories: Experiments in Reworking Cities." *International Journal of Urban and Regional Research* 38(2): 379–392.

Kelty, C. 2008. *Two Bits: The Cultural Significance of Free Software*. Durham, NC: Duke University Press.

Kitchin, R., Maalsen, S. and McArdle, G. 2016. "The Praxis and Politics of Building Urban Dashboards." *Geoforum* 77: 93–101.

Law, J. and Singleton, V. 2014. "ANT, multiplicity and policy." *Critical Policy Studies* 8(4): 379–396.

Le Dantec, C. A. and DiSalvo, C. 2013. "Infrastructuring and the formation of publics in participatory design." *Social Studies of Science* 43(2): 241–264.

Liegl, M., Boden, A., Büscher, M., et al. 2016. "Designing for Ethical Innovation: A Case Study on ELSI Co-design in Emergency." *International Journal of Human-Computer Studies* 95: 80–95.

Lodato, T.J. and DiSalvo, C. 2016. "Issue-oriented hackathons as material participation." *New Media & Society* 18(4): 539–557.

Mann, C., Voß, J.-P., Amelung, N., et al. 2014. *Challenging Futures of Citizen Panels: Critical Issues for Robust Forms of Public Participation*. Berlin: Technische Universität Berlin.

Marres, N. 2007. "The Issues Deserve More Credit: Pragmatist Contributions to the Study of Public Involvement in Controversy." *Social Studies of Science* 37(5): 759–780.

Perng, S.-Y., and Kitchin, R. 2018. "Solutions and Frictions in Civic Hacking: Collaboratively Designing and Predicting Wait Time for an Immigration Office." *Social & Cultural Geography* 19(1): 1–20.

Robinson, P.J., and Johnson, P.A. 2016. "Civic Hackathons: New Terrain for Local Government-Citizen Interaction?" *Urban Planning* 1(2): 65–74.

Schrock, A.R. 2016. "Civic Hacking as Data Activism and Advocacy: A History from Publicity to Open Government Data." *New Media & Society* 18(4): 581–599.

Voß, J.-P., and Amelung, N. 2016. "Innovating Public Participation Methods: Technoscientization and Reflexive Engagement." *Social Studies of Science* 46(5): 749–772.

13

SMART FOR A REASON

Sustainability and social inclusion in the sharing city

Duncan McLaren and Julian Agyeman

Introduction

Whether as a goal for cities, or a discourse on urban futures, the concept of the 'smart city' is central to established, perhaps even dominant, narratives. Although it has (more-or-less successfully) absorbed objectives of innovation, creativity and environmental efficiency, the 'smart city' has been consistently contested, particularly over its social and political dimensions. This chapter outlines an alternative concept or narrative, that of the 'sharing city', and explores the overlaps, contrasts and interactions between ideas of smart and sharing cities with the aim of proposing a more socially and environmentally sustainable future orientation for cities.

The chapter proceeds by briefly reviewing the development and contestation of smart cities discourses. It then outlines the sharing paradigm proposed by McLaren and Agyeman (2015), highlighting the ways in which this conceptual framework interprets cities as shared spaces, and the changing nature of sharing in cities, especially with the emergence of the so-called 'sharing economy'. It notes the diversity of approaches encompassed by the idea of sharing cities, and highlights the persistence of ideas of smartness. It subsequently contrasts such 'smart sharing city' models with those of social urbanism and the urban commons, exemplified in Latin American cities such as Medellín, highlighting the continued value of 'low-tech' civic and community sharing and the ways in which the smart cities discourse may be attempting to swallow the new concept of sharing cities. Conclusions are drawn regarding the potential for sharing cities approaches to bring justice and solidarity to the centre in urban futures.

We should note that our analysis seeks to sketch the interconnected public, corporate and political discourses of smartness, not just scholarly ones. This chapter therefore cites a range of literature from peer-reviewed books and journals, to newspaper articles, blogs and videos.

Smart city discourses

Smart city discourses and narratives have been in wide circulation now for more than a decade, building on and adopting elements of preceding narratives of wired, intelligent and creative cities (Hollands, 2008). As Vanolo (2014b) notes, there is no consistent definition, but "most commonly the idea relies on the implicit assumption that urban infrastructures and everyday life can/should be optimized and 'greened' through the technologies and innovations of global IT companies." Smart city proposals are typically partnerships between public authorities and corporate technology providers, involving the application of digital technologies to enhance the efficiency, functionality and control of urban infrastructures and services, supporting cost reductions and (increasingly) also environmental sustainability goals. With this background and these actors, it is perhaps unsurprising that smart city projects tend to focus on economic and entrepreneurial potential, although aspects of participatory governance and environmental and social sustainability have also long appeared in variants of the discourse (Caragliu et al., 2011; Ahvenniemi et al., 2017; Trindade et al., 2017). Perhaps the best contemporary example, and currently the most controversial is Sidewalk Toronto:

> [A] joint effort by Waterfront Toronto and Alphabet's Sidewalk Labs to create a new kind of mixed-use, complete community on Toronto's Eastern Waterfront, beginning with the creation of Quayside. Sidewalk Toronto will combine forward-thinking urban design and new digital technology to create people-centred neighbourhoods that achieve precedent-setting levels of sustainability, affordability, mobility, and economic opportunity.
>
> *(Sidewalk Toronto, 2018)*

Nonetheless, technology remains central to the concept, with the adoption and development of ICT, including ubiquitous web connectivity through broadband and WiFi, connected and real-time sensor and surveillance technologies, and RFID tagging of objects and devices. Technology is seen – largely uncritically – as a panacea, enabling and enhancing economic competitiveness, attractiveness to footloose businesses and innovators, efficiency in public services, participation in governance and environmental sustainability (Caragliu et al., 2011; Kramers et al., 2014; Ahvenniemi et al., 2017). With few exceptions – such as communal WiFi networks and community organised civic hacking – the technology of smart cities and smart city proposals is corporately sourced (if purchased by the city as a public service) through increasingly common public-private partnership arrangements (Hollands, 2015; Lee et al., 2014).

Smart city projects and rhetoric are found in every continent, typically seen as an essential aspect of responding to the challenges of fast growing urban populations, fiscal austerity, environmental constraints, and rising social and economic expectations (Trindade et al., 2017). They include both retrofit and new-build approaches, with India's aspirations to develop 100 smart cities (Sharma, 2018; Smart Cities Mission, 2016) embracing both approaches.

Critiques of smart cities

Smart cities run up against social critique on grounds of participation, inclusion and equality. There is a lively academic and popular literature challenging the central corporate narratives of the smart city (e.g., Hollands 2008; Townsend, 2013; Greenfield 2013). Recent analysis (Söderstrom et al., 2014; Hollands, 2015; Wolfram, 2012) tends to emphasize the extent to which the discourse is dominated by corporate and institutional actors, focused optimistically on technology, functionality and efficiency (in a world of increasing financial and environmental scarcity); but in tension with activists and citizens who seek to insert public interests, equity and social inclusion into smart city narratives. Critical analysis has exposed questions of civil liberties, especially with regard to surveillance; social exclusion and livability; social discipline and legitimation; and democracy, interests and power (Sennett, 2012; Greenfield, 2013; Provoost 2013; Vanolo 2014a; March and Ribera-Fumaz, 2014; Townsend, 2013; Luque-Ayala and Marvin, 2015).

The contrasts with more human-centred prescriptions from leading urbanists and placemakers such as Jan Gehl (2010), are striking. Gehl centres public life, and the need for welcoming shared public spaces at a human scale, enabling encounter, serendipity and cultural mixing. The idea of a turnkey, city-from-scratch consisting of robust technologies that, once deployed, will function consistently is mistaken, Greenfield (2013) argues. Ignoring the specifics of place and social milieu, and above all the inhabitants of cities, is a recipe for disaster. Greenfield (2014) calls instead for recognition of the value of democracy, "citizen cunning and unglamorous technology." Lefevre (2014) similarly highlights how promotional images of smart cities are typically "entirely devoid of human life," but he argues that in reality "cities succeed not because of how 'smart' they are, but because of how human they are."

March and Ribera-Fumaz (2014) argue that the smart cities ideology also acts to depoliticize urban planning and development, turning the process into a technical and managerial issue. Provoost (2013) similarly highlights the anti-democratic nature of smart cities. She argues that they have a deliberate social dark side; that smart infrastructure is being marketed to cities *intentionally* to construct a privatized, commercial platform for services, health, and education, replacing traditional community provision and enclosing the existing urban commons. From this perspective the smart city is platform capitalism on steroids, with every citizen as part of its captive market.

Provoost is also scathing about the *design* of stand-alone smart cities: often highway-oriented, car-based – with exclusive spaces and design drawing on US cul-de-sacs rather than inclusive ones learning from European neighbourhoods. She highlights a deep divide in architecture between 'starchitect' advocates of commercially motivated, privately financed smart cities; and those – like Jamie McGuirk – working with 'self-organized cities,' in which development possibilities are emerging from the slums and favelas through collaboration. Sennett (2012) similarly sees more potential in self-organization and a case for working with existing social capital in communities: "If they have a choice, people want a more open, indeterminate city in which to make their way; this is how they can come to take ownership over their lives."

In summary then, the dominant smart cities discourses are technologically simplistic, post-political, socially constraining, corporate and neo-liberal.

Sharing cities: An alternative discourse?

The sharing cities discourse is slightly newer, with a few examples of city-led and citizen-led designations (notably Seoul and Amsterdam), and also illustrated by contested sharing practices in a much wider set of cities including Barcelona, Berlin, San Francisco and Milan.

Seoul launched its city-funded Sharing City project in 2012, aiming to "bring the sharing economy to all Seoul citizens by expanding sharing infrastructure, promoting existing sharing enterprises, incubating sharing economy startups, utilizing idle public resources, and providing more access to data" (Johnson, 2013). Amsterdam adopted the Sharing City moniker in 2015 after a two-year campaign led by ShareNL, which brought together citizens, NGOs and local businesses, with the aim "as a city [to] utilize the opportunities that the collaborative economy offers in the areas of sustainability, social cohesion and economy" (ShareNL, 2017).

However, more widely, sharing cities are emerging at the intersection of two very different modalities of sharing: collaborative consumption in the so-called 'sharing economy'; and urban commoning in city spaces and communities (McLaren and Agyeman, 2015). Despite distinctive cultural roots, these sets of practices can be found to some degree in cities around the world, but with regionally distinctive forms of engagement. Our observations suggest that in Anglo-Saxon cultures, cities tend to seek to facilitate commercial collaborative consumption, with an 'Uber-for-X' model particularly to the fore in the USA. On the other hand, in Latin cultures, especially in South America, cities often actively facilitate urban commoning. Elsewhere in Europe and Asia, a range of hybrid forms seem to be more common, with state or civil society involvement alongside commercial actors. More research is needed to be clear what forms are emerging in Africa and the Middle East. Our understanding of sharing cities is therefore much broader than implied by the most salient models (found in the commercial sharing economy, and in self-labelled 'Sharing Cities' such as Seoul and Amsterdam), and reflects our understanding of sharing as a paradigm for human relations.

The sharing paradigm

Our understanding of 'sharing' encompasses processes whereby something is divided between multiple users or used, occupied, or enjoyed jointly with other users. We recognize a broad spectrum of things that can be shared, ranging from material resources and production facilities, to services, experiences and capabilities. In this we echo real life practice and common usage of the terms 'share' and 'sharing' in which there is also a clear and intended moral undertone of fairness. Sharing is an evolved human behaviour found in all societies, and it is cultural and political in nature as much as economic.

Despite the rapid growth of web-based sharing intermediaries, the models based on such intermediaries do not even represent the whole of the sharing economy, never mind the potential for a sharing society. In McLaren and Agyeman (2015) we present a broader scope for analysis of sharing, offering a four-fold categorization of modes of sharing (distinguished on dimensions of 'socio-cultural' to 'mediated', and 'communal' to 'commercial') (see Table 13.1).

The commercial mediated quadrant (lower left in the table) is dominated by modern sharing economy platforms such as Uber, Airbnb and Kickstarter – principally web-based intermediaries that, in one way or another, bring together people to facilitate collaborative consumption, more efficiently share resources, provide services or act collectively but monetize the process, taking a fee for facilitating or participating in the exchange.

Mediated forms of sharing need not be commercial – governments, not-for-profits, and communities can deliver them too. The communal mediated quadrant (upper left in the table) includes organizations such as Streetbank and Freecycle, timebanks that facilitate peer-to-peer sharing, and communal services such as libraries.

Nor does commercially motivated sharing need to be formally mediated. It can instead arise within communities of peers. Such commercial sociocultural approaches (lower right) include cooperatives, and novel forms of peer-production such as Linux,[1] Enspiral, and collaboration using blockchain technology. This quadrant has particularly blurred borders, as many of its occupants involve elements of intermediation, and their commercial goals are often secondary to social purposes.

The final quadrant (upper right) is where we find fewest formal organizations, and most traditional communal sociocultural sharing within families, traditional ethnic and religious groups, and close-knit geographic communities. Sharing here is often highly reciprocal, but rarely monetized. It includes much caring and domestic work, the coproduction of community facilities and services, and emanations such as co-housing and supper clubs.

This categorization helps us understand and illustrate how sharing is changing in contemporary society. In the global North we see a tendency for socio-cultural sharing to erode, while mediated commercial sharing is growing particularly fast. The former was often communal – or even communitarian – based on strong community level social capital and inter-personal trust. The new forms of sharing,

TABLE 13.1 Key dimensions of the sharing paradigm

	(Inter)mediated sharing	*Sociocultural sharing*
Communal sharing	Communal mediated (learned, intrinsically motivated)	Communal socio-cultural (evolved, intrinsically motivated)
Commercial sharing	Commercial mediated (learned, extrinsically motivated)	Commercial socio-cultural (evolved, extrinsically motivated)

by contrast, are typically web-based, and more cosmopolitan – based on weak links which cross community boundaries, backed by trust in the intermediary and its procedural tools such as rating systems, rather than by trust in the specific individuals involved (McLaren and Agyeman, 2015).

We think it important to note that experience with the internet suggests *cycles* of disintermediation and reintermediation (Chircu and Kauffman, 1999). We would not therefore expect the commercial models in which intermediaries reap profits from the labour of their participants to be the 'last-word' in online sharing approaches marked by marginal costs which are (arguably) declining to zero (Rifkin, 2014). New peer-to-peer models and post-commercial intermediaries, building on the experience of bodies such as Enspiral, and user or provider-owned cooperative sharing platforms, more ambitious than the taxi-coops that have grown in cities such as Austin in resistance to Uber, can already be foreseen (Bollier, 2016; Orsi et al., 2013). At the time of writing, debate over the insidious political role of social networks such as Facebook and Twitter has stirred new discussion of options for collective ownership of such platforms by their users.

Commonalities with smart city discourses

In self-designated 'sharing cities' such as Seoul and Amsterdam, and also San Francisco, the overlaps with smart cities are substantial and the technological dependencies involved bear restating.

Sharing economy analyses highlight the significance of a whole series of 'smart technologies' such as mobile internet, particularly with increasingly ubiquitous location, payment, identity and reputation services – notably those linked to social networks such as Facebook. These enable real-time transactional 'sharing' with strangers using web platforms such as Airbnb, Uber, Feastly, PetVacay, etc. The digital technology enables physical sharing or exchange of value, while providing the necessary reassurance to participants that the person who has booked to stay on your couch, agreed to look after your dog, cook your supper, or drive you to the airport is who they said they were ... not a scammer or axe-wielding maniac. For services such as bike- and car-sharing, location services are critical, supported by technologies such as RFID that enable the location of physical items, as well as of users, to be tracked.

The internet plays a central role also in modern forms of the peer-to-peer economy, whether for digital sharing of designs for 3D-printing, virtual collaboration tools, or accessing online finance through Kickstarter or using Bitcoin. And thus we see again ways in which technology is positioned as a source of economic or commercial advantage, a way to obtain market competitiveness through innovation or creativity.

Such a framing of the sharing economy, encouraged by the widespread adoption of neoliberal ideals of the entrepreneurial city (Hollands, 2015; Harvey, 1989) is however, highly problematic in other respects. It frames sharing as an 'economic', rather than a social, cultural or political activity. It thus perpetuates the myth that human society is founded on, and bounded by the economy, rather than vice versa, and that the environment is simply a source of economic resources, rather than the fundamental space in which humans and our societies and cultures evolved and coexist.

It also primes us to seek 'solutions' to our problems in markets, in monetized exchange, and in the production and consumption of goods and services, constrained by economic frames and drivers. Of course sharing has economic outcomes and functions. Sharing can deliver utility. But this is only a first step in understanding the possible contribution of sharing to human flourishing. Without the capabilities to transform them, neither materials nor goods nor services will necessarily deliver wellbeing or meet our needs (Sen, 2001). So, we argue that a sharing paradigm should begin from the question of how sharing approaches and shared resources can more directly enhance capabilities for all. We find fuller expression of that in narratives of social urbanism and the urban commons that often do not mention sharing explicitly.

Social urbanism

Our understanding of sharing cities and the sharing paradigm also encompasses alternative visions for cities, which enable the sharing of the city, its spaces, infrastructures and services without necessarily relying on commercial intermediaries, online technologies, or even the explicit discourse of sharing cities.

More often than not, such alternative visions arise outside of existing power structures, in citizens' movements, counter-cultural spaces and protest. But they can be state-led. For example, in Colombia's second city Medellín *'urbanismo sociale'* – social inclusion in a shared public realm – inspired by the philosophy of the Medellín Academy, has been the critical driving factor. Unlike the more conspicuous 'sharing city branding' of an Amsterdam, or Seoul, from the mid-1990s Medellín has focused on empowering citizens, beginning in the poorest neighbourhoods (see also Chapter 5). Library parks such as Parque Biblioteca España have been constructed in marginalized parts of the city, providing free access to computer and information technology, and educational classes, as well as space for cultural activities and recreation. The city has invested heavily in shared public transit and infrastructure – including bus rapid transit, nine cable car links and a huge outdoor escalator – to connect the poor hillside *comunas* with the centre. Public facilities, such as health centres and schools, have been developed at the cable-car stations. The major projects have been funded with revenue from the city's public services company, Empresas Públicas de Medellín (EPM) and developed through a participatory budgeting and planning process with the community.

What we see in Medellín is a particularly developed and coordinated – if still imperfect – process of building (or rebuilding) the urban commons of public spaces, facilities and culture that underlie the possibilities for sharing and cooperation in all cities. As David Harvey (2012) reminds us, the city is produced by commoning undertaken by citizens, as much or more than it is created by the commercial development industry. Economic framings of smart sharing, focused on commercial intermediaries, tend to overlook urban commons as shared spaces and commoning as a sharing practice.

Contrasting the discourses: Smart sharing or social urbanism?

There are multiple ways in which sharing city and smart city discourses could be contrasted. Here we focus on the nature and implications of some significant and illuminating contrasts highlighted by: the breadth of motivations; (in)dependence from 'smart' technology; the relative (un)importance of efficiency and controllability; and the different notions of ownership and governance embodied in the discourse.

Even amongst the cities actively pursuing smart goals and enabling commercial sharing, we see a much wider diversity of sharing behaviours than can be accounted for purely in individualistic economic terms. Communal, civic and peer-to-peer models reflect deliberate efforts at social inclusion and solidarity on various scales. They also treat technology merely as an instrumental add-on, rather than a fundamental enabler. In civic provision of infrastructures and services efficiency might be facilitated by online services – e.g. online ticketing and live timetabling for public transit; online searching and reservations for public libraries – but here the technology is best understood as an 'add-on', not fundamental. In informal communal sharing of care for children or the elderly, 'swishing', informal and formal timebanking and exchange schemes, or formal and informal coops, digital technologies may play no role at all, but such sharing behaviours are no less socially valuable for that. In other words, contemporary urban sharing can be facilitated by technology, but is not so dependent on it as smart city approaches imply. Even on-line approaches are often low-tech, like Freecycle, based on simple email lists, while some of the most inspiring community sharing initiatives are very basic, like Pumpipumpe's front door stickers for residents to display things they are able to lend out.

Nonetheless, there may be good social inclusion reasons for wanting to exploit technology and enable sharing between strangers, especially where this might span ethnic divisions in cities. Web intermediated sharing has the potential to be more cosmopolitan than communitarian in this respect. But that doesn't eliminate value in off-line sharing, and arguably the very foundation of sharing cities has to be in streets and public spaces, where urban design and public culture is far more important to the functioning of the urban commons than smart street lamps and digital surveillance.

The significance of differences in goals and motivations is even more far-reaching. Smart cities aim to be 'efficient', 'functional', and 'well-controlled' (FutureLab, 2017). By contrast social urbanism would seem to pursue 'effective', 'diverse', and 'resilient'. Indeed, arguably, sharing cities rooted in urban commoning would appear to actively reject 'well-controlled' (in favour of democratic), and 'efficient' (in favour of diverse, and experimental). Such goals flow from a very different understanding of what is 'functional' – a functional city in sharing cities parlance is one that is accessible to all inhabitants, not rationed and regulated by income; one which enhances possibility and serendipity, creating new outcomes and experiences, not simply efficiently delivering predetermined ones; and one that is diverse, and even chaotic, in the emergent sense of the term.

This inevitably recognizes and builds on the mutual interdependence of urban commoners. It acknowledges the importance and desirability of shared infrastructures and services – whether provided by public agencies or communal effort. This seems a world away from the smart city view of infrastructure, where the aim seems to be to minimize the provision and maintenance of infrastructure, rather than recognize it as underpinning basic capabilities. For instance, applications such as Waze have been touted by city authorities – in Boston, for example – as a solution to increasing gridlock when in reality they have become a means to cut back on planning, investment and maintenance of shared infrastructure. The difference might appear subtle, but in such contexts intention can be everything. Like David Cameron's advocacy of the 'Big Society' in the UK, such co-production can be a mechanism of austerity, dumping greater responsibilities on communities with less resources, rather than a genuine expression of community participation and solidarity. Involving the community as a means to build capacity, resilience and autonomy is radically different to the same intervention designed to delegate responsibility without building capacity.

Social urbanism and urban commoning extend sharing from *use* of urban resources to collective *ownership*. This can be seen as a push back against neoliberal ideals of private individual ownership (which are largely endorsed in smart city discourses). It might even be read as a challenge to foundational liberal ideals of 'self-ownership' insofar as social urbanism and sharing admit to interdependency and reliance on community or public agencies.

The expression of shared ownership is not always a literal one, but one of the role of citizens in decision-making and governance, sometimes expressed as a right to the city (Harvey, 2012), and even (in analysis of open-source approaches) as a right to infrastructure (Jiménez, 2014). In contrast to the role of public engagement in smart cities, instrumentally legitimating the use of technology and developing a 'smartmentality' (Vanolo 2014a) to cope with inevitable technological change, participation in social urbanism plays a substantive and normative role (in Fiorino's (1990) terms). This plays out further in practical contrasts in governance and participation. As we saw in Medellín, public ownership, participatory planning, and participatory budgeting all emphasize the collective ownership role of the public.

These contrasts in intent, purpose and governance might appear to create tensions between environmental goals and those of creating the lively shared city. But if goal-setting is taken out of the hands of the technocratic elite, this does not imply abandonment of environmental objectives. Despite widespread perceptions that publics prioritize consumption over conservation, the opposite seems to be true in emergent urban commoning (and similar initiatives such as transition towns, which demonstrate a willingness to engage in environmental behaviour which is fair and collective). And in social urbanism we see emergent environmental outcomes, even where such goals are not explicit, whereas in smart cities (and in some expressions of sharing) there is a very real risk that environments might be improved for elites, but not for everyone, with the creation of new divisions in addition to existing ones of race, class and income. More generally the ownership of objectives and discourses can be divergent. We need to ask which groups and interests promote which goals and discourses.

While for the city authorities in smart cities the key drivers for sharing might be efficient resource use (especially of constrained housing stock); the challenges of service provision in the face of aging populations and budgetary austerity; and growing recognition of the impacts of environmental problems (especially air pollution) on the urban economy: for *publics* and for social entrepreneurs there are clearly also motivations like social connectedness, inclusion and solidarity. In contrast, in social urbanist models, social inclusion is more typically a shared motivation of city authorities and publics, while environmental and efficiency goals are more incidental. And although financial resources are scarce, reducing expenditure rarely appears to be an ideological objective of policy, and more conventional social liberal, or neo-Keynesian investment approaches predicated on enhancing equity appear more normal (see Table 13.2).

This is not to argue that the creativity and innovation so valued by smart cities is irrelevant to sharing cities and the urban commons. But it points perhaps at the importance of social and grassroots innovation (Seyfang and Smith, 2007) rather than the scalable forms so sought after by venture capital. Social innovation targeted at community-identified needs is more typical of commons and peer-to-peer approaches, and has a key role in strengthening the economic and social resilience of cities, building the core economy (Miller, 2010) and sectors that directly deliver wellbeing and services (Engelen et al., 2014). In such models justice is pursued not primarily through redistribution but through an emphasis on building basic services

TABLE 13.2 A tale of two discourses

	Smart sharing cities	*Social urbanism*
Key driver	Economic development	Social inclusion
Cooperate or compete?	Cities compete with each other	Cities cooperate in networks and with neighbouring areas
Role of technology	Key to competitiveness	Enables collaboration
Politics of scarcity	Austerity largely a political construct	Genuine scarcity and need
People treated as:	Primarily consumers	Primarily citizens
Environmental objectives	Explicit (secondary) aims of resource efficiency and environmental benefit	Environmental benefits real but incidental
Sharing discourse	'sharing economy'	'urban commons'

and production in those parts of the economy that are not exposed to international competition (Engelen et al., 2014).

Yet as 'smart' discourses try to swallow sharing – as they previously absorbed innovation and creativity – app-based approaches and the quest for Uber-for-X take pride of place, and an economic focus on competition for inward investment and footloose hipsters (or 'creative' talent) is reproduced. Dangerously, such narratives dismiss the existing expertise of cities and of commoners, and encourage us to turn to Silicon Valley intermediaries and venture capitalists for 'sharing expertise'. This would seem to be a pernicious example of the smart storytelling identified by Söderström et al. (2014) in which corporate interests intentionally market a particular narrative for the future of cities, one which passes inevitably through the 'obligatory passage point' of their technology or consulting expertise.

But even while threatened, we see hope in the mobilization of discourses of sharing. They promise to reinvigorate values of community and normative principles of fairness around a restored conception of the urban commons. In other words, they offer an expression of 'just sustainabilities' (Agyeman, 2013). With a broad social, cultural and political understanding of the logics of urban sharing and urban commoning, technological smartness could be harnessed to social transformation of values and behaviour. Cities should therefore embed smart city activities within broadly defined sharing city objectives and programmes, co-produced with citizens.

Ultimately, truly 'sharing cities' are not just those which actively 'share' things – smartly or not – but those which are themselves 'shared' by all. Such cities may be smart, but not for the sake of smartness, rather for the sake of social inclusion.

Note

1 While Linux is open-source, its developers and many users deploy it commercially in provision of IT services.

References

Agyeman, J. 2013. *Introducing Just Sustainabilities: Policy, Planning, and Practice*. London: Zed Books.

Ahvenniemi, H., A. Huovila, I. Pinto-Seppä and M. Airaksinen. 2017. "What are the differences between sustainable and smart cities?" *Cities*, 60(A): 234–245

Bollier, D. 2016. "Transnational Republics of Commoning as a New Mode of Governance." Big Ideas Thinkpiece, Friends of the Earth. Online at: https://www.foe.co.uk/sites/default/files/downloads/transnational-republics-commoning-reinventing-governance-through-emergent.pdf. Last accessed 26 April 2018.

Caragliu, A., C. Del Bo and P. Nijkamp. 2011. "Smart Cities in Europe." *Journal of Urban Technology*, 18(2): 65–82.

Chircu, A.M. and R.J. Kauffman. 1999. "Strategies for Internet Middlemen in the Intermediation/Disintermediation/Reintermediation Cycle." *Electronic Markets*, 9(1–2): 109–117.

Engelen, E., S. Johal, A. Salento and K. Williams, 2014. "How to Build a Fairer City." *The Guardian*, 24 September. Online at: http://www.theguardian.com/cities/2014/sep/24/manifesto-fairer-grounded-city-sustainable-transport-broadband-housing.

Fiorino, D.J. 1990. "Citizen Participation and Environmental Risk: A Survey of Institutional Mechanisms." *Science Technology & Human Values*, 15(2): 226–243.

Future Lab, 2017. Website. http://www.futurelab.tuwien.ac.at/what-is-a-smart-city-the-concept-of-smart-city-from-a-global-perspective/ (Last accessed 20 October 2017).

Gehl, J. 2010. *Cities for People.* Washington DC: Island Press.

Greenfield, A. 2013. *Against the smart city.* New York: Do Projects.

Greenfield, A. 2014. "The Smartest Cities Rely on Citizen Cunning and Unglamourous Technology." *The Guardian*, 22 December. Online at http://www.theguardian.com/cities/2014/dec/22/the-smartest-cities-rely-on-citizen-cunning-and-unglamorous-technology.

Harvey, D. 1989. "From Managerialism to Entrepreneurialism: The Transformation in Urban Governance in Late Capitalism." *Geografiska Annale*, 71B(1): 3–17.

Harvey, D. 2012. *Rebel Cities: From the Right to the City to the Urban Revolution.* New York: Verso.

Hollands, R.G. 2008. "Will the Real Smart City Please Stand Up? Intelligent, Progressive or Entrepreneurial?" *City*, 12(3): 303–320.

Hollands, R.G. 2015. "Critical Interventions into the Corporate Smart City." *Cambridge Journal of Regions, Economy and Society*, 8: 61–77.

Jiménez, A.C. 2014. "The Right to Infrastructure: A Prototype for Open Source Urbanism." *Environment and Planning D: Society and Space*, 32(2): 342–362.

Johnson, C. 2013. "Is Seoul the Next Great Sharing City?" *Shareable*, 16 July. Online at http://www.shareable.net/blog/is-seoul-the-next-great-sharing-city.

Kramers, A., M. Höjer, N. Lövehagen and J. Wangel. 2014. "Smart Sustainable Cities – Exploring ICT Solutions for Reduced Energy Use in Cities." *Environmental Modelling & Software*, 56: 52–62.

Lee, J. H. M.G. Hancock and M.-C. Hu. 2014. "Towards an Effective Framework for Building Smart Cities: Lessons from Seoul and San Francisco." *Technological Forecasting and Social Change*, 89: 80–99. doi:10.1016/j.techfore.2013.08.033.

Lefevre, M. 2014. "Moving Beyond the 'Smart City' Paradigm." New Cities Foundation blog, 9 July. Online at http://www.newcitiesfoundation.org/moving-beyond-smart-city-paradigm.

Luque-Ayala, A. and S. Marvin. 2015. "Developing a Critical Understanding of Smart Urbanism?" *Urban Studies*, 52(12): 2105–2116.

March, H. and R. Ribera-Fumaz. 2014. "Smart Contradictions: The Politics of Making Barcelona a Self-Sufficient City." *European Urban and Regional Studies*, 20: 1–15.

McLaren, D. and J. Agyeman. 2015. *Sharing Cities: A Case for Truly Smart and Sustainable Cities.* Cambridge, MA: MIT Press.

Miller, E. 2010. "Solidarity Economy: Key Concepts and Issues," in *Solidarity Economy I: Building Alternatives for People and Planet*, edited by E. Kawano, T. Masterson and J. Teller-Ellsberg. Amherst, MA: Center for Popular Economics. (Chapter available online at http://www.communityeconomics.org/node/211, last accessed 26 April 2018.)

Orsi, J., Y. Eskandari-Qajar, E. Weissman, M. Hall, A. Mann and M. Luna. 2013. *Policies for Shareable Cities: A Sharing Economy Policy Primer for Urban Leaders.* Oakland, CA: Shareable and the Sustainable Economies Law Center. Online at http://www.shareable.net/blog/policies-for-a-shareable-city.

Provoost, M. 2013. "From Welfare City to Neoliberal Utopia." *Strelka Talk*. Online at http://vimeo.com/64392842. (Last accessed 20 October 2017).

Rifkin, J. 2014. *The Zero Marginal Cost Society: The Internet of Things, the Collaborative Commons, and the Eclipse of Capitalism.* New York: Palgrave Macmillan.

Sen, A. 2001. *Development as Freedom.* Oxford: Oxford University Press.

Sennett, R. 2012. "No One Likes a City That's Too Smart." *The Guardian*, 4 December. Online at http://www.theguardian.com/commentisfree/2012/dec/04/smart-city-rio-songdo-masdar.

Seyfang, G. and A. Smith, 2007. "Grassroots Innovations for Sustainable Development: Towards a New Research and Policy Agenda." *Environmental Politics*, 16(4): 584–603.

ShareNL. 2017. Website: http://www.sharenl.nl/amsterdam-sharing-city/ (last accessed 20 October 2017).

Sharma, A. 2018. "Demystifying the Current State of India's Ambitious Smart City Mission." *Digit*, 31 January. Online at: https://www.digit.in/internet-of-things/demystifying-the-current-state-of-indias-ambitious-smart-city-mission-39370.html (last accessed 26 April 2018).

Sidewalk Toronto. 2018. Website: https://sidewalktoronto.ca (last accessed 26 April 2018).

Smart Cities Mission. 2016. Website. Ministry of Housing and Urban Affairs, Government of India. http://smartcities.gov.in/content/ (last accessed 26 April 2018).

Söderström, O., T. Paasche and F. Klauser. 2014. "Smart Cities as Corporate Storytelling." *City*, 18(3): 307–320.

Townsend, A.M. 2013. *Smart Cities: Big Data, Civic Hackers, and the Quest for a New Utopia.* New York: WW Norton & Company.

Trindade, E.P., M.P.F. Hinnig, E.M. da Costa, J.S. Marques, R.C. Bastos and T. Yigit-canlar. 2017. "Sustainable Development of Smart Cities: A Systematic Review of the Literature." *Journal of Open Innovation: Technology, Market, and Complexity*, 3(11). doi:10.1186/s40852–40017–0063–0062.

Vanolo, A. 2014a. "Smartmentality: The Smart City as Disciplinary Strategy." *Urban Studies*, 51(5): 883–898.

Vanolo, A. 2014b. "Whose Smart City?" *Open Democracy*, 8 April. Online at: https://www.opendemocracy.net/opensecurity/alberto-vanolo/whose-smart-city.

Wolfram, M. 2012. "Deconstructing Smart Cities: An Intertextual Reading of Concepts and Practices for Integrated Urban and ICT Development." Proceedings REAL CORP 2012 Tagungsband, 14–16 May, Schwechat. Online at: http://www.corp.at (last accessed 20 October 2017).

14

PSEUDONYMISATION AND THE SMART CITY

Considering the General Data Protection Regulation

Maria Helen Murphy

Introduction

Smart cities, driven by big data, clearly pose significant data protection and privacy challenges (Kitchin 2016a; Kitchin 2016b). While the popular conversation around smart cities often focuses on their futuristic potential, data driven planning is common policy for many governments and has been for several years. Accordingly, the legal and ethical issues of smart cities are evident, and the data protection challenges are being tackled in the present – if not always in a satisfactory manner. At this point, it is almost trite to comment that data protection law is outdated and unsuited to the modern context (McCullagh 2009; Information Commissioner's Office 2008). While the original Data Protection Convention of 1981 and the Data Protective Directive of 1995 (DPD) both attempted to boldly address an emerging issue, there are clear shortcomings in how the data protection principles and rights enshrined in those documents have been implemented and enforced. The General Data Protection Regulation (GDPR) is designed as an update to these laws and endeavours to respond to the modern environment. With the Regulation set to apply from May 2018, it is an opportune time to consider its implications for the development of smart cities and to assess whether it is fit for purpose.

It should be noted that while the GDPR constitutes a significant change in the data protection landscape, Recital 9 of the GDPR states that the "objectives and principles of Directive 95/46/EC remain sound" (Kennedy and Murphy 2017: 100). Accordingly, the GDPR still operates by placing certain obligations on those who process data (data controllers and data processors) and by providing rights to those whose data is processed (data subjects). In order to process personal data, data controllers must have an adequate legal basis to process the data and must comply with the data protection principles at all times. The grounds for lawful processing under the GDPR are similar to those provided for under the DPD. Adequate bases for processing include: consent; necessary for the performance of a contract; necessary for compliance with a legal obligation; necessary for the protection of vital interests; necessary for a task in the public interest or in the exercise of official authority; or necessary for the legitimate interests of the data controller except where overridden by the rights of the data subject (GDPR: art 6(1)).[1] In addition to having an adequate basis for processing, the data controller must also follow the data protection principles. These principles require that personal data be:

a   processed lawfully, fairly and in a transparent manner in relation to the data subject
b   collected for specified, explicit and legitimate purposes and not further processed in a manner that is incompatible with those purposes;
c   adequate, relevant and limited to what is necessary in relation to the purposes for which they are processed
d   accurate and, where necessary, kept up to date; every reasonable step must be taken to ensure that personal data that are inaccurate, having regard to the purposes for which they are processed, are erased or rectified without delay
e   kept in a form which permits identification of data subjects for no longer than is necessary for the purposes for which the personal data are processed;
f   processed in a manner that ensures appropriate security of the personal data, including protection against unauthorised or unlawful processing and against accidental loss, destruction or damage, using appropriate technical or organisational measures.

The ePrivacy Regulation, designed to replace the existing ePrivacy Directive, was originally scheduled also to apply from May 2018, but that deadline will no longer be met.[2] It is important to note that once the ePrivacy Regulation is finalised and in force, it will "particularise" and "complement" the GDPR. While the final content of the ePrivacy Regulation is uncertain, the eventual text will have implications for the smart city – particularly as regards its extended application to non-traditional telecom operators, machine-to-machine communication, and terminal equipment. For example, Recital 12 of the European Commission Proposal states that "the principle of confidentiality enshrined in this Regulation should also apply to the transmission of machine-to-machine communications." In spite of this, significant uncertainty remains regarding how the proposed ePrivacy Regulation would apply in scenarios pertinent to the smart city. For example, the ePrivacy confidentiality principle applies only to "content" or "metadata" and Härting argues that the "raw data" captured by IoT devices is unlikely to qualify as either category under the definitions set out in the proposed Regulation (Härting 2017: 6–7; ePrivacy Regulation: art 4(3)). Due to the continued uncertainty on this and other issues, this chapter focuses on the potential impact of the agreed text of the GDPR.

Key changes and challenges in the smart city

A number of changes in the GDPR will impact the smart city and its component parts. The provision for enhanced data subject rights, for example, raises questions of feasibility in the smart city context. Among the additional rights are an express right to be forgotten and data portability (GDPR: arts 17 and 20). Challenges also remain with the concept of purpose limitation due to the unpredictability of smart city data use; in fact, purpose limitation appears "antithetical to the rationale of big data and the functioning of data markets which seek to hoard data in case they have possible future value" (Kitchin 2014: 178; Mayer-Schonberger and Cukier 2013). While consent is not the only legal basis for lawful data processing, it is often the stated ground (Sadowski and Pasquale 2015). The difficulty of obtaining freely given and informed consent in the smart city context is well recognised (Luger and Rodden 2013; Edwards 2016). Flaws with the traditional model of notice and consent are magnified for an individual moving through a smart city (Kitchin 2016a). The experience is not conducive to providing effective choice or even awareness of the amount of data being collected (Jones and Leta 2015). The truly smart city depends on the interconnection of a multitude of devices and ubiquitous computing. While the embedded and seamless nature of such technologies makes the obtaining of initial consent a challenge, the continued and often automated re-sharing of data presents an obstacle to authentic consent that may be insurmountable in the absence of a technological breakthrough. As pointed out by the Article 29 Working Party, the "possibility to renounce certain services or features of an IoT device is more a theoretical concept than a real alternative" (Article 29 Working Party 2014a: 7). Accordingly, it is uncertain whether consent can be a meaningful ground for processing information in the smart city (Edwards 2016; Kosta 2013).

The consent conundrum will persist under the framework of the GDPR which straitens the criteria for valid consent. Under the GDPR, data controllers will not only be required to demonstrate that consent was specific, informed, and freely given, but must also show that it was unambiguous on the basis of a statement or clear affirmative action (GDPR: recital 32). In spite of the aforementioned weaknesses of consent as a lawful basis, the proposed ePrivacy Regulation places significant emphasis on the concept of consent and adopts the same definition and conditions of consent as those laid out in the GDPR (ePrivacy Regulation: art 9 and recital 18). As data collected as part of a smart city apparatus is likely to disperse in complex ways, it will be particularly challenging to ensure that a data subject's right to withdraw consent "at any time" will be as easily exercised as the giving of consent. Moreover, the GDPR states that consent may not be considered "freely given" where consent is a precondition for the provision of a service that is not necessary for the performance of that contract (GDPR: art 7). While there is some promise in the "tagging" of personal data with metadata describing the consents associated with that information and enabling the withdrawal of that consent, the difficulty of obtaining "meaningful consent" and the big data capacity to draw inferences remain (ENISA 2015: 46). Others argue that consent is a poor basis for legal processing and that a shift to a "responsible use framework" is more logical at this point (Executive Office of the President 2014: 56; Edwards 2016).

Data protection by design and by default

It seems clear that the Article 17 DPD requirement to adopt appropriate technical and organisational data security measures is a forerunner of "data protection by design and by default" as mandated by Article 25 GDPR (Brown 2014; Murphy 2015). Due to the Article 17 requirement being contained in a Directive as opposed to a Regulation, it is unsurprising that the mandate has been interpreted differently by Member States. Some countries have not elaborated on what "appropriate technical and organisational measures" entail, while others have set out in detail what appropriate security measures should be implemented in specific circumstances (Hon, Hörnle, and Millard, 2012; Esayas 2015).

The GDPR's development of the requirement originally introduced under the DPD takes guidance from privacy-by-design principles (Cavoukian 2009a). In reflection of privacy-by-design's dictum that privacy risks should be considered from the outset, Article 25 GDPR states that data controllers must implement appropriate technical and organisational measures in order to protect data protection principles in an effective manner "both at the time of the determination of the means for processing and at the time of the processing itself" (GDPR: art 25(1)). It is notable that Article 25 specifically highlights pseudonymisation as an example of a technology designed to implement data protection principles, a practice considered in more detail with respect to the smart city below.

The categorisation of data

Whether or not a datum is considered "personal" determines whether data protection law – with its processing restrictions and data subject rights – applies. The GDPR is explicit as regards its application to "the protection of natural persons with regard to the processing of personal data" (GDPR: art 1(1)). In the GDPR "personal data" is defined as "any information relating to an identified or identifiable natural person ('data subject')". According to the Regulation an identifiable natural person is "one who can be identified, directly or indirectly, in particular by reference to an identifier" such as a name, an identification number or "to one or more factors specific to the physical, physiological, genetic, mental, economic, cultural or social identity of that natural person" (GDPR: art 4(1)). As a result, data protection rights and responsibilities do not apply to information deemed not to be personally identifiable and Recital 26 clarifies that data protection rules do not apply to anonymous information (GDPR: recital 26). The logic of this exclusion appears to be based on the reasoning that there is no privacy harm – and as a result no privacy interest – implicated in the processing of non-personally identifiable data. Under the cloak of anonymity, individuals can act free from scrutiny and by virtue of that freedom can engage in free expression and thought without fear of reprisal (Nissenbaum 1999).

It should be noted, however, that while smart cities may often rely on ostensibly anonymous data, the ease with which data points can be correlated across different databases means that "it is now rare for data generated by user activity to be completely and irreversibly anonymised" (European Data Protection Supervisor 2014; Ohm 2010; Edwards 2016). As pointed out by Kitchin (2014: 172), "in an age of big data the strategy of de-identification provides only a weak form of privacy because it is possible to reverse engineer the process by combing and combining data sets" (Narayanan and Shmatikov 2010). In fact, evidence suggests that just four "spatio-temporal points" are required in order to uniquely identify 95 per cent of individuals (de Montjoye et al. 2013: fig. 2; see also Ohm 2010). In spite of its intuitive appeal, "the notion of perfect anonymisation has been exposed as a myth" (Rubinstein and Hartzog 2016: 703). While certain more labour-intensive anonymisation techniques are very difficult to reverse, it is clear that many previously trusted techniques are vulnerable (Ohm 2010).

Notwithstanding re-identification risks, the GDPR attempts to respond to the oft-expressed concerns of data controllers by setting some limits as to what can reasonably be considered "re-identifiable" data. While in keeping with a tradition of favouring a pragmatic approach to anonymisation, the approach of the Regulation is unsatisfactory from a data protection perspective (Walden 2002). To assist in determining whether data is "reasonably likely to be used to identify the natural person", the GDPR refers to so-called "objective factors", including cost and time required for identification (GDPR: recital 26). Such an approach is, of course, in the interests of data controllers who wish to use de-identified data outside of the scope of data protection law. While the practical standard appears to be designed to head off broad-brush claims that all information can be re-identified, the requirement to consider the "available technology at the time of the processing" ignores the reality that technology evolves and new capabilities are being developed constantly.

As data is considered by many to be a valuable commodity, the honeypot effect increases the likelihood that data currently impenetrable to re-identification techniques may not always be so. Once such a method is developed, or once a re-identification attack is successful, the previously anonymised data should properly be considered personal data. At that point, however, it may be too late for the protection of the fundamental rights of the data subject. This will be particularly problematic where the data has already been transferred outside of the European Union. Moreover, such an approach completely upends the GDPR's apparent commitment to the principle of privacy-by-design which requires privacy consideration to be built-in from the planning stages. While some risk is created by the pragmatic formulation, it should be noted that similar accommodations for "reasonableness" in the DPD have been interpreted strictly by the Article 29 Working Party. Even though the DPD states that in order to be considered anonymised, data should not be re-identifiable by any "means likely reasonably to be used", the

Working Party has clarified that re-identification must be "'reasonably' impossible" in order to be exempt from the DPD (Article 29 Working Party 2014b: 8). As pointed out by Rubinstein and Hartzog (2016: 746), "'reasonably' impossible is clearly a self-contradictory notion". As a result of the legislative distinction between personal and non-personal data, the categorisation of information is a crucial threshold question that has multifarious implications for the collecting entity, in terms of both compliance costs and the freedom to innovate without restraint.

Pseudonymisation as solution?

The decision to explicitly acknowledge within the text of the legislation a new category of pseudonymised data is representative of the search for compromise that is characteristic of this area of law. Even though the institutions of the European Union have increasingly embraced their human rights role, the original goals of the Union remain prominent as evidenced by the EU's "Big Data Strategy" which references the importance of stimulating research, innovation, and competitiveness in data (Commission of the European Communities 2014). The search for balance is evident from Article 1 of the GDPR which recognises the "right to the protection of personal data", but also states that the "free movement of personal data within the Union shall be neither restricted nor prohibited for reasons connected with the protection of natural persons with regard to the processing of personal data" (GDPR: art 1(2)(3)). Where data is hailed as the new oil, a boon for the economy, the cure for cancer, and the end of traffic jams, those who seek to put restrictions on how data is used are sometimes written-off as protectionists, tin-foil hatters, and dinosaurs (Yakowitz 2011).

For some, the potential of pseudonymisation represents an alternative to the failed promise of anonymisation (Barocas and Nissenbaum 2014). The approach taken in the GDPR to the question of pseudonymisation appears to attempt to reconcile the fears of the data protection advocates – wary of excessive collection – with the desires of the big data evangelists – hungry for more data and less restrictions. "Pseudonymisation" is defined in the GDPR as a means of processing personal data

> in such a manner that the personal data can no longer be attributed to a specific data subject without the use of additional information, provided that such additional information is kept separately and is subject to technical and organisational measures to ensure that the personal data are not attributed to an identified or identifiable natural person.
>
> *(GDPR: art 4(5))*

In contrast to truly anonymised data, this definition clearly states that pseudonymised data continues to be personal data as defined by the Regulation. While pseudonymised data – amenable as it is to the singling out of data subjects and cross dataset linkability – is already subject to the DPD, misconceptions on this point appear common among data controllers (Article 29 Working Party 2014a; Esayas 2015). Pseudonymisation comes in various forms of course, but pseudonymised data may be vulnerable to reidentification through the key-holder directly reidentifying the data, brute force attacks, and data breaches (Article 29 Working Party 2014a; Esayas 2015). As a result, the concession to the data protection advocates in the GDPR is the recognition of the perils of a "pseudonymisation as solution" mentality and the explicit acknowledgement that pseudonymised data is still personal data that falls within the scope of the Regulation. Recital 28 describes pseudonymisation as a tool that can both assist data controllers in meeting their obligations and protect data subjects.

A major purpose behind the introduction of the category of pseudonymised data in the Regulation is the incentivisation of data controllers to implement the privacy enhancing technique. The GDPR encourages adoption of the measure in a number of ways. For example, whether or not data has been pseudonymised will be relevant to the question of whether a form of processing is incompatible with the purposes for which it was initially collected (GDPR: art 6(4)). As data stores can be viewed as a gold mine, loosening the purpose limitation when data is pseudonymised paves the way for additional uses, and assuages some concerns of those wishing to capitalise on the big data potential.

Due to the serious repercussions of a data breach for the personal data rights of a data subject, the GDPR introduces more stringent and far-reaching rules on notification than existed previously in the general data protection sphere.[3] Under the new regime, data controllers will be required to notify the appropriate supervisory authority "without undue delay and, where feasible, not later than 72 hours after having become aware of it" (GDPR: art 33). There is an important proviso to this requirement, however, that discharges the duty to notify where the controller is able to demonstrate that the data breach is "unlikely to result in a risk to the rights and freedoms of natural persons" (see also GDPR: recital 85). While we await further guidelines regarding the circumstances in which a data controller is required to notify, some data controllers may wish to avoid such disclosure where the data breach includes personal but pseudonymised data. If the key that would enable the data to be reidentified was not exposed in the breach, for example, a controller may argue that such data is "unlikely to result in a risk to the rights and freedoms of natural persons". Even if the controller chooses to notify the relevant supervisory authority, they are likely to argue against notifying data subjects – or indeed the general public – due to the reduced privacy risk associated with pseudonymised data. Article 34 GDPR states that data subjects need not be notified if "appropriate technical and organisational protection measures" have been implemented that "render the personal data unintelligible to any person who is not authorised to access it". As data breaches cause significant reputational damage and undermine customer confidence, such an outcome would clearly be desirable from the perspective of data controllers.

Another incentive is provided with the assurance that the pseudonymisation of data can be used as evidence of data protection by design and the implementation of appropriate security measures within an organisation (GDPR: arts 25(1) and 32 (1)(a)). Recital 78 states that data controllers should be able to demonstrate compliance with the Regulation by adopting internal policies and measures in accordance with the principles of data protection by design and default. The fact that pseudonymisation is the only technical or organisational measure explicitly mentioned in Article 25 strongly signals that pseudonymisation of personal data will be considered good practice under the GDPR (GDPR: art 25(1)). Interestingly, the GDPR anticipates that "an approved certification mechanism" may be used to demonstrate compliance with the data protection by design and default mandate (GDPR: art 25(3)).

Compliance through concession

The construal of anonymisation and pseudonymisation has been a major area of divergence under the Data Protection Directive (European Council 2012; Polonetsky, Tene, and Finch 2016). The Article 29 Working Party has typically taken quite a rigid view of what data can be considered exempt from data protection requirements by reason of de-identification (Article 29 Working Party 2014b; El Emam and Alvarez 2015). Some have suggested that this is due to the Working Party being comprised of regulators with an unrealistic idea of what level of anonymity can be achieved (Esayas 2015). It has been suggested that the "all or nothing" approach can discourage the adoption of technological solutions that can have genuinely privacy enhancing effects (Strobl, Cave, and Walley 2000; Walden 2002). The reasoning implies that if a data controller does not believe they will be given credit for the adoption of privacy enhancing technologies, they may simply decide to allocate resources elsewhere.

In some ways, this reasoning conflicts with a key underlying premise of privacy-by-design as originally articulated by Ann Cavoukian (2009b). A central foundation of privacy-by-design is the notion that "positive-sum" solutions – that enable privacy protection and facilitate progress – are possible. The type of cost benefit analysis that would lead to a data controller eschewing privacy controls like anonymisation runs contrary to the philosophy of privacy-by-design. The GDPR attempts to address this conundrum and incentivise data controllers into embracing the privacy-by-design approach. In addition to recommending the adoption of certain technical measures, including encryption and pseudonymisation, the Regulation also endorses the adoption of a privacy-by-design "mindset" by encouraging data controllers to

> take into account the right to data protection when developing and designing such products, services and applications and, with due regard to the state of the art, to make sure that data controllers and processors are able to fulfil their data protection obligations.
>
> *(GDPR: recital 78)*

In addition to placing data protection by design on a mandatory footing, the GDPR also aims to incentivise its embrace by lessening certain obligations when privacy enhancing technologies are utilised. Encouraging the use of pseudonymisation techniques was a prominent aspect of this effort in the text of the Regulation and has, as a result, served as a particular point of focus in this chapter. The emphasis on pseudonymisation as a minimising technique suggests awareness by the drafters of the failure of anonymisation as a catch-all privacy solution (Polonetsky, Tene, and Finch 2016; Rubinstein and Hartzog 2016; Ohm 2010). In fact, from a certain perspective, pseudonymisation may appear to reflect the perfect promise of privacy-by-design. If data is pseudonymised, privacy is better protected and data controllers are rewarded with more freedom to process data while remaining within the bounds of data protection law. On closer inspection, the promise does not hold up.

There are several technical weaknesses with pseudonymisation as the smart city solution, but there are also key issues of ethics and understanding. While transparency is a fundamental value endorsed in the GDPR, telling data subjects that their data is pseudonymised has the potential to be misleading and even deceptive (see GDPR: arts 5(1)(a) and 12, and recitals 39 and 58). For one, describing data as "pseudonymous" sounds very similar to "anonymous" to the average person. "Anonymous" is a term with significant rhetorical power (Sweeney 1997: 100; Rubinstein and Hartzog 2016). As a result of this association, individuals may be more likely to agree to and support a vast array of processing types that they might not approve of if they truly understood the distinction (Ohm 2010).

Edwards (2016) has criticised the introduction of the term pseudonymisation into the GDPR as the "sudden invention of an ill thought out category". The decision of the European Union to persist with the category of personal data and to endorse pseudonymisation as an important technological solution indicates an unwillingness to forgo the existing model. While this is not surprising in light of the lengthy and heavily lobbied institutional process, it is concerning from a privacy perspective, and is suggestive of privacy theatre (Ohm 2010; Schwartz 2008). This is problematic for a number of reasons but it is particularly concerning where it may result in differing choices and behaviours among a citizenry under the illusion that their data is protected.

This chapter does not dispute the merit of pseudonymisation as a beneficial part of a larger approach to protecting the privacy of data subjects. Nor does it disavow the merits of privacy-by-design. In fact, the author welcomes the introduction of a mandate requiring the implementation of data protection by design and by default. Notwithstanding this, while the legal requirement in support of privacy-by-design is likely to encourage greater adoption of privacy enhancing measures, it is certainly not a panacea. Implementing privacy-by-design in complex systems is a significant challenge and comprehensive solutions are unlikely. The history of the anonymisation debate should inform our expectations and while guidelines and technical specifications will have an important role to play under the new regime, a critical privacy-by-design mindset must be maintained at all times (Koops and Leenes

2014). Most crucially, where anonymisation or pseudonymisation techniques are utilised, it is incumbent on data controllers to put in place robust internal governance structures that facilitate the continual review of their data's reidentifiability alongside consistent application of all data protection principles. While the GDPR appears to strive for such an outcome, its formulation is liable to varied and unsatisfactory interpretation.

Notes

1 Public organs cannot rely on "legitimate interests" as a legal basis for data processing.
2 Proposal for a Regulation of the European Parliament and of the Council Concerning the Respect for Private Life and the Protection of Personal Data in Electronic Communications and Repealing Directive 2002/58/EC (Regulation on Privacy and Electronic Communications).
3 Although see the notification requirements under the existing ePrivacy Directive. It should also be noted that the Irish Data Protection Commissioner issued a Code of Practice on personal data security breaches in 2011.

References

Article 29 Working Party. 2014a. *Opinion 8/2014 on the recent developments on the Internet of Things*. http://ec.europa.eu/justice/data-protection/article-29/documentation/opinion-re commendation/files/2014/wp223_en.pdf.
Article 29 Working Party. 2014b. *Opinion 05/2014 on data anonymisation techniques*. http:// ec.europa.eu/justice/dataprotection/.
Barocas, S., and H. Nissenbaum. 2014. "Big data's end run around anonymity and consent." In *Privacy, Big Data, and the Public Good Frameworks for Engagement*, edited by J. Lane, V. Stodden, S. Bender and H. Nissenbaum, 44–75. New York: Cambridge University Press.
Brown, I. 2014. "Britain's smart meter programme: A case study in privacy by design." *International Review of Law, Computers & Technology* 28(2): 172–184.
Cavoukian, A. 2009a. *Privacy by design*. Information and Privacy Commissioner. http:// www.ipc.on.ca/images/resources/privacybydesign.pdf.
Cavoukian, A. 2009b. *The 7 foundational principles*. Information and Privacy Commissioner. https://www.ipc.on.ca/images/Resources/7foundationalprinciples.pdf.
Commission of the European Communities. 2014. *Towards a thriving data-driven economy*. COM (2014)442. http://ec.europa.eu/transparency/regdoc/rep/1/2014/EN/1-2014-442-EN-F1-1. Pdf.
de Montjoye, Y., C. Hidalgo, M. Verleysen and V. Blondel. 2013. "Unique in the crowd: The privacy bounds of human mobility." *Scientific Reports* 3(1376): 1–5.
Edwards, L. 2016. "Privacy, security and data protection in smart cities: A critical EU law perspective." *European Data Protection Law Review* 2(1): 28–58.
El Emam, K., and C. Alvarez. 2015. "A critical appraisal of the Article 29 Working Party Opinion 05/2014 on data anonymization techniques." *International Data Privacy Law* 5(1): 73–87.
ENISA. 2015. "Privacy by design in big data." https://www.enisa.europa.eu/news/enisa-news/privacy-by-design-in-big-data-an-overview-of-privacy-enhancing-technologies-in-the-era-of-big-data-analytics.
Esayas, S. 2015. "The role of anonymisation and pseudonymisation under the EU data privacy rules: beyond the 'all or nothing' approach." *European Journal of Law and Technology* 6(2).

European Council. 2012. *Evaluation of the implementation of the Data Protection Directive, Annex 2.* http://lobbyplag.eu/governments/.

European Data Protection Supervisor. 2014. *Preliminary opinion of the European Data Protection Supervisor on privacy and competitiveness in the age of big data: The interplay between data protection, competition law and consumer protection in the digital economy.* https://edps.europa.eu/sites/edp/files/publication/14-03-26_competitition_law_big_data_en.pdf.

Executive Office of the President. 2014. *Big data: Seizing opportunities, preserving values.* https://obamawhitehouse.archives.gov/sites/default/files/docs/big_data_privacy_report_may_1_2014.pdf.

Härting, N. 2017. *Study on the impact of the proposed ePrivacy Regulation.* https://www.informationpolicycentre.com/uploads/5/7/1/0/57104281/epr_-_gutachten-final-4.0_3_.pdf.

Hon, W., J. Hörnle and C. Millard. 2012. "Data protection jurisdiction and cloud computing – when are cloud users and providers subject to EU data protection law? The cloud of unknowing, part 3." *International Review of Law, Computers & Technology* 26(2–3): 129–164.

Information Commissioner's Office. 2008. "UK privacy watchdog spearheads debate on the future of European privacy law." http://www. ico.gov.uk/upload/documents/press-releases/2008/icoleads-debate_070708.pdf.

Jones, A., and M. Leta. 2015. "Privacy without screens and the internet of other people's things." *Idaho Law Review* 51(3): 639–660.

Kennedy, R., and M.H. Murphy. 2017. *Information and communications technology law in Ireland.* Dublin: Clarus.

Kitchin, R. 2014. *The data revolution: Big data, open data, data infrastructures and their consequences.* London: Sage.

Kitchin, R. 2016a. *Getting smarter about smart cities: Improving data privacy and data security.* Data Protection Unit, Department of the Taoiseach, Dublin, Ireland. http://www.taoiseach.gov.ie/eng/Publications/Publications_2016/Smart_Cities_Report_January_2016.pdf.

Kitchin, R. 2016b. "The ethics of smart cities and urban science." *Philosophical Transactions* 374(2083): 1–15.

Koops, B., and R. Leenes. 2014. "Privacy regulation cannot be hardcoded. A critical comment on the 'privacy by design' provision in data-protection law." *International Review of Law Computers & Technology* 28(2): 159–171.

Kosta, E. 2013. *Consent in European data protection law.* Hague: Brill/Nijhoff.

Luger, E., and T. Rodden. 2013. "An informed view on consent for Ubicomp." In *Proceedings of the 2013 ACM international joint conference on pervasive and ubiquitous computing.* New York: ACM.

Mayer-Schonberger, V., and K. Cukier, 2013. *Big data: A revolution that will transform how we live, work, and think.* New York: John Murray.

McCullagh, K. 2009. "Protecting 'privacy' through control of 'personal' data processing: A flawed approach." *International Review of Law, Computers and Technology,* 23(1–2): 13–24.

Murphy, M.H. 2015. "The introduction of smart meters in Ireland: Privacy implications and the role of privacy by design." *Dublin University Law Journal* 38(1): 191–207.

Narayanan, A., and V. Shmatikov. 2010. "Privacy and security myths and fallacies of 'personally identifiable information.'" *Communications of the ACM* 53(6): 24–26.

Nissenbaum, H. 1999. "The meaning of anonymity in an information age." *The Information Society,* 15(2): 141–144.

Ohm, P. 2010. "Broken promises of privacy: Responding to the surprising failure of anonymization." *UCLA Law Review* 57: 1701–1777.

Polonetsky, J., O. Tene and K. Finch. 2016. "Shades of gray: Seeing the full spectrum of practical data de-identification." *Santa Clara Law Review* 56(3): 593–629.

Rubinstein, I., and W. Hartzog. 2016. "Anonymization and risk." *Washington Law Review* 91: 703–760.

Sadowski, J., and F. Pasquale. 2015. "The spectrum of control: A social theory of the smart city." *First Monday* 20(7).

Schwartz, P. 2008. "Reviving telecommunications surveillance law." *University of Chicago Law Review* 75(1): 287–315.

Strobl, J., E. Cave and T. Walley. 2000. "Data protection legislation: interpretation and barriers to research." *British Medical Journal* 321: 890–892.

Sweeney, L. 1997. "Weaving technology and policy together to maintain confidentiality." *Journal of Law, Medicine, and Ethics* 25(2–3): 98–110.

Walden, I. 2002. "Anonymising personal data." *International Journal of Law and Information Technology* 10(2): 224–237.

Yakowitz, J. 2011. "Tragedy of the data commons." *Harvard Journal of Law and Technology* 25(1): 1–67.

15

THE PRIVACY PARENTHESIS

Private and public spheres, smart cities and big data

Leighton Evans

Introduction

The motivation for this chapter is to address how the smart city as a set of technological interventions in the everyday life of urban citizens may reposition and reconceptualise everyday privacy. The concept of the smart city deployed here is as an amalgamation of the processes and techniques of big data deployed to increase the efficiency of city processes through the provision of continuous streams of data and real-time regulation of city systems (Townsend, 2013). The fundamental logic and essence of big data, to transform everyday objects and entities into sites of data production for quantitative analysis, sits uneasily with notions of privacy in a "traditional" spatial sense as spaces away from authoritative gaze. Smart cities, driven by big data, clearly pose significant data protection and privacy challenges (Kitchin, 2016: 1). Indeed, the technologies deployed in smart city solutions have profound social, political and ethical effects. This includes the introduction of new forms of social regulation, control and governance; the extension of surveillance and eroding of privacy; and the enabling of predictive profiling and social sorting (Kitchin, 2016; Vanolo, 2014). The desire to achieve efficiency and control through smart city technologies then is in a tense relationship with the very concept of private space and private citizenhood. Indeed, the use of computational technique (to borrow the usage from Ellul, 1973) and the ontotheological status of computation in society (see Berry, 2011; 2015) both predicts and necessitates an invasion and structural change of private space in order for such a computational worldview to operate. The all-pervasive data mining and data processing that is the essential element of computation (and the smart city concept) requires a coding of activities that translates the activities of the private sphere so they can be encoded as data, and for that data to be processed. It is true that data protection and other legal constraints work to shape the kind of activity permitted (and to hide and obfuscate activities that are not permitted). However, the acceptance of the digital into the private and the normalisation of the relationship between digital devices, software and the activities of the private sphere have reduced such protection to post-hoc solutions that ignore the reality that the private sphere has been transformed by the presence of new technologies.

This chapter argues that a fundamental aspect of the private – its separateness – has been compromised by the emergence, use and proliferation of digital technology, and that the result of this is a re-spatialisation of the private away from the spatial and into the phenomenological, behavioural, epistemological and practical. This marks a major departure from the changes to privacy in previous epochs, which have privileged its spatial differentness. Here, the nature of parenthesis as a bracketing off is especially useful, with particular regards to Husserl's (1976) use of the term in his phenomenology. While this does not argue that privacy lies with the privileging of mental objects, it does contend that privacy becomes a property not of spatial boundaries but of orientation towards technology and orientation to privacy as a mode of everyday existence. This turn in privacy is therefore substantially different to the spatial privacy of the modern age, but in itself retains a parenthetic relationship with other realms of human activity.

Drawing on Arendt's exegesis of the development of the private sphere and notions of different epochs of the private sphere and their importance in citizenship, this chapter argues that the comparison between the privacy desired by critics of the current situation and the privacy afforded to persons in the digital world constitutes a dialectic that reveals an emerging – but currently undefined – epoch of private space and the private sphere (as a sector of societal life in which an individual enjoys a degree of authority unhampered by interventions by state, government or other institutions). The private has always been a separate sphere, delineated by spatial and affective factors that gave it clear difference from the political, social and public domains. The computational logic of digital media, with industrial level big data collection fuelling algorithmic governance of spaces and citizens, is fundamentally incompatible with the private sphere as detached from the public sphere (Papacharissi, 2010). Technologies that are critical to the functioning of the smart city are part of this algorithmic governance, in part because the concept of the smart city promotes a strong emphasis on creating technical solutions and overly promotes top-down technocratic forms of governance, rather than political or social solutions to identified issues in civic governance (Greenfield, 2013). For example, smartphones continuously communicate their location to telecommunications companies through cell mast connection, GPS or connection to wi-fi spots. At home or on the move, locational data is now collected at all times, in a pervasive, continuous, automatic and cheap manner. Moreover, applications on smartphones access and transfer this information and share the information with third parties (Leszczynski, 2016: 240). A smart city that accesses this data flow to rationalise footfall in the city is – no matter how anonymised the data may be – involved in the blurring of public and private through their use and legitimisation of such data. Notions of social or ethical responsibility, or political responsibility, may be elided by the efficiencies afforded by the technological solutions which draw on this data.

Being watched and watching others (veillance) through continuous connectivity and opaque algorithmic functioning of computational devices in what was termed private space is a familiar current situation. This continual veillance (or auto-veillance) forces a transparency or openness upon spaces and places that were once considered private. The effect of this presence of technologies that reformat everyday life into data and the desire of private and governmental organisations (through processes and techniques of veillance that create transparency) to accrue, store and process this data to understand the data subject have irrevocably altered both the meaning and phenomena of privacy. However, claims to the "death of privacy" simplify the unfolding processes of remediation that are underway. The logic of computation does not eliminate privacy through forced transparency but instead repositions privacy as an affordance of living in a digitally-infused world that is realised through individual practices and orientations. The points of con-testation and resistance are scaled at the individual rather than societal level and constitute a negotiation with the expectations of being-digital in the world. The digital citizen is always moving between the private and public as a function of engagement with digital media that affords veillance and transparency (such as the smartphone continually bleeding out data outside of the circumspection of the user), and this indicates a coming or already-present epoch where privacy is not defined by property but by knowledge, awareness and caution of digital media.

This chapter concludes by outlining three ways in which privacy is reshaped away from spatial privacy by new smart city technologies. Privacy becomes a function of focal practices of technology usage (following Borgmann), epistemol-ogies of privacy, and orientation to computational devices (following Ihde and Heidegger). However, while these practices and knowledge-based attitudes to technology are indicative of a practice-based privacy, they are in a continual ten-sion with big data processes that are characterised by greater accessibility, usability and convenience. Privacy as a practice rather than spatial phenomenon therefore becomes a challenge rather than a given based on spatial positioning. The continual pressure to acquiesce to big data processes as a factor of their increasing presence gives a parenthetic character to privacy, where privacy is an active, chosen practice amidst processes of big data. No longer a given based on spatial practices, privacy requires phenomenological, epistemological, discursive and practical elements in opposition to normative practices of everyday media use that afford veillance and force transparency.

Parenthetic structure of privacy historically: The "bracketing away" of the private

The conceptualisation of the private realm, and contextualisation of its develop-ment, here is provided by the work of Hannah Arendt and to a lesser extent Jürgen Habermas. Arendt's extensive argument on the development of the private in *The*

Human Condition contextualises the bracketing off of the private that this chapter argues is a structural necessity of privacy that computation and computational technique threatens. While human life is always rooted in being with others (an observation rooted in Heideggerian thought and the concept of *mitsein*) (Arendt, 1998: 22), the private sphere serves to delineate activities into specific spheres of human action. Away from the private sphere, the politics sphere was the Greek instantiation of public life, and the social sphere (the coming together of people for a specific purpose that was non-political) a development of Roman society (Arendt, 1998: 23). The political and social stand in a direct opposition to the "natural association" whose centre is the home (Arendt, 1998: 24). In the Greek city-state, being social with others was not a "human" characteristic; the rise of the city-state gave rise to a distinction between the political and public, and of all human activities only action and speech constituted political action out of which rose human affairs (at least for Plato and Aristotle). The distinction between the private and the public sphere corresponds to the distinction between the household and political spheres, with the social sphere emerging in the modern age. Arendt makes much of the observation that freedom (and therefore the political being-with) was critical to Eudemonia, as freedom is essential to the achievement of the state of flourishing. With equality in the polis, historically it can be seen that the private was seen as a state of being that is significantly inferior to the public life – indeed, a state of privation compared to the public life, separated from and without the virtue of a life in public.

Such conceptions of the public life in this history are, of course, deeply problematic. A patriarchal polis like that outlined in Arendt's account is not desirable in the modern age. However, it serves to illustrate how the private sphere was both constructed by a comparative position with the political and seen as less desirable than the political. Through the Enlightenment and into modernity, the separateness of the private sphere is maintained while its status goes from privation to superiority over the public. This change in status begins with the structure of the family being absorbed across society (Arendt, 1998: 40), and the notion of a harmonious society that emerges from the structure of the household (Arendt, 1998: 44). The growth of the behavioural sciences (anthropology, sociology, politics) works to normalise this domination of the household, and legitimise the structures of the private in society (arguments familiar in the work of Heidegger, Foucault and others). The effect of this is to transform labour into the defining characteristic of public life, as politics spans the private and public spheres. This transformation of the public sphere (into a commons) is signified by the visible: dependent upon appearance and perceptions rather than actions and speech. Most critically though, the private sphere became held in property which results in wealth. Arendt argues that wealth had never been sacred to the common man before modernity (Arendt, 1998: 61), but the rise of the social sphere coincided with the private care for property that made wealth into a public concern. Society became organised around the concerns of property owners that demanded protection from the "public" because of this wealth (a concept that owes much to Locke). While private possessions and wealth may have undermined the prestige of the public sphere, they have also served to maintain the separation between the two even though the private has ascended to a position of dominance over the public. The parenthesis of the private sphere is spatial, political, economic and affective in that the conventions and logics of the private inform the politics and expectations of other spheres of human activity. As the private realm has become concerned with wealth and sovereignty, this has become the only concern left in modern society (Arendt, 1998: 68). The result is that a life spent in the public realm is shallow (Arendt, 1998: 71), where once it was rich in comparison with the private (or privation).

While the perception of the private over time has varied from privation to dominance in society according to Arendt's account, the separateness of this sphere has always been maintained. Habermas (1992) famously laments the structural transformation of the public sphere to a debased version of its former self, partially thanks to the advent and use of electronic media. It can be argued that at the time Habermas identifies this debasement occurring in the bourgeois public sphere, a similar transformation begins with the private sphere through the same influence. The structural transformation of the public sphere involved the intermingling of the private and public to such an extent that the domains of the private (economy, family, affect and emotion) became part of that public sphere to the detriment of the bourgeois sphere of rational, critical debate. In parallel, the separate nature of the private sphere was affectively altered by the dissolution of the parenthesis between private and public too, obtrusively bringing the concerns of public life into the private sphere (Papacharissi, 2010).

The digital erasing of the bracket

The parenthetic metaphor used here to describe the private sphere implies a separation from the public and social spheres, while maintaining an affective relationship on those spheres. To describe the dissolution of this parenthesis, I follow a line of thought which posits that the dominance of the morality and politics of the private over the public spheres could not be destroyed by a removal of privacy alone. To achieve this alteration of the private, there must be another set of concerns that replace the private as the key structuring ideas for the public sphere. As White (2015: 44) argues, it is difficult to conceive of the public and political spheres of today without the private. White (2015: 56) contends that the shift of epistemological authority from the archives and libraries of the public sphere to the databanks of the internet accessible in the private has fundamentally altered the balance of power and the boundaries between the spheres. The emergence of networked, digital technologies that reorganise human affairs along a logic of computational (or "big") data processing pose the transformative threat to this historically developed private parenthesis (Papacharissi, 2010). While digital devices seamlessly integrate themselves into everyday life, the presence of digital technology in everyday life itself alters the perception of what is private.

The presence of digital media that contribute to big data in everyday life results in an altered orientation to both everyday life and the processes of big data accrual and processing. Underpinning the present data revolution, van Dijck (2014: 197) describes the belief that people and behaviours can be known through the abstractive processes of quantification as "dataism": an ideological position on epistemology of human behaviour, but one that is reliant on the premise that data itself is unproblematic. As Drucker (2011) argues, data is assumed to be a given but data itself collapses the critical distance between the phenomenal world and its interpretation. The effect of this is to undo the interpretive stance on which humanistic interpretation of the world is based, and offer a Cartesian view of self, where the self is divorced from the body which can be measured, disciplined and quantified. This positioning of the corporeal as something that can be quantified and objectified has a similar interpretive turn for privacy. Instead of discrete spaces, private space is transformed into a measured, observed and surveilled space that has an altogether different character to the private space of modernity. This transformation is closely related to the phenomenological experience of being-with (see Evans, 2015) digital technology, as well as to the structural change in private space that the presence and functioning of digital technologies work to transform.

The kind of interpretive stance taken to the world is altered once data and its visualisation become a key part of understanding the world, and a change of the status and site of privacy is an effect of this change. Markham (2013) notes that data is assumed to be "beyond argument", objective and unquestionable. Ruckenstein (2014: 68) argues that such an assumption (when considering technology that quantifies the body) affects one's relationship to the body. For Dean (2010: 54), the product of this is "a gaze, or the perspective of another before the subject imagines itself". This preeminent subjective gaze is the view from data harvesting and visualisation, not knowledge and reflection. In effect, digital technologies position the user for the sake of the production of data on that user. The notion of a private self is therefore problematised; if knowledge of the position of the self in the world is the product of a computational gaze that provides data for analysis, then the idea that the subject of this (the self) can be outside this gaze is problematic – particularly in an environment optimised for the provision, harvesting and analysis of data such as the computationally-infused smart city. If the effect of the presence of computational digital media in everyday life is to comport one's own orientation to self towards the objective, data-influenced position then the environment and space one occupies can also be considered to be subject to this shift. In essence, an affected private self would see an accordingly affected private space and sphere.

If the essence of digital media technologies is the abstraction of environmental or human phenomena as data, then one effect is to hermeneutically position this information as an objective truth. The process of abstraction reveals processes that then become both the conscious concern of the user and a commodity that can be used to reshape behaviour and potentially be used in the commodity form as a source of revenue or profit. The technologies are of course increasingly popular; networked gadgets that are part of the nascent "Internet of Things" or "Internet of

Everything" enable data collection on an industrial scale through the close integration of networked technology to human activities. Such devices are an integral part of the smart city vision, providing a means of leveraging a sensor network within urban infrastructures and another means to track individuals moving through cities (Vincent, 2014), such as the vision of Sidewalks Labs (a division of Alphabet, the parent company of Google) in the Quayside district of Toronto (Crawford, 2018). It is this continual data harvesting that is complicit in the collapse of the parenthesis of the private sphere. These technologies operate across all spheres of human action, and make no differentiation between public, social or private space. The collection of spatial data and data on activities that take place in spaces that were considered private effects a perceptual, phenomenological and structural change on the private sphere, a flattening of that sphere into the sphere of data collection. Berry (2015: 14) argues that such technology is indicative of the emergence of a new industrial internet, "a computational, real-time streaming ecology that is reconfigured in terms of digital flows, fluidities and movement". The constant harvesting of information about everyday actions and the sharing and representation of that data can be seen as a form of capitalism of its own, such as in Foster and McChesney's (2014) concept of surveillance capitalism. While a user may receive information on their behaviours that can assist in behavioural changes or adaptations, the information garnered from the total users of a device can be used in aggregated form to inform decision making, planning or predictions on behaviour and movement in emergent "smart cities" where "big data" informs the everyday management of the environment – and the private or public nature of the space of activity is not a consideration (Greenfield, 2013; Townsend, 2013). This transformation re-shapes the private, from separated from but affecting public activity to being enrolled in the public. If the collection, processing and presenting of data become the organising principle of the public sphere, subsuming the private in the process, then the private has been both displaced as the key concern of society and as the sphere that organises the function of other spheres in society (Greenfield, 2013; Townsend, 2013).

Wilson (2011: 857) argues that processes of data production in cities are afforded legitimisation through processes of standardisation and objectification, and that these processes in turn are involved in the process of transduction of space (Dodge and Kitchin, 2011). While Wilson's argument concerns the physical characteristics of the city, rather than the processes that underlie human physical presence in the world, the two processes identified are useful in identifying the logic underpinning digital technologies. Standardisation refers both to the use of standardised technological artefacts and standardised processes used in the abstraction and collection of data concerning a physical entity. Digital technologies are critical in the production, processing and furthering of data as an objectification of phenomena. Kittler's (1999: 158–68) argument that media structures "human affairs" through the production, processing, transmission and storage of data is useful in linking this to privacy. The standardisation of process through the concretisation of the form of the device and the standard encoding and storage of data is in itself a standardisation of the abstraction of data. Objectification is the product of this standardisation; the abstraction of data from the private sphere (such as activity on social media) objectifies information that was previously beyond public conspicuousness and presents that data in a form that can be operationalised. The internal logic of this technology is both to harvest and share information.

The logic of the creation and continuation of a data stream that shapes human affairs à la Kittler (1999: 158–68) in effect argues that the media device is responsible for an ordering of the human in the world. In the case of big data technologies and the private sphere, the ordering is threefold: the human perception of the world is reordered; the human perception of the private sphere is reordered through the alteration of the perception of the world and through the role of the digital media in private spaces; and subjective notions of private spatiality are altered as the user is enrolled into the role of connected consumer and data producer that comes from the use of digital media. Digital technology is both co-existing with the user in private spaces but also responsible for a transformation of the activities of people in private spaces that renders the private public, and erases the parenthesis of the private in a general flattening of all spheres of human activity as data-producing. The product of this for the smart city – as an environment where data accumulation and processing is integral to fulfilling the purpose of the environment – is the erosion of the private sphere as a bracketed physical and phenomenological space from the circumspection of public and private authorities.

Remaking the bracket: The de-spatialisation of privacy

The presence of digital technologies in all spheres of everyday life, and the functioning of these technologies as data harvesting machines, performs a flattening of space that erodes the parenthesis of the private. The presence of data harvesting technologies in private space denies those spaces the parenthetic apartness from public or social space, and flattens all spaces of human activity into a homogenised space for data production, collection and processing. However, the idea of the end of the parenthesis is by no means meant to signal the end of privacy. The panoptical vision of the digital world is by no means a given, and privacy is still a critical aspect of human experience. Concerns about the erosion of private space are not erroneous or hyperbolic, but they do fail to recognise that privacy has an affective as well as spatial dimension, and these aspects of privacy need to be attended to if we are to understand privacy in an age of ubiquitous computing. Here, I want to outline briefly three possible approaches to understanding privacy that acknowledge that privacy is becoming de-spatialised, but allows for the affective dimension of privacy to be acknowledged and the parenthesis to be reconsidered along affective, epistemological and phenomenological dimensions.

Firstly, privacy can be thought of as a function of focal practices of technology usage, following the work of Albert Borgmann (1984). Focal practices refer to the holistic usage of technologies where not only the technological aspect of the device is considered, but also the environment and the possibilities of understanding the situation through technology usage are considered. With regards to privacy, the use of the device in a situation where the user or other people are oriented towards privacy will result in particular practices of usage (or non-usage) which can characterise privacy in a performative sense. The focal practice of privacy will characterise privacy in a particular way, and an understanding of such practice will allow for a performative, behavioural, pragmatic concept of privacy in an age of digital ubiquity. Such an approach to privacy requires both an appreciation of how to "be private" in using technology, and affordances on the part of designers and companies to allow for private usage if desired. While this kind of affordance can be seen in internet browsers (with incognito windows or private browsing tabs) how this relates to or could work with smart city technologies through a temporary opt-out model remains to be seen.

Secondly, and closely related to this, an understanding of a phenomenological orientation to computational devices (Ihde, 1990; Heidegger, 1977, Evans, 2015) can also help understand how deeply embodied technologies, and technologies that are present in private spaces but withdrawn from circumspection, can be encountered in a free manner. Here, technology is recognised as an ordering influence in the world, but its ordering of the world can be aligned to the aims and objectives of the user if that user takes the technology as a conduit to their own goals, rather than acting passively in the face of such technology. With regards to privacy, the understanding of the technology by the user and assimilation of the technology with the orientation to being-private are critical. This positions privacy as a mode of being, a bracketing off of the public world with technology rather than against it. This appears to be incommensurate with the current modes of smart city technology, but privacy-by-design principles (Hustinx, 2010) would aid in this orientation to privacy while maintaining technological use.

Thirdly, with a very different basis and conceptualisation of the private, epistemologies of privacy (see Kitchin, 2014: 168–174) become very important. This refers to how privacy operates as a known condition of human existence, and indeed how well known the threats to the sanctity of the private sphere are amongst the technology-using public. Advocating self-responsibility with regards to knowledge about privacy is problematic due to the vast number of and largely hidden nature of techniques of data collection. An understanding of the levels of knowledge of these techniques allied to an understanding of how this knowledge impacts on behaviour would bring another contour to the understanding of privacy as an affective rather than spatial phenomenon. Such an approach to educating and improving knowledge on the smart city and big data in general relies upon greater transparency (both in terms of cities and the technologies used), education on big data and smart cities for citizens and a continual provision of information on the uses of data. Whether the inclination or ability to force this change exists is questionable, although on-going revelations on social media data and psychological profiling regarding elections (Cadwalladr and Graham-Harrison, 2018) may provide an impetus for further public education and awareness on this issue.

These practices and knowledge-based attitudes to technology are in a continual tension with big data processes that are characterised by greater accessibility, usability and convenience. To "turn away" from technology in an epistemological, phenomenological or behavioural sense is not a given, and the means and methods of how people do and will do this need to be understood in greater detail than at present. Research that concentrates on how privacy has been violated can tell us only so much; how it is preserved after violation is the gap that needs to be filled. The private citizen of the data world is not yet an entity that is fully drawn; it is being moulded as the processes and presence of big data become both more apparent and more ingrained in everyday life. The idea of a space "away" from such processes becomes more fanciful by the day, and because of this the spatial parenthesis of private space is being challenged and removed. In a "smart city" environment, where the continual sensing and collection of data feed the operational systems that regulate the operations of the city as a space, this space "away" becomes even more difficult to comprehend. The affective dimension of privacy as the key to how to be private is the challenge on the horizon for understanding privacy in a world of big data; a new affective parenthesis of privacy is the goal in the giant control system of the smart city.

Acknowledgements

The research for this paper was funded by a European Research Council Advanced Investigator grant, The Programmable City (ERC-2012-AdG-323636).

References

Arendt, H. 1998. *The Human Condition* (2nd Ed.). Chicago, IL: University of Chicago Press.
Berry, D.M. 2011. *The Philosophy of Software: Code and Mediation in the Digital Age*. Basingstoke: Palgrave Macmillan.
Berry, D.M. 2015. *Critical Theory and the Digital*. United States: Bloomsbury Academic USA.
Borgmann, A. 1984. *Technology and the Character of Contemporary Life: A Philosophical Enquiry*. Chicago, IL: University of Chicago Press.
Cadwalladr, C. and Graham-Harrison, E. 2018. "Revealed: 50 Million Facebook profiles harvested for Cambridge Analytica in major data breach". *The Guardian*. https://www.theguardian.com/news/2018/mar/17/cambridge-analytica-facebook-influence-us-election (last accessed 4 April 2018).
Crawford, S. 2018. "Beware of Google's intentions." *Wired*. https://www.wired.com/story/sidewalk-labs-toronto-google-risks/ (last accessed 5 April 2018).
Dean, J. 2010. *Blog Theory: Feedback and Capture in the Circuits of Drive*. Cambridge: Polity Press.
Dodge, M. and Kitchin, R. 2011. *Code/space: Software and everyday life*. Cambridge, MA: MIT Press.
Drucker, J. 2011. "Humanities Approaches to Graphical Display." *Digital Humanities Quarterly*, 5(1). http://www.digitalhumanities.org/dhq/vol/5/1/000091/000091.html (last accessed 4 April 2018).
Ellul, J. 1973. *The Technological Society*. New York: Knopf Doubleday.
Evans, L. 2015. *Locative Social Media: Place in the Digital Age*. Basingstoke: Palgrave Macmillan.

Foster, J.B. and McChesney, R. 2014. "Surveillance capitalism." *Monthly Review*. Available at: http://monthlyreview.org/2014/07/01/surveillance-capitalism/ (accessed: 24 March 2016).

Greenfield, A. 2013. *Against the Smart City*. New York: Do Publications.

Habermas, J. 1992. *The Structural Transformation of the Public Sphere: An Inquiry into a Category of Bourgeois Society*. Cambridge: Polity Press.

Heidegger, M. 1977. *Question Concerning Technology and Other Essays, Vol. 1* (Trans. Lovitt, W.). New York: HarperCollins Publishers.

Husserl, E. 1976. *Ideas: General Introduction to Pure Phenomenology*. London: Humanities Press Intl.

Hustinx, P. 2010. "Privacy by Design: delivering the promises." *Identity in the Information Society*, 3: 253–255.

Ihde, D. 1990. *Technology and the Lifeworld: From Garden to Earth*, Bloomington and Indianopolis: Indiana University Press.

Kitchin, R. 2014. *The Data Revolution: Big Data, Open Data, Data Infrastructures and their Consequences*. London: Sage.

Kitchin, R. 2016. "The ethics of smart cities and urban science." *Philosophical Transactions A* 374(2083): 1–15.

Kittler, F.A. 1999. *Gramophone, Film, Typewriter*. San Francisco: Stanford University Press.

Leszczynski, A. 2016. "Geoprivacy." In Kitchin, R., Lauriault, T. P. and Wilson, M. M. (eds.) *Understanding Spatial Media*. London: Sage, pp. 235–244.

Markham, A. 2013. "Undermining 'data': A critical examination of a core term in scientific inquiry." *First Monday*, 7 October, 18(10). http://uncommonculture.org/ojs/index.php/fm/article/view/4868/3749.

Papacharissi, Z. 2010. *A Private Sphere: Democracy in a Digital Age*. Cambridge: Polity.

Ruckenstein, M. 2014. "Visualized and interacted life: Personal analytics and engagements with data doubles." *Societies*, 4(1): 68–84.

Townsend, A.M. 2013. *Smart Cities: Big Data, Civic Hackers, and the Quest for a New Utopia*. New York, NY: W.W. Norton & Company.

Van Dijck, J. 2014. "Datafication, dataism and dataveillance: Big data between scientific paradigm and ideology." *Surveillance & Society*, 12(2): 197–208.

Vanolo, A. 2014. "Smartmentality: The smart city as disciplinary strategy." *Urban Studies* 51(5): 883–898.

Vincent, J. 2014. "London's bins are tracking your smartphone." *The Independent*. 10 June 2014. www.independent.co.uk/life-style/gadgets-and-tech/news/updated-londons-binsa re-tracking-your-smartphone-8754924.html (last accessed 4 April 2018).

Wilson, M. W. 2011. "Data matter(s): legitimacy, coding, and qualifications-of-life." *Environment and Planning D: Society and Space*, 29(5): 857–872.

White, A. 2015. *Digital Media and Society: Transforming Economics, Politics and Social Practice*. Basingstoke: Palgrave Macmillan.

16

THE CHALLENGES OF CYBERSECURITY FOR SMART CITIES

Martin Dodge and Rob Kitchin

Introduction

Over the past three decades there has been a concerted move to digitally augment existing infrastructures, roll out new networked infrastructures, and utilize computational systems to tackle urban problems and deliver city services more efficiently. Such endeavours are now encapsulated within the notion of "smart cities", which advocates claim can help address urban resilience and sustainability in a time of population increases, climate change, and deepening socio-economic inequalities (White, 2016). In other words, smart city technologies are seen to offer an effective way to counter and manage uncertainty and risk. However, as with previous rounds of technological adoption and adaptation in cities – such as those related to energy supply, transportation, and telecommunication – they also create a paradoxical situation wherein the promised benefits (such as convenience, economic prosperity, safety, sustainability) are almost always accompanied by negative consequences and new variances of traditional problems (e.g., reproducing inequality, creating security and criminal risks, environmental externalities) (Greenfield, 2013; Singh and Pelton, 2013; Townsend, 2013). Importantly, this paradoxical relationship and the reproduction of urban problems and risks in a new guise is for the most part ignored in the promotional discourse for smart cities driven by commercial and governmental interests, or is present as a potential new issue to be "solved" by a further round of technological innovation and capital spending.

This chapter examines the implications of this paradoxical relationship, detailing how smart city technologies designed to produce urban resilience and reduce risks are actually opening up systems they are meant to augment to new forms of vulnerability and risk. The discussion considers the balancing point between reward and risk when previously relatively "dumb" systems are made "smart" through the introduction of networked computation, and are thus opened up to software bugs, data errors, network viruses, hacks, and potential criminal and terrorist cyberattacks (Little, 2010; Cerrudo, 2015).

For as long as there have been urban societies there have been criminal activity and attempts to steal property, disrupt city infrastructure, and defraud public services. Attempts to thwart such criminality have been built into the fabric of cities themselves through architecturally enacted defences, including strong doors, high walls and fences, and latterly security alarms and CCTV. Historical evidence and contemporary experience, however, show that all such security measures have some vulnerabilities which criminals are quick to identify and exploit. With time, all security, even sophisticated or well-designed solutions, will be defeated (especially if the reward of success provides sufficient motivation). There is thus a perennial struggle between defenders and attackers to secure city space, infrastructures and systems that provide adequate protection but are not so restrictive that they seriously inconvenience users or inhibit essential economic urban functions.

Smart city technologies are no different, being afflicted with a range of security vulnerabilities and risks, and an ongoing struggle is now evident between the cybersecurity industry and criminals and variously motivated hackers. However, while the base motivations to break into these systems might remain timeless (e.g., theft, extortion, impersonation, vandalism, malicious disruption), the nature of their performance is different. Because smart city technologies rely on networked digital computation, exploits of their vulnerabilities can be undertaken at distance and attacks can be masked, reducing the risk of detection and capture for perpetrators. Moreover, the use of software tools to automate hacking has greatly lowered costs and "super empowered" individual actors to conduct virtual criminality against multiple targets simultaneously, potentially affecting thousands of systems in different cities. Unauthorized access is often made easier because the so-called "attack surfaces" – the set of ways that a system might be susceptible to a breach – are multiplied due to a system's many interlocking parts, which are owned and controlled by a diverse set of stakeholders, making it difficult to secure every aspect of a large infrastructure or utility network. The rewards for success can also be significant, for example in the case of a data breach providing access to millions of user details, or in the case of vandalism/terrorism shutting down the entire electricity supply to a city, and can garner large amounts of publicity.

The nature of cyberattacks

Cyberattacks seek to "alter, disrupt, deceive, degrade, or destroy computer systems and networks or the information and/or programs resident in or transiting these systems or networks" (Owens et al., 2009: 1). There are three distinct forms of cyberattack against operational systems: *availability attacks* that seek to close a system down or deny service use; *confidentiality attacks* that seek to extract information and monitor activity; and *integrity attacks* that seek to enter a system to alter information and settings (and plant malware and viruses) without being noticed by the legitimate operator/owner (Singer and Friedman, 2014).

Cyberattacks can be performed by multiple different actors, from nation-state intelligence agencies and militaries, terrorist groups, organized criminals, hacker collectives, political and socially motivated activists, to "lone wolf" hackers, "script kiddies" and bored teenagers. It is estimated that over 100 nations have government-funded and directed cyberattack units, many capable of targeting critical urban infrastructure (Goodman, 2015). Anecdotal evidence from media reporting indicates a significant increase in organized criminals conducting thefts and frauds by targeting online systems, including so-called "ransomware" attacks that are a virtualized means of monetary extortion against organizations (Hern, 2016).

Cyberattacks try to exploit one of five major vulnerabilities of digital technologies that are central to smart city systems.

Weak software security and data encryption: Research has detailed that, on average, there are 30 errors or possibly exploitable bugs for every 1,000 lines of code (Li et al., 2004). In typical large systems being deployed in cities there are millions of lines of code that produce hundreds of potential 'zero-day' exploits (as yet unknown security vulnerabilities) for network viruses, malware, and directed hacks. Moreover, research by cybersecurity specialists has revealed that many smart city systems have been constructed with no or minimal security (such as no user authentication, or using default or weak passwords, e.g., "admin", "1234") (Cerrudo, 2015). Further, city governments and vendors of smart city technologies too often deploy them without undertaking thorough cybersecurity testing and where encryption is used, security issues can arise regarding how it is operated (Cerrudo, 2015).

Use of insecure legacy systems and poor ongoing maintenance: Many smart city technologies are layered onto much older infrastructure that relies on software and technology created 20 or 30 years ago, which has not been upgraded for some time, nor can they be migrated to newer, more secure systems (Rainie et al., 2014; Cerrudo, 2015). These technologies can create inherent vulnerabilities to newer systems by providing so-called "forever-day exploits" (holes in legacy software products that vendors no longer support and thus will never be patched). Even in the case of newer technologies, it can be difficult to test and rollout patches onto critical operational systems that need to be always on (Cerrudo, 2015).

System interdependencies and large and complex attack surfaces: The complexity of smart city systems means that it can be difficult to know which components are exposed and in what ways, to measure and mitigate risks, and to ensure end-to-end security (Cerrudo, 2015). Even if independent systems are secure, linking them to other systems can potentially open them to risk, with the level of security only guaranteed by the weakest link. Moreover, the interdependencies between technologies and systems mean that they are harder to maintain and upgrade. Beyond being hacked, the complexity of systems also increases the chances of "normal accidents" (e.g., programming bugs, human errors) that cause unanticipated failures (Perrow, 1984; Townsend, 2013).

Cascade effects: The interdependencies between smart city technologies and systems have the potential to create cascade effects, with failures or disruption having knock-on impacts that result in the failure of other critical utilities or services (cf. Little, 2010). For example, a cyberattack on telecommunications infrastructure could cascade into an urban operating system that then cascades into the other systems, such as traffic management or emergency response. This is one of the key security risks of an urban operating system, wherein several systems are linked together to enable a "system of systems" approach to managing city services and infrastructures thus undoing the mitigating effects of using a siloed approach (i.e., fully separate system with physically independent telecommunications cabling and sources of power, etc.) (Little, 2010). A successful cyberattack on the electricity grid has huge cascade effects as it underpins so many activities such as powering homes, workplaces, and a plethora of other essential infrastructures. For example, a sophisticated cyberattack on the software controlling parts of Ukraine's electricity grid switched off the power to about a quarter of a million consumers for several hours in December 2015 (Zetter, 2016).

Human error and deliberate malfeasance of disgruntled (ex)employees: Technical exploits can be significantly aided by human error, for example, employees responding to phishing emails and installing viruses or malware, or naively inserting infected datasticks into computers (Singer and Friedman, 2014). In some cases, there are weaknesses in software system designs, such that they can be easily and surreptitiously sabotaged by disgruntled present and ex-employees.

These vulnerabilities are exacerbated by a number of factors, not least that it is often unclear who is responsible for maintaining security across complex systems and infrastructures when several companies and stakeholders collaborate in their design, supply hardware and software, and operate and use various elements (US DHS, 2016). This is exacerbated with respect to urban management, where city administrations are under increasing pressure for year-on-year "efficiency" savings that leads to an under-investment in infrastructure and its security maintenance, an over-reliance on legacy systems, outsourcing that minimizes in-house knowledge, and difficulties in recruiting and retaining skilled IT staff. With respect to the latter, there is a lack of investment in dedicated cybersecurity personnel and leadership (in the form of Chief Information Officer or Chief Technology Officer) and Computer Emergency Response Teams (CERTs) in city governments (Cerrudo, 2015). Any cybersecurity plans cities do possess are often siloed with respect to particular systems and departments so that cross-function assessment and response is lacking (Cerrudo, 2015).

In addition, it is clear that many smart city vendors have little or no experience in embedding security features into their products – despite claims made in their marketing literature – and many systems possess significant vulnerabilities. These vendors can impede security research by limiting access to their systems for testing, thus enabling them to continue to release unsecured products without oversight or accountability (Cerrudo, 2015). Moreover, too many cities have been lax in insisting on strong security controls and response within the procurement process for new systems.

Risks to smart city infrastructure

There is a growing body of well documented, real-world examples of malicious cyber-attacks aimed at city infrastructures. Many of these are relatively inconsequential, such as randomly directed probes of connected computers and scans across publicly available Internet addresses, and are unsuccessful. However, a small number are much more significant and involve a security breach. Between 2010 and 2014, the US Department of Energy (that oversees the power grid, regulates power generation, and manages the nuclear weapons arsenal) documented 1,131 cyberattacks, of which 159 were successful (Reilly, 2015). In 53 cases, these attacks were "root compromises", meaning that the attackers gained administrative privileges to computer systems, stealing various kinds of personnel and operational information, and potentially doing other damage (Reilly, 2015). There have been a range of cyberattacks on transport management systems, as well as proof-of-concept demonstrations of possible attacks. While the idea of crippling a city by disrupting the flow of traffic by hacking its management is not new – for example, it was a central plot device in the 1969 heist movie, *The Italian Job* – it can now be done remotely and is harder to defend against. For example, a cyberattack on a key toll road in Haifa, Israel, closed it for eight hours causing major traffic disruption in 2013 (Hodson, 2014); (for details on widespread vulnerabilities in wireless-accessible traffic signals see Ghena et al., 2014). A ransomware attack on the San Francisco municipal rail network led to ticketing machines being removed from service for several days (Gibbs, 2016). A teenager in Lodz, Poland, managed to hack the city's tram switches, causing four trams to derail and injuring a number of passengers (Nanni, 2013). In the United States, air traffic control systems have been hacked and Federal Aviation Administration servers compromised, with malicious code installed onto control networks (Goodman, 2015). Vehicles are also open to being hacked given that new cars contain so many digital controls and sensors and are connected to wireless networks (Greenburg, 2015).

All essential urban services including the electricity grid, water supply, and road traffic control rely on Supervisory Control and Data Acquisition (SCADA) systems that are used to control functions and material flows. These systems measure how an infrastructure is performing in real-time and enable either automated or human operator interventions to change settings. Many deployments are from the 1980s onwards and some contain "forever-day" exploits. A number of SCADA systems have been compromised, with hackers altering how the infrastructure performs or causing a denial-of-service. The most infamous documented SCADA hack to date was the 2009 Stuxnet attack on Iran's uranium enrichment plant (Zetter, 2015).

Smart city technologies are linked together via a number of communications technologies and protocols such as Long Term Evolution (4G LTE), Global System for Mobile Communication (GSM), Code Division Multiple Access (CDMA), WiFi, bluetooth. All of the modes of networking and transferring data are known to have security issues that enable data to be intercepted by third parties and provide unauthorized access to devices. Some of these protocols are so complicated that they are difficult to implement securely. Likewise, telecommunication switches that link together the local and long distance Internet infrastructure are known to have vulnerabilities, including manufacturer and operator back-door security access and access codes that are infrequently updated (Singh and Pelton, 2013).

Securing smart cities

Given the scale and diversity of security flaws in the smart city, and their growing number of cyberattacks, how can vulnerabilities in smart cities technologies be addressed to minimize risk? To date, the strategy adopted for securing the smart city has largely been the use of technical mitigation solutions, such as access controls, encryption, IT industry standards and security protocols, and software patching regimes, along with staff training. While this has had some effect, given the vital nature of smart city technologies and infrastructures to urban life, it has become obvious that securing such systems requires a wider set of systemic interventions that encompass mitigation (lessening the force or intensity of something occurring) and prevention (stopping something from happening or arising), and ensure enactment through both market-led initiatives and governance-led regulation and enforcement.

Conventional mitigation

The common approach to securing smart city systems has been to utilize well-known software security tactics to try and prevent access and to enable restoration if a compromise occurs – for example, the use of access controls (username/password, two-stage authentication, biometric identifiers), properly maintained firewalls, virus and malware checkers, end-to-end strong encryption, and procedures to ensure routine software patching and the ability to respond with urgent updates to close vulnerabilities as they occur, audit trails of usage and change logs, and effective offsite backups and emergency recovery plans. Where feasible, systems should have built-in redundancy to ensure that if the primary delivery of a critical system fails, a secondary system automatically takes its place. Such redundancy might include the use of decentralized cloud-based solutions or a completely separate technological solution. While an optimal solution, it is also the case that creating genuine redundancy is often difficult and expensive.

The extent to which the protections are available varies across technologies and vendors; and the application across different institutions and companies is also inconsistent. Moreover, in complex, distributed systems with many components these solutions need to work equally across the complete system since the whole infrastructure/enterprise is only as strong as the weakest link. Further, it is often the case that these kinds of solutions are layered on after a system has been developed rather than being integral to the design.

These technical solutions are often bolstered by a vigilant IT staff whose job it is to oversee the day-to-day maintenance of these systems, including monitoring security issues and reacting swiftly to new cyberattacks and breaches. In addition, non IT-staff across an organization can be trained to maintain good practices with respect to security, such as adopting stronger passwords, routinely updating software, encrypting files, and avoiding phishing attacks. However, training is often conducted only once and ongoing staff compliance with best practice is hard to achieve.

While these security measures have genuine utility, they are far from a complete solution, particularly as smart technologies become ever more critical to the smooth functioning of cities. Instead, a more systemic approach needs to be adopted in relation to both technical design and training. In particular, a security-by-design approach that is proactive and preventative, rather than reactive and remedial, needs to be employed by city governments and key institutions responsible for urban management and infrastructure provision. Security-by-design seeks to build strong security measures into systems from the outset rather than attempting to layer them on after initial development. This requires security risk assessment to be a fundamental part of the design process and all aspects of security systems to be rigorously tested before the product is sold, including a pilot phase testing the security when deployed in real-world contexts and operating as part of a wider network of technologies (to ensure end-to-end security). It also means having in place an ongoing commitment to cybersecurity, including a mechanism to monitor products throughout their life cycle, a process of supporting and patching them over time, and a procedure for notifying customers when security risks are identified. With respect to existing city software systems and control infrastructure, all vendors should be asked for full security documentation and procedures, and a comprehensive testing of their security should be undertaken to identify weak points, undertake remedial security patching, and to upgrade future service level agreements with respect to enhanced security. This is especially the case for legacy systems. If systems cannot be remedially fixed and forever-day exploits remain that could bring down critical systems, then firm plans need to be put in place for upgrades or replacement. It should be noted that there are cost implications in mandating better security and this needs to be factored into smart city investment strategies.

With respect to overseeing the security aspects of smart city technologies a core security team is essential within urban administrations with specialist skills and responsibilities above and beyond day-to-day IT administration. The work of this team would include: undertaking threat and risk modelling; actively testing the security of smart city technologies (rather than simply monitoring and trusting vendor reassurances); conducting ongoing security assessments; preparing and reviewing detailed plans of action for different kinds of cybersecurity incidents; liaising with the city departments and companies administering smart city initiatives; and coordinating staff training on security issues. The staff would also constitute a city's Computer Emergency Response Team to actively tackle any on-going cyber-security incidents (Cerrudo, 2015). As a routine part of their work, the core security team should consult with cybersecurity vendors to stay up-to-date on potential threats and solutions (Nanni, 2013). In addition, the team creates a formal channel for security feedback and ethical disclosure, enabling bugs and security weaknesses to be reported by members of the consultants, academics, and allied technology companies. Initial security assessments would be carried out as early as possible, for example in the scoping and procurement phases of technological adoption, to ensure the solutions developed conform to expectations. Part of any assessment should be a consideration of whether systems should be kept in siloes to limit cascade effects. Given cost constraints and lack of strategic foresight, very few cities presently have core cybersecurity teams and are therefore underprepared to deal with a serious cyberattack.

Enactment and enforcement

While it is one thing to advocate for stronger mitigation measures, it is another to ensure that a more systemic approach to cybersecurity for smart cities is widely implemented and enforced. More attention needs to be paid to the mechanisms to incentivize participation by both the public and commercial sector, and to penalize those who fail to improve security of their products, systems, and services. There are two routes to improving mitigation measures: market-led adoption and government-led regulation and legal enforcement.

The market-led approach consists of commercial vendors developing smart city technologies taking a proactive, self-regulatory stance to security. Here, software companies choose to adopt security-by-design as a de facto standard, collaborate with each other to create effective industry-wide standards, and establish best practices. They ensure security across complex, interdependent systems, and work more closely with the rapidly growing cybersecurity industry in order to improve their products. In so doing, security becomes an expected norm and the adoption of a serious approach to security by companies provides competitive advantage over those that do not comply. In part, the market-led approach is driven by competition; fear of reputational damage and litigation caused by a major security scandal; and the benefits of self-regulation, rather than the approach of statutory enforcement with legal prosecution and fines.

While a market-led approach to security does presently exist, it predominantly adopts the weak mitigation approach detailed above and not security-by-design. In part this is because there has been weak pressure from buyers for enhanced security, mainly due to a poor understanding of security vulnerabilities and their potential consequences and inadequate procurement practices. Moreover, the imperatives to get product to market as quickly as possible (often to pre-empt a competitor) and turn a profit mean that security corners are being cut. As such, market-led responses will need to be accompanied by more "top-down" regulation and better management practices by city authorities and utility operators.

The regulation and management-led approach seeks to encourage secure deployment of smart city technologies through compliance measures and active oversight. The former requires the formulation of security standards, directives, and best practices that smart city deployments must comply with or face some form of penalty, such as prosecution, fines, or loss of contract. There are now a host of smart city standards initiatives underway – by bodies such as the International Standards Organization, British Standards Institute, American National Standards Institute, and City Protocol – aimed at defining minimum specifications for technical development and deployment of core technologies. The latter necessitates setting up management structures and procedures for ensuring compliance is being met and enforced. In addition, city administrations must call for security-by-design and integral life-long security maintenance (including on-time patching and 24/7 incident response) into the procurement process and subsequent service level contracts. They should also support whistle-blowers who wish to expose security vulnerabilities and require the public reporting of security breaches.

A preventative approach

Even with a strong mitigation strategy and effective enforcement procedures, it is not possible to eradicate all the security vulnerabilities and associated risks from the smart city. There is, therefore, a case to be made for considering a preventative approach, one that involves building some urban infrastructure and control systems that are deliberately "deaf" (not networked and remotely accessible) and "dumb" (i.e., not automated by code), which would elide many software security overheads. A preventative approach is quite straightforward to articulate – simply put, "do not adopt smart city technologies as presently conceived"; the best way to prevent risks from materializing is not to create vulnerabilities in the first place.

Yet making the case for such an approach is much more difficult in practice because of the perceived benefits of creating a smart city. Such a cautious, preventative approach, that questions seriously the commercial logics and profit streams of many hardware vendors and software developers, will be derided as "backward looking" and having a neo-Luddite mentality (see Jones, 2013). Advocating a preventative approach is considered a radical means of securing smart cities as it requires a reframing of the value around technology in regards to convenience/efficiency and security/safety. It requires a counter-narrative against "smarter is better" and advocacy for conventional electro-mechanical components and systems that run reliably without additional software monitoring and network access.

There is a case, however, to be made that the greater potential risks networked infrastructure poses, plus the higher cybersecurity overheads, outweigh the efficiency and functionality gains promised. In the era of ubiquitous wireless connectivity, cloud-computing and remote control, the notion of having so-called "air-gapped" systems might seem counter-intuitive. However, it can be an effective method of security that prevents hacking and cascade effects and significantly reduces vulnerabilities.

Equally, there are reasons to be sceptical of the benefits claimed by advocates (who are often self-interested) for new cyber-physical systems as it is well noted that they tend to oversell the promises of smart city technologies while ignoring their threats. Many existing smart city system deployments have not delivered the anticipated gains in efficiency, flexibility, productivity and convenience. In regards to the Internet of Things, presently there is little perceivable gain or real benefits to the functioning and management of cities in many sensor-net deployments (though they benefit vendors through their sale/servicing and potential monetization of data streams). In fact, if anything, some newly software-enabled systems make routine tasks more complex to complete, error-prone, unreliable, costly in time and cognitive attention, and less secure, as well as raising issues with respect to excessive data surveillance and personal privacy (Greenfield, 2013; Kitchin, 2016). In other words, networking city infrastructure and introducing new systems do not necessarily improve performance, yet they do make them more vulnerable to cyberattacks.

Nonetheless, at present, implementing preventative measures will be difficult to promote and promulgate given the widespread adoption of techno-utopian discourses of "progress" enacted by smart urbanism. This is especially the case in the current neoliberal climate that encourages cities to form public-private partnerships with companies and to outsource or privatize services, and where access to government grants will be difficult without claiming to create and implement innovative and cutting-edge smart city solutions. This may change though if the "cutting-edge" of city management becomes recognized as the "bleeding-edge" of cyber insecurity.

Conclusion

This chapter has examined issues around the security of smart cities. In an ironic twist, smart city technologies are promoted as an effective way to counter and manage uncertainty and risk, yet they paradoxically induce new risks, including making city infrastructure and services more vulnerable and open to extensive forms of digital vandalism, network disruption and cyber-criminal exploitation. This paradox has largely been ignored by commercial and governmental interests or tackled through conventional mitigation approaches. While the majority of cyberattacks are presently being repulsed by software tools and management practices there is real potential for much more disruptive and damaging impacts on critical systems. Criminals and other actors are developing more sophisticated methods of hacking, and security measures fail to keep pace. It may be that more severe disruption of critical infrastructure has so far been avoided because nation-state actors do not want to reveal their capabilities and they fear retaliation from adversaries (Rainie et al., 2014).

Present strategies for addressing the vulnerabilities and risks posed by the mass adoption of networked technologies for city management are inadequate and predominantly rely on existing technical and training mitigation strategies and market-led solutions. Instead, there needs to be a widening and deepening of mitigation strategies to include security-by-design as a de facto approach for all future smart city procurement, a comprehensive assessment of existing urban infrastructures and information systems and remedial security patching or replacement, the formation of core security and computer emergency response teams within city administrations with specialist skills. This should be complemented by a management and regulation approach to smart city technologies and implementation, rather than simply a market-led approach, to ensure active oversight and compliance with security standards, best practices, municipal policy, and third-party service contracts. Moreover, serious consideration should be given to a preventative approach to security, wherein critical infrastructure is air-gapped or not given the "smart" treatment when it is not really needed.

It is not feasible to halt the smart city agenda, and much of the adoption of networked technologies and software systems by municipal authorities across the world cannot simply be removed. However, it is not too late to recognize the extent of the new cybersecurity vulnerabilities and risks posed by these technologies and to put in place strategies and approaches to mitigate and prevent them.

Acknowledgements

This chapter is a modified version of Kitchin, R. and Dodge, M. 2017. "The (in) security of the smart cities: vulnerabilities, risks, mitigation and prevention", *Journal of Urban Technology*. Rob Kitchin's contribution is based on research funded by a European Research Council Advanced Investigator grant, The Programmable City (ERC-2012-AdG-323636).

References

Cerrudo, C. 2015. "An emerging US (and world) threat: cities wide open to cyber attacks", *Securing Smart Cities*. http://securingsmartcities.org/wp-content/uploads/2015/05/Cities WideOpenToCyberAttacks.pdf.

Ghena, B., Beyer, W., Hillaker, A., Pevarnek, J. and Halderman, J.A. 2014. "Green lights forever: analyzing the security of traffic infrastructure", *Proceedings of the 8th USENIX Workshop on Offensive Technologies*. http://www.usenix.org/system/files/conference/woot14/woot14-ghena.pdf

Gibbs, S. 2016. "Ransomware attack on San Francisco public transit gives everyone a free ride", *Guardian*, 28 November. http://www.theguardian.com/technology/2016/nov/28/passengersfree-ride-san-francisco-muni-ransomeware (accessed 5 October 2017).

Goodman, M. 2015. *Future Crimes*. New York: Bantam Press.

Greenburg, A. 2015. "Hackers remotely kill a Jeep on the highway, with me in it", *Wired*, 21 July. http://www.wired.com/2015/07/hackers-remotely-kill-jeep-highway (accessed 5 October 2017).

Greenfield, A. 2013. *Against the Smart City*. New York: Do Press.

Hern, A. 2016. "Ransomware threat on the rise", *Guardian*, 3 August, http://www.theguardian.com/technology/2016/aug/03/ransomware-threat-on-the-rise-as-40-of-businesses-attacked (accessed 5 October 2017).

Hodson, H. 2014. "Gridlock alert", *New Scientist*, 9 August, https://www.sciencedirect.com/science/article/pii/S0262407914615323 (accessed 30 May 2018).

Jones, S.E. 2013. *Against Technology: From the Luddites to Neo-Luddism*. London: Routledge.

Kitchin, R. 2016. "The ethics of smart cities and urban science", *Philosophical Transactions A*, 374(2083): 1–15.

Kitchin, R. and Dodge, M. 2017. "The (in)security of the smart cities: vulnerabilities, risks, mitigation and prevention", *Journal of Urban Technology*. https://www.tandfonline.com/doi/abs/10.1080/10630732.2017.1408002.

Li, P.L., Shaw, M., Herbsleb, J., Ray, B. and Santhanam, P. 2004. "Empirical evaluation of defect projection models for widely-deployed production software systems", *ACM SIG-SOFT Software Engineering Notes*, 29(6): 263–272.

Little, R.G. 2010. "Managing the risk of cascading failure in complex urban infrastructures", in Graham, S. (ed.), *Disrupted Cities: When Infrastructure Fails*. London: Routledge, pp. 27–39.

Nanni, G. 2013. *Transformational "Smart Cities": Cyber Security and Resilience*. Mountain View, CA: Symantec.

Owens, W.A., Dam, K.W. and Lin, H.S. 2009. *Technology, Policy, Law, and Ethics Regarding US Acquisition and Use of Cyberattack Capabilities*. Committee on Offensive Information Warfare; National Research Council. Washington DC: National Academic Press.

Perrow, B. 1984. *Normal Accidents: Living With High-Risk Technologies*. New York: Basic Books.

Rainie, L., Anders, J. and Connolly, J. 2014. "Cyber Attacks Likely to Increase", *Digital Life in 2025*. Pew Research Center. http://www.pewinternet.org/files/2014/10/PI_Futureof Cyberattacks_102914_pdf.pdf (accessed 5 October 2017).

Reilly, S. 2015. "Records: Energy Department struck by cyber attacks", *CNBC*, 10 September. http://www.cnbc.com/2015/09/10/records-energy-department-struck-by-cyber-attacks. html (accessed 5 October 2017).

Singer, P.W. and Friedman, A. 2014. *Cybersecurity and Cyberwar*. Oxford: Oxford University Press.

Singh, I.B. and Pelton, J.N. 2013. "Securing the cyber city of the future", *The Futurist*, 47(6): 22.

Townsend, A.M. 2013. *Smart Cities: Big Data, Civic Hackers and the Quest for a New Utopia*. New York: Norton.

US DHS. 2016. *Strategic Principles for Securing the Internet of Things*, 15 November. http:// www.dhs.gov/sites/default/files/publications/Strategic_Principles_for_Securing_the_Inter net_of_Things-2016–1115-FINAL.pdf (accessed 5 October 2017).

White, J.M. 2016. "Anticipatory logics of the smart city's global imaginary", *Urban Geography*, 37(4): 572–589.

Zetter, K. 2015. *Countdown to Zero Day: Stuxnet and the Launch of the World's First Digital Weapon*. New York: Broadway Books.

Zetter, K. 2016. "Inside the cunning, unprecedented hack of Ukraine's power grid", *Wired News*, 3 March, http://www.wired.com/2016/03/inside-cunning-unprecedented-hack-ukraines-power-grid (accessed 5 October 2017).

PART III
Conclusion

17

REFRAMING, REIMAGINING AND REMAKING SMART CITIES

Rob Kitchin

Introduction

A principal aim of this book has been to critically examine the creation of smart cities *and* to try and formulate new visions of smart urbanism that seek to gain the promises of smart cities while minimizing their perils; to explore the various critiques of smart city rhetoric and deployments *and* to suggest social, political and practical interventions that would enable better designed and more equitable and just smart city initiatives. Of course, producing a form of smart urbanism that realizes promises while curtailing perils is no easy task – and is perhaps impossible at a deep ideological level given the many stakeholders and vested interests involved and their differing politics, approaches, aims and ambitions. Nonetheless, trying to negotiate across these interests and ambitions is necessary if critique is to transition, even if in partial and limited ways, into the reframing, reimagining and remaking of smart cities so that they are more emancipatory, empowering and inclusive. It is also required if the present adoption gap for smart city technologies, wherein solutions are not being taken up by city administrations as hoped and expected by the smart city advocacy coalition, is to be overcome (Kitchin et al. 2017). In this concluding chapter, I contend that the reframing, re-imagining and remaking of smart city thinking and implementation needs to occur in at least six broad ways. Three of the transitions concern normative and conceptual thinking with regards to goals, cities and epistemology; and three concern more practical and political thinking and praxes with regards to management/governance, ethics and security, and stakeholders and working relationships.

Recasting normative and conceptual concerns

Goals

At one level, the goals of creating smart cities are already established – to improve quality of life and create more efficient, productive, competitive, sustainable and resilient cities (see Table 1.2). At a more profound, normative level, however, the goals of smart cities are less well defined and cogently established (Luque-Ayala and Marvin 2015). Beyond addressing instrumental concerns (e.g., optimizing traffic flows, reducing energy consumption, lowering crime rates, making service delivery more efficient), for whom and what purpose are smart cities being developed? Are smart cities primarily about – or should be about: creating new markets and profit, facilitating state control and regulation, addressing their anticipatory logics (demographic shifts, global climate change, fiscal austerity; Merricks White 2016) or improving the quality of life of citizens? Or are they about all of these, but with varying emphases depending on local context? And if they are about all of these goals, then how are these framed conceptually and ideologically?

The fundamental question of 'what kind of cities do we want to create and live in?' is largely reduced to the instrumental level within smart city discourse, in which it is assumed that tackling such issues is inherently of universal benefit. More profound framings with respect to fairness, equity, justice, citizenship, democracy, governance and political economy are either ignored or are understood in a pragmatic way within a neoliberal framing that renders them post-political in nature – that is, commonsensical and beyond challenge and contestation (Swyngedouw 2016; Cardullo and Kitchin 2018). And yet, each of these framings can be understood and practised in a variety of ways – for example, there are many theories of social justice (e.g., egalitarianism, utilitarianism, libertarianism, communitarianism, contractarianism, etc.; Smith 1994) and which one someone subscribes to makes a big difference to whether a particular approach to, or action in, the smart city is seen as being just (Smith 1994). Adopting an approach to smart cities rooted in the notion of 'The Right to the City' (Lefebvre 1996) will produce a very different kind of smart city to one rooted in the ideas and ideals of the free market and entrepreneurial urbanism (Hall and Hubbard 1997).

Rather than start with these kinds of fundamental, normative questions and then formulating a strategy to realize its principles, the impression one gains from encountering many smart city initiatives is that the starting point is the technology. Then there is an attempt to think about what the technology might be applied to (e.g., reducing traffic) and then a move to frame the approach with respect to a core issue (e.g., sustainability, safety, security, economic competitiveness). In other words, the means is post-justified by ends, rather than the ends shaping the means. In so doing, the core issue is framed and understood in a shallow, limited sense. For example, developers might state that a technology can make a system more sustainable, without saying what 'being sustainable' means beyond instrumental targets. Like social justice, there are many conceptions of sustainability, and adopting the principles of different positions might lead to the development of alternative solutions.

Similarly, developers might say that the technology is 'citizen-focused', but as Shelton and Lodato (this volume) have highlighted the citizen is often an empty signifier, reduced to a vacuous notion of a generic figure which is served through stewardship or civic paternalism. This generic figure is presupposed to hold certain characteristics, such as digital literacy and middle-class sensibilities (Datta, this volume). Even as an archetypal generic smart citizen, Cardullo and Kitchin (2018) show through their unpacking of citizen participation in smart cities that citizens almost exclusively occupy passive positions in smart city initiatives – they are data points, users, recipients, consumers, testers and players; occasionally they provide feedback, but are rarely creators, decision-makers or leaders. In other words, 'citizen-focused' simply means citizens are the target audience or supposed beneficiaries in systems designed and administered by state bodies and companies. Smart citizenship, Cardullo and Kitchin (2018) conclude, is underpinned by a neoliberal ethos that favours consumption choice and individual autonomy within a framework of constraints that prioritize market-led solutions to urban issues; it is not grounded in civil, social and political rights and the common good. A smart city framed by alternative notions of citizenship would then be quite different with respect to how they were implemented, as the recent re-orientation of Barcelona from a neoliberal approach to one underpinned by the concept of technological sovereignty is making clear (Galdon 2017; March and Ribera-Fumaz 2017).

Grappling with more normative questions is important because they set the wider framework within which smart city agendas and initiatives are formulated, deployed and run. At present, few cities or companies can coherently articulate their smart city vision and goals in normative terms beyond technical, aspirational statements (e.g., Dublin will be 'open, connected, engaged'; Cork will be 'innovating, creating, connecting'). Instead, smart cities are somewhat haphazard, uncoordinated and opportunistic – what Dourish (2016: 37) refers to as the accidental smart city, wherein:

> the city becomes smart … [in a] piecemeal, gradual, disparate manner … little by little, one piece at a time, under the control of different groups, without a master plan, and with a lot of patching, hacking, jury-rigging and settling.

In cases where a more fully realized strategy has been formulated it can be contradictory with respect to other urban policies. City administrations, in particular, as the core bodies driving and implementing smart city initiatives need to start the process of divining their smart city agenda and strategies by considering these normative questions, not simply by holding workshops to consider which urban problems to prioritize for smart city solutions.

Cities

For the most part, smart city advocates frame the city as a technical entity which consists of a set of knowable and manageable systems (or system of systems) that act in largely rational, mechanical, linear and hierarchical ways and can be steered and controlled through technical levers, and that urban issues can be solved with technical solutions (see Kitchin et al. 2015; Mattern 2017). Moreover, 'the city' is treated as a generic analytical category, meaning a solution developed for one city can be transferred and replicated elsewhere. While cybernetic approaches recognize the complexity and emergent qualities of city systems, they are still understood as being machinic and largely closed and bounded in nature. Such a view of cities is limited and limiting; not only does this narrow, technical view fail to capture the full complexity of cities, but it also constrains the potential benefits that smart city technologies might produce by creating solutions that are not always attuned to the wider contexts in which urban problems are situated. Indeed, such technical interventions can often be 'sticking plaster solutions'. For example, technical solutions to traffic congestion usually seek to optimize flow or re-route vehicles; they do not address the deep-rooted problem that there are too many vehicles using the road system, or provide a solution that shifts people onto public transport or encourages more cycling and walking.

Cities are not simply technical systems that can be steered and controlled in the same way that a car or plane can be. Nor can urban issues be simply solved with technical solutions. Cities are complex and ever-evolving, jam-packed with a multitude of inter-dependent, contingent and relational actors, actants, processes and relationships. Cities have a range of different, often competing, actors and stakeholders – government bodies, public sector agencies, companies, nongovernmental bodies, community organizations and so on – that have different goals, resources, practices and structures and are trying to address and manage various issues. Cities are full of culture, politics, competing interests and wicked problems. No two cities hold the same qualities, having different histories, populations, cultures, economies, politics, legacy infrastructures and systems, political and administrative geographies, modes of governance, sense of place, hinterlands, interconnections and interdependencies with other places, and so on. In other words, cities are places not simply systems. Consequently, their messiness is not well captured in computational logic and is difficult to model, predict, and manage through technocratic governance.

Understanding cities from a relational, place-based perspective, it is clear that smart city technology will not be a silver bullet to solve urban issues. Yet, while intrinsically city administrations know that cities are complex, open, multiscalar, contingent and relational, when they pursue a smart city agenda they often practise a form of strategic essentialism, seeking to tackle urban issues through narrow technical fixes that ignore wider interdependencies. Likewise, companies developing smart city technologies perform the same strategic essentialism, though they often have less appreciation of the full complexities, processes, practices and politics of managing and governing a city (I have been asked several times by companies to explain how cities and city administration work). For smart city initiatives to work well they need to be conceptualized and contextualized within a broader and richer understanding of what a city is and how it works in practice. In other words, smart city advocates need to recognize and accommodate a more nuanced, relational understanding of cities and to appreciate and take into account the diversity and complexity of cities in their formulations. This also requires smart city advocates to recognize that their technical solutions will not work on their own and need to be positioned alongside and integrated with other solutions that are more social, political, legal, fiscal and community-orientated, and they should articulate and promote what that *suite* of solutions might be.

Epistemology

How can we know the city? To understand and explain it? And then act on this knowledge? These are epistemological questions. In general, smart city technologies, and associated rhetoric and science (urban science and urban informatics) are founded on big data analytics (Kitchin 2014). In short, this means algorithms are used to process vast quantities of real-time data in order to dynamically manage a system and to make future predictions. There are two issues with this approach. The first is that these data are typically quantitative and one-dimensional in nature, limited in scope (e.g., sensor readings, camera images, clickstreams, admin records), and do not provide a full, multispectral picture of the city. They provide a very narrow, selective view of city systems and life, prioritizing data that are machine-readable and excluding far more information than they include (Mattern 2013). The second is that the scientific approach adopted for data generation, analysis (e.g., statistics and modelling) and communication (e.g., data visualizations via urban dashboards) is reductionist, mechanistic, atomizing, essentialist and deterministic in how it produces knowledge about cities (Kitchin et al., 2015). It is an approach that decontextualizes a city and its systems from history, its politics and political economy, its culture and communities, the wider set of social, economic and environmental relations that frame its development, and its wider interconnections and interdependencies that stretch out over space and time. Moreover, with its claims to objectivity and neutrality, such an approach tends to marginalize and replace other ways of examining the city (such as through focus groups, interviews, surveys, etc.) and other forms of knowing such as phronesis (knowledge derived from practice and deliberation) and metis (knowledge based on experience) (Kitchin et al., 2015).

This is not to say that this approach does not produce useful or valuable knowledge. If it did not, I would not have co-developed the Dublin Dashboard and Cork Dashboard for those respective cities.[1] Rather it is to recognize that such knowledge is partial, based on a narrow realist epistemology and instrumental rationality, and that it needs, on the one hand, to reframe its epistemology to openly acknowledge its situatedness, positionality, contingencies, assumptions and shortcomings, and on the other hand, to complement such knowledge with other forms of knowing, such as phronesis and metis (Kitchin et al., 2016). Such an epistemological move dovetails with the reframing of cities to recognize their multiple, complex, interdependent nature. Without this change in epistemology, the underlying scientific rationalities of smart city technologies and approach will remain anaemic, partial and open to significant underperformance and failure (Flood 2011).

Recasting practical and political concerns

Management/governance

Smart city technologies enact algorithmic governance and forms of automated management – city systems are measured, analysed, and outcomes assessed and acted upon in an automatic, automated and autonomous fashion (Kitchin and Dodge 2011). Such automated management facilitates and produces instrumental and technocratic forms of governance and government, that is, rote, procedural, rule-driven, top-down, autocratic means of managing how a system functions and how it processes and treats individuals within those systems. Algorithmic governance is a technically-mediated means to manage a city, wherein there is a belief that the city can be steered and controlled through algorithmic levers. For its advocates, such a data-driven, algorithmic approach ensures rational, logical and impartial governance and optimal performance. It is a means to objectively and impartially nudge, steer, discipline and control people to act in certain ways.

Such algorithmic, technocratic forms of governance have been critiqued in a number of ways. The use of algorithmic systems that generate and process streams of big data greatly intensifies the extent and frequency of monitoring people and shifts forms of governance from regimes of discipline towards social control (Kitchin and Dodge 2011; Gabrys 2014; Sadowski and Pasquale 2015). In control regimes, people become subject to constant modulation through software-mediated systems in which their behaviour is directed explicitly or implicitly reshaped, rather than being (self)disciplined. Governance is modified so it is no longer solely about moulding subjects and restricting action, but about modulating affects, desires and opinions, and inducing action within prescribed comportments (Braun 2014; Krivy 2018). Calculative regimes of control are more distributed, interlinked, overlapping and continuous, enabling institutional power to creep across technologies and pervade the social landscape (Martinez 2011). At the same time, the technological systems underpinning them are narrow in scope and reductionist and functionalist in approach; that is, they ignore wider cultural, social and political contexts and processes and simplify complex phenomena into code rather than taking a more holistic or negotiated approach to managing an issue (Kitchin 2014). The smart city thus produces a particular form of governmentality, what Vanolo (2014) terms 'smartmentality'. Relatedly, the exhaustive and indexical nature of data generation converts every city system adopting such technologies into a surveillance machine, with the interlinking of such systems and the processing and analysing of such data raising a number of ethical concerns (Kitchin 2016). As such, far from being impartial and objective, smart city technologies have built-in normative values and judgements about how systems should perform, and how they assess and manage outcomes, with these hardcoded into the underlying software. And they have normative effects in terms of how they are deployed to shape and modify systems, citizens, and institutional behaviour.

Far from creating a more democratizing landscape of governance, smart city systems are mostly top-down, centrally-controlled and managerialist in orientation, and are produced and deployed for government by companies. For many critics this raises a number of concerns about the process of introduction within cities and the corporatization of urban governance. Within city administrations smart city initiatives are often introduced by bureaucrats rather than elected officials or being developed in conjunction with local communities. Indeed, local communities (and depending on location, politicians) are often little consulted in decision-making processes concerning smart city technologies and their form, implementation and operation (and certainly not as they would be with respect to planning and development plans). In terms of the corporatization of city governance there are three concerns. First, it actively promotes a neoliberal political economy and the marketization of public services wherein city functions are administered for private profit (Hollands 2008). Second, it creates a technological lock-in that leaves cities beholden to particular technological platforms and vendors (Hill 2013) and creates a corporate path dependency that cannot easily be undone or diverted (Bates 2012). Third, it leads to 'one size fits all smart city in a box' solutions that take little account of the uniqueness of places, peoples and cultures and thus works sub-optimally (Townsend et al. n.d.).

Just as cities need to be conceptualized in a broader and more synoptic way by smart city advocates, so does city management and governance. While it is undoubtedly the case that many smart city technologies do enable more efficient and effective management of city systems, and provide convenience and improve services, they are not sufficient solutions on their own to the diverse range of issues facing cities and themselves cause some concerns. Instead, they need to be introduced and implemented through processes of co-creation and co-production between city administrations, companies and citizens; be open and transparent in their formulation and operation, including using open platforms and standards where possible; and be used in conjunction with a suite of aligned interventions, policies and investments that seek to tackle issues in complementary ways, blending technical, social, political and policy responses. Not enough work has been done to consider how best to achieve such a blended, open, and co-produced form of urban management and governance, though the approaches being undertaken by cities such as Amsterdam (Netherlands), Barcelona (Spain), Bristol (UK), and Medellín (Colombia) provide some examples.

Ethics and security concerns

Smart city technologies generate huge quantities of data about systems and people, much of them in real-time and at a highly granular scale. These data can be put to many good uses; however, generating, processing, analysing, sharing and storing large amounts of actionable data also raise a number of concerns and challenges. Key amongst these are privacy, predictive profiling, social sorting, anticipatory governance, behavioural nudging, control creep, data protection and data security. Indeed, many smart city technologies capture personally identifiable information and household level data about citizens – their characteristics, their location and movements, and their activities – link these data together to produce new derived data, and use them to create profiles of people and places and to make decisions about them. As such, there are concerns about what a smart city means for people's privacy and what privacy and predictive privacy harms might arise from the sharing, analysis and misuse of urban big data (Kitchin and Dodge 2011; Baracos and Nissenbaum 2014; Edwards 2016; Kitchin 2016; Taylor et al. 2016; Leszczynski 2017; Murphy, this volume, Evans, this volume). In addition, there are questions as to how secure smart city technologies and the data they generate are from hacking and theft and what the implications of a data breach are for citizens (Cerrudo 2015; Dodge and Kitchin, this volume).

To date, the approach to these issues has been haphazard, uncoordinated and partial. As suggested with respect to city management and governance in general, addressing privacy and security issues requires a multi-pronged set of interventions that ideally are coherently aligned and implemented in conjunction with one another. In a recent report for the Irish Government's Data Forum I outlined such an approach, suggesting four types of intervention, each consisting of a number of mediations (Kitchin 2016). First, market-driven solutions: including the development of industry standards, stronger self-regulation, and the reframing of privacy and security as a competitive advantage. Second, technological solutions: including end-to-end encryption, access controls, security controls, audit trails, backups, up-to-date patching, and privacy enhancement tools. Third, policy, regulatory and legal solutions: including revised fair information practice principles, privacy by design, security by design, and education and training. Fourth, governance and management solution at three levels: vision and strategy – smart city advisory boards and published strategies; oversight of delivery and compliance – smart city governance, ethics and security oversight committees; and day-to-day delivery – core privacy/security teams, smart city privacy/security assessments, and computer emergency response teams.

Using these solutions together would provide a balanced, pragmatic approach that enables the rollout of smart city technologies and initiatives, but in a way that is not prejudicial to people's privacy, actively work to minimize privacy and predictive privacy harms, curtail data breaches, and tackle cybersecurity issues. They also work across the entire life-cycle (from procurement to decommissioning) and span the whole system ecology (all its stakeholders and components). Collectively they promote fairness and equity, protect citizens and cities from harms, and enable improved governance and economic development. Moreover, they do so using an approach that is not heavy handed in nature and is relatively inexpensive to implement. They are by no means definitive, but would enable a more ethical, principle-led approach to the design and implementation of smart cities. Failing to tackle these issues will undermine and curtail smart city initiatives and public support for them.

Stakeholders and working relationships

As detailed in Chapter 1, smart city protagonists are often divided into those who develop, implement and promote smart city technologies and initiatives, and those who critique such endeavours. While the former have been starting to respond to critique, albeit in rather limited ways, and the latter have started to make more active interventions, there is still much more work to be done to bring different stakeholders into dialogue and working relationships. There is certainly a lot of learning that needs to be done: by city administrations with respect to developing smart city strategies and procuring and deploying smart city technologies; by companies with respect to how cities are managed and function and balancing private gain with public good; by communities involved in or living with smart city initiatives; and by researchers and consultants who are seeking to understand what is unfolding in different cities and contexts. This learning will progress most effectively through co-creation and co-production, with stakeholders working together.

This requires all stakeholders to be open to working and learning from one another for the common purpose of improving the quality of lives for citizens and how cities are managed and governed. With respect to academia, this means critical scholars have to become more applied in orientation: to give constructive feedback and guidance and to set out alternatives and to help develop strategies, not just provide critique. This does not mean that critique is not valuable in and of itself. Nor does it mean dumbing down or abandoning a critical position or emancipatory politics or 'getting into bed with the enemy'. It means putting principles into action – to translate them into practical and political outcomes. Our own endeavours on The Programmable City project have demonstrated that smart city stakeholders are open to robust exchanges and are prepared to rework initiatives and change direction, especially if we are willing to work with them and others to realize any reframing, reimagining and remaking involved. That said, not all city administrations or companies want such collaborations, or it might be very difficult to align differing ideological beliefs, in which case external critique might be the only option. However, in my view, such critique ideally also needs to suggest alternatives – whether ideological or practical – and to support the work of other oppositional groups (such as local communities or NGOs).

Conclusion

The purpose of this chapter has been to set out some of the key shortcomings, challenges and risks associated with smart city technologies and initiatives and to suggest how smart city thinking and implementation might be productively reframed, reimagined and remade in six ways. The aim has not been to be definitive or comprehensive, but rather to provide some initial ideas and contentions – some more conceptual and philosophical, some more practical and political – that act as provocations for discussion and debate. As such, while the six interventions detailed offer a set of initial entry points, my hope is that they are creatively reworked and extended by those working in smart city endeavours.

How likely such a recasting of smart cities is is an open question. The smart cities epistemic community and advocacy coalition remains strong, with a reasonably coherent and stable narrative, and many city administrations are deploying smart city solutions in a largely pragmatic, instrumental way rather than it being underpinned by a strategy rooted in normative concerns and principles. That said, there is a persistent adoption gap in the take up of smart city technologies, with many deployments remaining at the experimental stage or being confined to 'smart districts' or city centres rather than being rolled out across entire urban areas. As outlined in Kitchin et al. (2017) there are good reasons for this gap including:

- a lack of *momentum*, with government being somewhat like an oil-tanker and difficult to shift direction;
- an aversion to *risk*, with city administrations charged with providing stability, certainty and reliability in delivery of city services not unproven disruption with solutions that are not mature;
- a lack of *trust* that new initiatives will work, with city administrations cognisant of previous investments that failed;
- a lack of clarity on *value for money*, return on investment, finance models and when to enter the market;
- a set of *competing demands* that all require investment, so if a proposed solution is not aimed at a critical problem it will find it difficult to compete for attention and resources;
- a set of *procedural issues* concerning regulations regarding procuring services and technologies and working with other bodies;
- a body of *inertia and resistance* within city administrations, with already existing practices and legacy systems and internal politics, fiefdoms, competing interests, and siloed departments and systems;
- *weak staffing* and *skills capacity* with respect to implementing smart city technologies; and,
- a fragmented local administration landscape, with cities divided up into autonomous municipalities causing *coordination* and *economy of scale* issues.

Overcoming these issues requires flexibility in approach and a more convincing argument – one that addresses the kinds of criticism detailed in this chapter and across the entire volume – that a smart cities approach is the answer to urban issues. Corporations and cities did change their narrative in relation to critique concerning citizen participation and focus. However, while the rhetoric shifted in tone to declare the focus was now to create citizen-orientated smart cities, the underlying logic, ethos and position of citizens was little changed (Kitchin 2015). In other cases, cities have moved beyond lip-service to take a more proactive approach to reimaging, reframing and remaking smart cities, actively engaging with deeper, more normative notions of what kind of smart city they want to create and the principles underpinning this: for example, Barcelona's 'technological sovereignty' (Galdon, 2017) and Medellín's 'social urbanism' (Talvard, this volume; McLaren and Agyeman, this volume). The chapters in this book collectively illuminate the many issues that still plague the drive towards smart cities, but also suggest ways to address them and alternative visions. The challenge is to realize these alternative visions to create ethical and principled smart cities that serve all citizens.

Note

1 http://www.dublindashboard.ie and http://www.corkdashboard.ie.

Acknowledgements

The research for this paper was funded by a European Research Council Advanced Investigator grant, The Programmable City (ERC-2012-AdG-323636).

References

Baracos, S. and Nissenbaum, H. 2014. "Big data's end run around anonymity and consent." In Lane, J., Stodden, V., Bender, S. and Nissenbaum, H. (eds), *Privacy, Big Data and the Public Good*. Cambridge: Cambridge University Press, pp. 44–75.

Bates, J. 2012. "'This is what modern deregulation looks like': Co-optation and contestation in the shaping of the UK's Open Government Data Initiative." *The Journal of Community Informatics* 8(2). http://www.ci-journal.net/index.php/ciej/article/view/845/916 (last accessed 6 February 2013).

Braun, B.P. 2014. "A new urban dispositif? Governing life in an age of climate change." *Environment and Planning D: Society and Space* 32: 49–64.

Cardullo, P. and Kitchin, R. 2018, online first. "Being a 'citizen' in the smart city: Up and down the scaffold of smart citizen participation in Dublin, Ireland." *GeoJournal*. doi:10.1007/s10708–10018–9845–9848.

Cerrudo, C. 2015. "An Emerging US (and World) Threat: Cities Wide Open to Cyber Attacks." Securing Smart Cities, securingsmartcities.org/wp-content/uploads/2015/05/CitiesWideOpenToCyberAttacks.pdf (last accessed 12 October 2015).

Dourish, P. 2016. "The Internet of urban things." In Kitchin, R. and Perng, S.-Y. (eds) *Code and the City*. London: Routledge, pp. 27–46.

Edwards, L. 2016. "Privacy, security and data protection in smart cities: A critical EU law perspective." *European Data Protection Law Review* 2(1): 28–58.

Flood, J. (2011) *The Fires: How a Computer Formula, Big Ideas, and the Best of Intentions Burned Down New York City–and Determined the Future of Cities*. New York: Riverhead.

Gabrys, J. 2014. "Programming environments: Environmentality and citizen sensing in the smart city." *Environment and Planning D: Society and Space* 32(1): 30–48

Galdon, G. 2017. "Technological Sovereignty? Democracy, Data and Governance in the Digital Era." CCCB Lab, http://lab.cccb.org/en/technological-sovereignty-democracy-data-and-governance-in-the-digital-era/ (last accessed 6 April 2018).

Hall, T. and Hubbard, P. (eds) 1997. *The Entrepreneurial City*. Chichester: John Wiley.

Hill, D. 2013. "On the smart city: Or, a 'manifesto' for smart citizens instead." City of Sound, 1 February.www.cityofsound.com/blog/2013/02/on-the-smart-city-a-callfor-smart-citizens-instead.html (last accessed 5 February 2013).

Hollands, R.G. 2008 "Will the real smart city please stand up?" *City* 12(3): 303–320.

Kitchin, R. 2014. "The real-time city? Big data and smart urbanism." *GeoJournal* 79(1): 1–14.

Kitchin, R. 2015. "Making sense of smart cities: addressing present shortcomings." *Cambridge Journal of Regions, Economy and Society* 8(1): 131–136.

Kitchin, R. 2016. *Getting Smarter about Smart Cities: Improving Data Privacy and Data Security.* Data Protection Unit, Department of the Taoiseach, Dublin, Ireland. http://www.taoiseach.gov.ie/eng/Publications/Publications_2016/Smart_Cities_Report_January_2016.pdf.

Kitchin, R. and Dodge, M. 2011. *Code/Space: Software and Everyday Life.* Cambridge, MA: MIT Press.

Kitchin, R., Coletta, C., Evans, L., Heaphy, L. and MacDonncha, D. 2017. "Smart cities, urban technocrats, epistemic communities, advocacy coalitions and the 'last mile' problem." *it – Information Technology* 59(6): 275–284.

Kitchin, R., Lauriault, T. and McArdle, G. 2015. "Knowing and governing cities through urban indicators, city benchmarking and real-time dashboards." *Regional Studies, Regional Science* 2: 1–28.

Kitchin, R., Maalsen, S. and McArdle, G. 2016. "The praxis and politics of building urban dashboards." *Geoforum* 77: 93–101.

Krivy, M. 2018. "Towards a critique of cybernetic urbanism: The smart city and the society of control". *Planning Theory* 17(1): 8–30.

Lefebvre, H. 1996. "The right to the city." In Kofman, E. and Lebas, E. (eds), *Writings on Cities.* Cambridge, MA: Blackwell.

Leszczynski, A. 2017. "Geoprivacy." In Kitchin, R., Lauriault, T. and Wilson, M. (eds), *Understanding Spatial Media.* London: Sage, pp. 235–244.

Luque-Ayala, A. and Marvin, S. 2015. "Developing a critical understanding of smart urbanism?" *Urban Studies* 52(12): 2105–2116.

March, H. and Ribera-Fumaz, R. 2017. "Against, for and beyond the smart city: Towards technological sovereignty in Barcelona." Paper presented at the Association of American Geographers, Boston. April 5–9.

Martinez, D.E. 2011. "Beyond disciplinary enclosures: Management control in the society of control." *Critical Perspectives on Accounting* 22(2): 200–211.

Mattern, S. 2013. "Methodolatry and the art of measure: The new wave of urban data science." *Design Observer: Places.* 5 November.http://designobserver.com/places/feature/0/38174/ (last accessed 15 November 2013).

Mattern, S. 2017. *Code and Clay, Data and Dirt.* Minneapolis: University of Minnesota Press.

Merricks White, J. 2016. "Anticipatory logics of the smart city's global imaginary." *Urban Geography* 37(4): 572–589.

Sadowski, J. and Pasquale, F. 2015. "The spectrum of control: A social theory of the smart city." *First Monday* 20(7). http://journals.uic.edu/ojs/index.php/fm/article/view/5903 (accessed 6 January 2017).

Smith, D.M. 1994. *Geography and Social Justice.* Oxford: Blackwell.

Swyngedouw, E. 2016. "The mirage of the sustainable 'smart' city. Planetary urbanization and the spectre of combined and uneven apocalypse". In: Nel-lo, O. and Mele, R. (eds), *Cities in the 21st Century.* London: Routledge, pp. 134–143.

Taylor, L., Richter, C., Jameson, S. and Perez del Pulgar, C. 2016. *Customers, Users or Citizens? Inclusion, Spatial Data and Governance in the Smart City.* University of Amsterdam. https://pure.uvt.nl/portal/files/12342457/Customers_users_or_citizens_Taylor_Richter_Jameson_Perez_de_Pulgar_2016.pdf (last accessed 16 August 2016).

Townsend, A., Maguire, R., Liebhold, M. and Crawford, M. *A Planet of Civic Laboratories: The Future of Cities, Information and Inclusion.* Palo Alto: Institute for the Future.

Vanolo, A. 2014. "Smartmentality: The smart city as disciplinary strategy." *Urban Studies* 51(5): 883–898.

INDEX

Page numbers in **bold** refer to figures, page numbers in *italic* refer to tables.

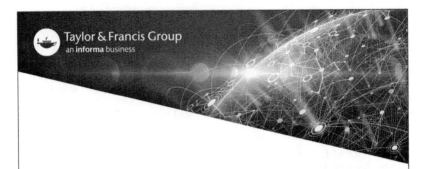